MAFIA III
OFFICIAL STRATEGY GUIDE

BASICS
THE MENU

The pause menu is accessed by pressing the Menu (Xbox) or Options (PS4) button on the controller. You can find the time, current cash in hand, the amount of money in your safe, and the current amount of TL-49 Fuses you're holding. You have access to many different features on this menu: the Kill List, Assets, Journal, Collection, Options, and Game. Details on these features are covered in this chapter.

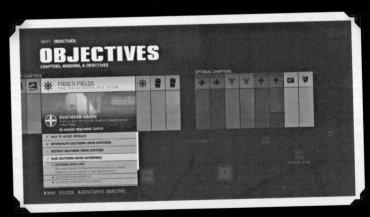

XBOX CONTROL	PS4 CONTROL	COMMAND
B	◎	Back
LT	L2	Zoom Out
RT	R2	Zoom In
X	▢	Objectives Menu
LS	L3	Toggle Wiretap Visibility (grays out areas of the map covered by wiretaps)
A	✕	Set Waypoint

MAP OBJECTIVES

The map menu's Objectives Panel is a popular stop when browsing through the pause menu. Here you can scroll through all available chapters, missions, and objectives using the Left Control Stick or the D-pad. There are two categories of objectives: Story Chapters and Optional Chapters. Optional Chapters unlock as you complete Story Chapters and can be played at any point in the game. You can always go back and play the Optional Chapters (unless you complete the game… then it's too late).

MAP ZOOM REVEALS

Chapters, missions, and objectives are all revealed on the maps with unique icons. These icons remain visible on the map no matter what zoom percentage is used. However, smaller icons such as health, fuses, junction boxes, and collectibles will not materialize until you zoom into the map at least 50%.

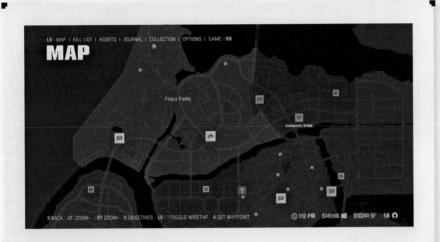

Reveal details of each chapter by scrolling to it and then navigate up and down through the objectives using the Left Control Stick. Press the **Ⓐ** or **Ⓧ** button to activate or deactivate the objective. This sets a waypoint on the map to the objective location and draws a route for easy navigation.

These same objectives can be singled out on the map by moving the map reticle directly over the matching icon at the objective location. You can also activate or deactivate the objective here, thus activating or deactivating the waypoint route.

Routes

To set a route, first open your map and manually select a mission. Press **Ⓐ** or **Ⓧ** to expand/select Chapters, and use the Right Control Stick to scroll through available objectives. Select an objective, and a route is created to help you navigate to that objective location. The route only appears on the Minimap when you're behind the wheel of a vehicle.

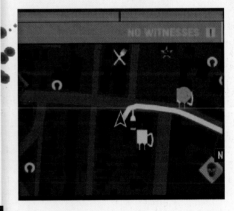

ROAD SIGNS

When a marker is set on an objective location, not only is a route drawn on the Minimap but you will also see turn signs on street corners along the route while you're driving. This allows you to keep your eyes on the road and off the Minimap.

KILL LIST

The Kill List is accessible through the pause menu. Scroll to the right from the map view to find this graphic list of enemies, starting with your number one target, Salvatore "Sal" Marcano. Below him in the criminal tree are his three capos, and below each capo are two lieutenants. Here you can see who has been eliminated and who remains on your hit list. Highlight Sal's photo and select View Intel, and then select "More" to read John Donovan's expanded dossier on the kingpin of New Bordeaux. Scroll to see intel about his criminal rackets as well. As you progress through the game, the Kill List will add profiles of Marcano's minions as well.

ASSETS

Scroll to the right of the Kill List in the pause menu to discover Assets. This is a great place to review your information on all your allies. Once introduced in the story, you can access info on Cassandra, Vito Scaletta, Thomas Burke, Emmanuel Lazare, Alma Diaz, and Nichole "Nicki" Burke.

When you select one of the three partners (Cassandra, Vito, or Burke), you can read a short bio. More importantly, if you page over to the right with the Left Control Stick or the D-pad, you can access a menu that details the associate's favors. This is a very convenient way of viewing upgrades available through the associates and how much money must be earned to unlock their upgrade options.

Cassandra's Favors

EARN	AVAILABLE FAVORS
0	Basic Arms Dealer: Buy Weapons On The Go
30,000	Screaming Zemi: A Throwable Distraction Device
60,000	Gunsmith: Improved Accuracy
100,000	Operator: Shut Down Phones For 5 Mins.
140,000	Gunsmith: Increased Ammo Capacity
180,000	Screaming Zemi: (Smoke)
220,000	Gunsmith: Improved Stability (Reduced Recoil)
270,000	Operator: Shut Down Phones for 10 Mins.
320,000	Screaming Zemi (Exploding)
370,000	Gunsmith: Faster Reload
420,000	Operator: Kill Phones & Call Your Backup

Vito's Favors

EARN	AVAILABLE FAVORS
0	Consigliere: Stash Your Cash On The Go
30,000	Hit Squad: Call In Armed Backup
60,000	Mob Doc: Add A Health Bar
100,000	Mob Doc: Add Another Adrenaline Shot
140,000	Consigliere: Show Enemy Locations, Collect Kickback
180,000	Mob Doc: Faster Health Bar Recovery
220,000	Enforcer Hit Squad: Call In Heavier Backup
270,000	Mob Doc: Add Health Bar
320,000	Mob Doc: Adrenaline Shot Fully Restores Health
370,000	High-Impact Hit Squad: Call Four-Man Kill Crew
420,000	Mob Doc: Max Health Bars

Thomas Burke's Favors

EARN	AVAILABLE FAVORS
0	Vehicle Delivery: Have Fresh Rides Brought To You
30,000	Clears Blue Police Zones: Cops Ignore Crimes For 30 Sec.
60,000	Cops Nearby: Mark Nearby Cops on Your Map
100,000	Explosives Supply: Arms Dealer Sells Explosives
140,000	Clears Blue Police Zones: Cops Ignore Crimes For 2 Mins.
180,000	Covert Car Theft: Steal Cars Undetected
220,000	Clears All Police Zones: Cops Ignore Crimes for 2 Mins.
280,000	Additional Explosives: Increase Carrying Capacity
320,000	Clears All Police Zones: Cops Ignore Crimes for 5 Mins.
370,000	Occupied Car Theft: Quietly Steal Occupied Cars
420,000	Clears All Police Zones: Cops Ignore Crimes for 10 Mins.

JOURNAL

The Journal can also be accessed in the pause menu; it's one click away from the Assets. This feature allows you to catch up on the story, or as much of the story as you've revealed through story chapter progression.

COLLECTION

In *Mafia III*, you are tasked with collecting many different objects. Similar to *Mafia II*, you'll be searching for vintage *Playboy* Magazines. But that's not all, you'll also be looking for Vargas Paintings, Albums, *Hot Rod* Magazines, Communist Propaganda Posters, and *Repent* Magazines. We extensively cover the locations of these collectibles in the Collectibles chapter of this guide, but just a quick tip: wiretapping reveals all collectibles within range of each hacked junction box. So, if you can find and hack all the junction boxes, then you can find all the collectibles.

Your collection progress is tracked in the pause menu. Simply scroll to the right of Assets to land on "Collection." Here you can scroll through all the individual pieces you've collected in each category and look inside the magazines and even read some vintage articles, like an interview with The Beatles.

OPTIONS

You'll find the Options to the right of Collection in the pause menu. In this menu, you can access control settings and adjust Look Inversion or alter the Aim Assist feature. You can also visit this area to assign commands to different buttons. In the Game Options, you can adjust the difficulty setting and turn on subtitles, among other things. And lastly, you can tweak the Display and Audio settings.

GAME

The final menu inside the pause menu is Game. This is where you go to load, start a new game, retry a chapter, or exit the game.

MOVEMENT

WALKING & RUNNING

Tilting the Left Control Stick controls walking and running. The further you tilt the stick the faster you will move. You should know that there are some heavy weapons that can slow Lincoln's running speed. When not in a gunfight, you should get into the habit of holstering your weapons, as not to draw attention to yourself.

CLIMBING & VAULTING

Lincoln can climb or vault over small objects. The speed at which the object is approached determines if a vault is performed or a climb. To climb over a fence or small object, walk up to the object and press **Y** or **△**. To vault over an object, run up to the object and just before reaching it, press **Y** or **△**. The **Y** or **△** is also used to initiate a climb up a ladder.

CROUCHING & STALKING

Press the Right Control Stick or **R3** to enter a crouched position. Lincoln can stalk around while crouched but he can't enter a full run. Use the stalk position to sneak around stealthily while taking out enemies. Press the same button to exit the crouching stance.

Enemy Awareness

The white indicator in the center of the screen displays enemy awareness. Get too close or make noise and the enemy awareness indicator expands. Draw too much attention and they'll come looking for you. The enemy awareness meter only appears when unnoticed or while in stealth mode. When enemies are looking for you, stay out of sight. When they've stopped looking, the enemy awareness indicator disappears.

Enemy Turf

Enemy Turf is territory controlled by criminal Rackets. Meaning the crooks there don't appreciate unwelcome guests. Overstay your welcome and they'll draw down on you. A "Trespassing" prompt appears onscreen when you enter one of these enemy occupied areas.

PICKING UP BODIES

If you need to move a victim to avoid nearby wandering eyes, stand over the fallen body and press down on the D-Pad. You can carry the body as long as you wish, and you can also carry the body while in the crouched position. You cannot enter buildings that require you to open the door or enter vehicles while carrying a body. You also have no access to weapons or projectiles while carrying a body. Press down on the D-Pad again to place the body on the ground in a less visible area.

TAKING COVER

Push up against walls and objects to avoid detection and flying bullets. To cover behind objects and walls, press your body against them and press **A** or **X**. While your back is against the object, you can strafe left or right (Lincoln will duck under open windows or clearings as you strafe) and shoot from around or over the covered object. When you release the Aim button, Lincoln automatically returns to cover.

You can also blind fire from cover by pressing the Fire button without pressing the Aim button (this keeps you in cover while shooting, but greatly reduces shot accuracy). You can also throw projectiles from cover. If an enemy is nearby, you can also stealthily attack from around a tall object or around or over a low object. When this type of attack is made available (when the target is within reach), the **B** or **◎** button will appear over the enemy.

SWIMMING

Tread water by tilting the Left Control Stick in the direction you want to swim. There's no underwater exploration. To exit the water, find a gradual slope to walk out of the water or find a low dock, ledge, sidewalk, or boat to pull up onto using the **Y** or **▲** button. Be careful in the bayou, the waters are infested with alligators. One chomp can kill you. It's also a good location to dump bodies—drop them in and watch them become alligator bait within seconds.

DRIVING

Behind The Wheel Controls

XBOX ONE	PLAYSTATION 4	ACTION
Click Left Stick	L3	Horn
Click Right Stick	R3	Look Behind
RB	R1	Drive-By Shoot
LT	L2	Brake/Reverse
RT	R2	Accelerate
✕	▢	Steal, Enter & Exit Vehicle
Left Stick	Left Analog	Steering
Right Stick	Right Analog	Camera
B	◎	Emergency Brake
D-Pad Left & Right	D-Pad Left & Right	Change Radio Station
D-Pad Right (Hold)	D-Pad Right (Hold)	Turn Radio Off/On
LB	L1	Pull up targeting UI to take out opposing vehicles
A	✕	Ram Vehicle

Tailing

You can follow some enemies back to Targets of Opportunity by tailing them. The target vehicle appears with a "Follow" message floating above. This vehicle appears as a red vehicle blip on the Minimap.

A Tailing Meter under your rearview mirror measures how suspicious the target is getting. Keep an eye on the Tailing Meter—driving too close to your target or drawing attention to your vehicle will fill the Tailing Meter and cause the target to flee. Things that draw attention to your vehicle are driving recklessly, driving in the opposite lane, tire skidding noises (yours or others you cause to brake hard), honking the horn or causing others to honk theirs. These warnings appear as a message above the Tailing Meter as they occur.

Drive-By Shooting & Target Selection

While carrying a handgun and while behind the wheel of a vehicle, tap **LB** or **L1** to cycle through targets in and around the target vehicle. Targets will cycle through vulnerable tires, engine, driver, and passengers. Green circles appear in the selection when you

have acquired a lock-on shot. Press **RB** or **R1** to shoot. Once an enemy has exited the vehicle, he is no longer a selectable target—you must use free aim to hit targets outside of vehicles.

Instead of manually moving the camera to look behind your vehicle while shooting at vehicles behind you, simply press and hold the Right Control Stick or **R3** button and you'll achieve a back camera view while all the available enemy vehicle drive-by features remain available to you. When you release the Right Control Stick button or **R3,** the forward view returns instantaneously.

Ram

Steer into enemy vehicles and press **A** or **✕** to take them out with a Ram move, causing major damage that can disable the target vehicle.

WIRETAPPING

You first need to complete the "Story Mission: Smack" before attempting to wiretap a junction box. Next, you need three TL-49 Fuses; it takes three fuses to wiretap one junction box. There's usually at least one fuse in the vicinity of each junction box. (Fuses are also revealed in district sectors whose junction box has already been wiretapped.) Next, look for the nearest untapped junction box icon on the map. If you are headed to that district early and its icon is not revealed on the map, use our map to find the junction boxes. Look for a large green utility box attached to a wall in the environment. Walk up to it and press ✗ or ◼ to begin the jimmying mini-game to pry the doors open.

JUNCTION BOX LOCK

The junction box lock will appear with a red "no-sign" icon over it if you do not have at least three fuses in your possession. Find three fuses before attempting a wiretap.

Step 1: Finding The Sweet Spot

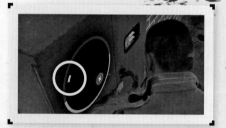

Rotate the Left Control Stick until a green highlight bar appears along the white circle covering the junction box. Move the control stick until you achieve the smallest green bar possible, and then press ✗ or ◼ to confirm the sweet spot. The smaller you can make the green sweet spot icon, the easier the next step will be.

Step 2: Prying The Doors Open

Now that a very small green bar (representing the sweet spot) is locked onto the circular white prying indicator, a much larger green bar appears in its place. The smaller the green sweet-spot bar you lock, the larger the pry area in this second step will be, and the slower the prying needle moves, making it easier to execute the break-in.

Now, the very thin white prying needle bounces across the white circle from the right to the left. The smaller the sweet spot you created, the slower this needle moves. Stop the needle in the green bar. The easiest and quickest way to nail this step is to quickly press ✗ or ◼ as soon as it touches the green area, instead of waiting for the needle to reach the green bar's middle.

AUTOMATIC JUNCTION BOX REVEAL

When you are sent to a new district through a story mission, all of that district's junction boxes are revealed on your map automatically.

Step 3: Wiretap

The third step is an automatic action. Clay takes the fuse and wires it into the junction box, creating a wiretap. After you close the doors, a green light on the fuse appears inside the junction box (seen through a small window), indicating that box has been wiretapped. If you access the Map Menu, you'll see enemies (if any are near) and collectibles are now revealed on the map in the district's sector where that junction box is located. There are many junction boxes and fuses scattered throughout New Bordeaux. Find and tap them all to reveal the collectibles on the entire map.

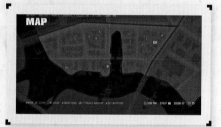

WHAT WIRETAPS REVEAL

Once you wiretap a sector's junction box, the in-game map reveals all of the collectibles, shops, Medicine Cabinets, TL-49 Fuses, and other key items and locations in that sector. Donovan marks each "Target of Opportunity" with an icon as well. These targets are the people, goods, and operations that contribute to the racket's Earn total.

After wiretapping, your Minimap reveals all enemies (red blips) within its radius. In addition, your Intel View reveals all nearby foes (highlighted red)—even through walls and around corners, including those you haven't yet spotted directly.

MENU MAP TOGGLE WIRETAP FEATURE

When a sector of a district has been wiretapped, that area will glow a brighter shade of green when you click on the Toggle Wiretap button. As you can see in this picture, the sector to the left has an untapped junction box, and the sector on the left has been wiretapped and is brighter. This is a good tool to use to quickly see the areas that you've yet to wiretap.

Using Wiretaps to Recruit Bosses

Each wiretapped node also reveals sensitive information about the rackets in the district. Lincoln Clay can leverage this information to convince certain bosses (though not all) to work for him when he takes over their rackets. Recruiting experienced bosses increases the Earn of your rackets. Note that without wiretapped info, Lincoln has no choice but to kill racket bosses when he confronts them.

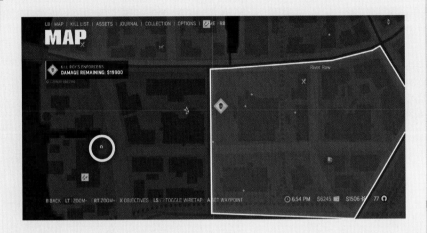

COMBAT

COMBAT KNIFE

You can use your Combat Knife to neutralize enemies—permanently—during Takedowns. However, you do have a Non-Lethal option for Takedowns. To select between Lethal and Non-Lethal, go to the Pause Menu > Options > Game > Melee Takedowns > Lethal or Non-Lethal. No matter what takedown method you choose, the outcome is the same: the fallen stay down permanently. The only difference is the amount of blood and violence you'll witness. Lincoln is always armed with the Combat Knife even though it does not appear in the weapon wheel. The knife is automatically taken out during a stealthy, lethal takedown.

MELEE

Tapping 🅱 or ◉ while facing a pedestrian puts them on the ground with one punch. In a combative situation with an armed gunman, multiple punches are required to subdue your opponent. If you are holding a weapon, your melee attacks are stronger. The same is true for the attacking enemy. You should avoid all face-to-face melees if you can help it. By using stealth, you can take anyone down with one attack. Sneak up behind them and preform a silent takedown. It is also possible to get a one-hit-kill while running at someone head-on. To achieve this, bolt out of cover and run at the enemy (that's facing you) from a short distance, ending your encounter with a punch, which becomes a takedown if done correctly.

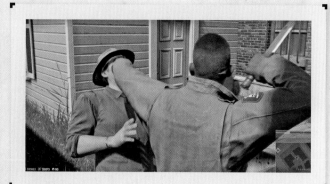

COUNTER

During a melee with armed enemies, you may be prompted to execute a counterattack. If you successfully press the 🅨 or △ button when prompted, Lincoln performs a finishing move that wins the battle. This often results in Lincoln flipping the enemy over, slamming him to the ground, and hitting him with whatever weapon is in hand or stomping on their head. This prompt may also appear on the enemy when you rush them before any engagement at all, but it's not as predictable as a melee prompt; so be ready, and be quick to hit 🅨 or △ when and if it appears to achieve a one-hit kill.

BRUTAL TAKEDOWNS

When you want to take out an enemy and briefly stun all his nearby buddies, use a Brutal Takedown. Notice when engaged in melee with an enemy that the 🅱 or ◉ attack button's outer edge is actually a gauge. This gauge fills red as you press and hold the Attack button. The trick for executing a Brutal Takedown is similar to the feature used to pry open doors, but a little less complicated. During a melee, simply press and hold the Attack button until the red line in the attack gauge enters the white zone (the white zone covers the 6 o'clock to 9 o'clock location on the attack gauge), and then quickly release the Attack button. If vibration is activated, the controller will vibrate to cue you when to quickly release the button.

Lincoln performs a Brutal Takedown and you get to enjoy the unique attack animation that coincides with the weapon currently held. If no weapon is held, Lincoln will stab the enemy multiple times in the face with his knife, for example.

It's not always as easy as it sounds, since the enemy can disrupt your attack while you're attempting to fill the Brutal Takedown gauge. If you continue to attack the enemy without executing the Brutal Takedown, Lincoln will eventually defeat the enemy with a finishing move or be pushed back. Also look for the counterattack prompt to finish the fight quickly. If you're thrown back and have already lost your stealth, you could also choose to shoot the enemy to finish him off before he pulls the trigger on his own weapon.

DRAW ATTENTION (WHISTLE)

Whistling draws enemy awareness. Use it while stalking to thin out groups of enemies or to draw them away. Hold left on the D-pad to whistle. Most enemies (excluding cops) will typically investigate a noise one at a time. With patience, you can lure multiple enemies into a kill zone killing each with a silent takedown, one after the other. With intel and thoughtful positioning, you can often draw attention to your number one target first and avoid a lot of violence.

THE DOS AND DON'TS OF KICKING IN DOORS

You have two choices when breaking into locked buildings. Use the slow and silent method using a crowbar to jimmy the door, or go in

fast and furious by kicking in the door. Your predicament should determine the method used. Jimmying the door is a more silent approach, and using this method maintains your stealth. Even if there are enemies on the other side of the door, you can quickly sidestep to the side of the doorway to quickly hide. Search mode may be triggered and someone may investigate, but you can use a silent takedown to preserve your anonymity.

On the other hand, kicking in doors with enemies within earshot immediately puts theses enemies in search or combat mode. In other words, you've blown your cover. When would you choose this option? Well, when you are in a hurry and don't care about stealth, when you are fleeing serious trouble, or if you can see inside the building (using intel) that no one is within earshot.

SHOOTING

To select a weapon, bring up the Weapon Wheel and select a weapon. Or simply tap **LB** or **L1** to draw a weapon. Press and hold the Left Trigger or **L2** to raise a weapon to aim and press the Right Trigger or **R2** to fire. Press ❌ or ⬜ to reload your weapon. If you have the ammo, all weapons automatically reload when the last round is shot and the trigger is pulled again. Some slow-loading weapons may only auto-load one more round (such as shotguns) to keep you fighting until you have time for a lengthy reload.

Weapon Wheel

Press and hold **LB** or **L1** to bring up the Weapon Wheel. While in this menu, time slows down around you so you can make your selection without getting annihilated in the heat of battle. Use the Right Control Stick to move the selector through the weapon slots around the wheel. Release **LB** or **L1** to confirm your selection and to instantly return to the game. Your selected weapon or projectile will be in your hands upon return.

WEAPON WHEEL LIMITATIONS

You cannot bring up the weapon wheel while in water and some friendly interiors.

WEAPON WHEEL FEATURES

WEAPONS EXCHANGE

Picking up or purchasing a weapon in the same class as one you hold forces you to drop the current weapon in your possession.

Quick Weapon Swap

To select your weapons and explosives in the Weapon Wheel, hold **LB** or **L1**, scroll to your weapon of choice and then let go of **LB** or **L1** to return to the game holding the new weapon of choice. Or to quickly swap between weapons without entering the weapon wheel, tap **LB** or **RB** or **L1** or **R1**. This toggles between the handgun in the left slot and the heavy weapon in the right slot.

Switch Aim Stance

Lincoln defaults to raising a weapon on his right side and aiming with his right eye. However, this is not always a safe stance. If you are on the right side of a doorway looking inside a building or looking around a corner to your left, shoot from the left side of your body so you don't expose a lot of Lincoln. To switch aim stance, simply click down on the Left Control Stick (or **L3** on the PlayStation 4 controller).

NUMBER	SLOT CONTENTS	NOTES
1	Grenades	The number under the grenade represents how many you are currently holding. Favors from Burke can increase this max hold amount.
2	Molotovs	The number under the Molotov represents how many you are currently holding. Favors from Burke can increase this max hold amount.
3	Submachine Guns, Rifles, Shotguns, or Special Weapons	You can only hold one handgun plus one heavy weapon at a time. This slot can contain only one of a number of heavy weapon types. The number below the weapon graphic displays the amount of ammo in your current cartridge and the max amount of ammo you are carrying.
4	Screaming Zemi	Screaming Zemis are a distraction projectile and can be upgraded to smoking and exploding. The number under the icon displays the amount you are currently holding. These can be purchased from the Weapons Delivery van.
5	Handguns	You can only hold one handgun plus one heavy weapon at a time. This slot can contain only one Handgun type. The number below the weapon graphic displays the amount of ammo in your current cartridge and the max amount of ammo you are carrying.
6	C4	C4 can be purchased from the Weapons Delivery van. To place, select the C4, select a plant location, press X or I to confirm your choice, and press RB or R1 to detonate from a safe distance.
7	Weapon Stats	The selected weapon's name and stats appear in the middle of the weapon selection wheel.

AUTOMATIC AIM STANCE SWITCH

Lincoln automatically switches aiming stance to the appropriate shooting side when pressed against the corner of an object while in cover mode. Manual switch aim is used when you are not in cover mode.

Hold Breath

Click the Right Control Stick or **R3** to enter and exit scope mode on scoped weapons. When staring down the scope, click down and hold the Left Control Stick (or **L3** on the PlayStation 4 controller) to take a deep breath and hold it. This steadies your aim making that distant target easier to shoot. You can only hold your breath for a handful of seconds, so take your shot as soon as possible.

THROWING PROJECTILES

Press and hold **RB** or **R1** to bring up a throwing arc graphic. Move the far end of the arc to the intended destination of the projectile and then release **RB** or **R1** to throw the projectile. You can cancel the throw during the aiming sequence by pressing 🅱 or ◉. The same throwing procedure can also be executed while you're in weapon aim mode (while holding the Left Trigger or **L2**).

PLANT & DETONATE C4

C4 can be used to explode vehicles when commanded, or as a trap for enemies by being placed on the ground or by a doorway at a pinch point. You can purchase C4 from the weapons delivery van. Press **RB** or **R1** to bring up a yellow highlighted rectangle (the C4 silhouette) that can be positioned over objects. Once you've found the desired location, press ❌ or ◼ to plant. Get into a safe location far away from the blast radius, and then press **RB** or **R1** to detonate. If you do not explode the C4, hold down on the D-pad to pick up the explosive while standing over it to disarm it and return the explosive to your inventory.

ASSOCIATES' SERVICES

ASSOCIATES SELECTION WHEEL

As you take over Rackets and Districts, your Underbosses introduce you to their criminal Associates who you can call using the radio provided by Donovan.

The Associates' Services selection wheel consists of six sections (once all of the features are unlocked). The services are Operator, Concigliere, Hit Squad, Vehicle Delivery, Police Dispatcher, and Arms Dealer. To use Associates' services, open the Weapon Wheel by holding **LB** or **L1**.

Markers

Markers provide a single free Service from an Associate in the Weapon Wheel. Markers are earned when you finish side jobs for your Underbosses or when you assign them districts. You can earn one Marker for each completed side job (such as delivering one vehicle for Burke), and one Marker for assigning a district to an Underboss. You can use these Markers to pay for Associate favors. When you are out of Markers, you can then pay cash for certain favors.

ASSOCIATE SELECTION WHEEL DETAILS

NUMBER	SLOT CONTENTS	NOTES	COST
8	Operator	A Cassandra Favor: Shut down phones for 5 (Level 1) or 10 (Level 2) minutes. Kill phones & call your backup (Level 3).	$1000 or 1 Marker
9	Consigliere	A Vito Favor: Betty Johnson is the Consigliere. When called, she will take the money you give her and deposit it into your safe to keep you from losing it if you die.	Free
10	Hit Squad	A Vito Favor: Bobby "Ducks" Navarro and his team of three shooters come to support you almost the moment you call. There are three levels of brutality you can unlock. Each level increases the Hit Squad's resistance to attacks and damage inflicted to the enemy.	$1000 or 1 Marker
11	Vehicle Delivery	This is a Burke favor: Valet, Hank McGahee will make his "livery" available to you. Select a vehicle from his collection and have it delivered to your location.	Free
12	Police Dispatcher	This is a Burke favor: Fiona Davidson works for the New Bordeaux police on Burke's behalf. As a radio operator she can spread some cash around to get the heat off your tail. There are five levels of this feature with increasingly beneficial features.	$6000 or 1 Marker
13	Arms Dealer	This is a Cassandra favor: Jackie DuVernay runs a mobile weapon shop from the back of his van. Call him when you need ammo, weapons, explosives, health, armor, or to apply upgrades.	Free to call but supplies cost money.
14	Selected Service Details	This displays whichever service is selected in the Associate Wheel.	N/A

OPERATOR

The Operator feature is an Associate favor from Cassandra. There are three levels of Operator to unlock. Calling the Switchboard Operator, Jennifer "Clicks" Moran shuts down all phones for a certain amount of time (depending on the level you have unlocked). Use this feature just before you suspect trouble with Witnesses or if the amount of Witnesses grows out of control. Call the Operator and Witnesses' attempts to call the police will not go through.

CONSIGLIERE

If you die, you lose about half of the money you are holding. This makes it imperative that you regularly drop money in the safe at your safe house. The easiest way to do this is to call the Consigliere. Betty Johnson will drive to your location, take your money, and make the delivery to your safe for free. This is a Vito Scaletta favor. The second level of this feature reveals enemy locations on the map and allows you to collect your Kickbacks without driving to your Associates' hideouts.

HIT SQUAD

The Hit Squad can be called when you feel like you could use an extra gunman on your side (or three to be exact). This is a Vito Scaletta favor with multiple levels of increasing strength. Call the Hit Squad from the Associates Wheel and three wise guys in a Potomac Gallant come speeding up to your location. If there are no enemies in sight, they will hang with you and protect you. If you start a fight, they will try to finish it. If an enemy hangout is nearby, they will attack preemptively, or you can fire the first shot to get them charging. The Hit Squad can clear an entire enemy hideout without you ever firing a single shot, but they will leave the boss for you.

Call them when enemy reinforcements have been called on you; your Hit Squad can distract this threat, and depending on the matchup, wipe them out without you lifting a finger. As you unlock higher levels of the Hit Squad, they become almost unstoppable. The higher the level unlocked (by continuing to give Vito territories), the more resilient to damage they become and the weapons they carry are more deadly. The final level gives you one extra man, increasing the squad to a four-man team.

VEHICLE DELIVERY

Your personal Valet, Hank McGahee is a Burke perk. Call Vehicle Delivery when you find yourself without a vehicle (or without the right vehicle for the job). After selecting this feature, you are presented with the option to select from a list of unlocked vehicles. After the selection is made, Hank arrives in your vehicle at your current location. Vehicle upgrades are unlocked similar to weapon upgrades: by assigning Associates territories. These vehicle upgrades apply only to these vehicles the valet delivers. Vehicle Upgrades are presented for the second and fourth districts.

VEHICLE INVENTORY

VEHICLE	DETAILS	UNLOCKING INFO
Berkley Executive	Father James' car	Unlocked when you get the Vehicle Delivery Service
Samson Drifter	Lincoln's personal muscle car	Unlocked after "Get Grecco"
Pinkerton Titan	Butcher's armored truck	Unlocked after "Kill The Butcher"
Armored Majesty	Tony's armored sedan	Unlocked after "Kill Tony"
De'Leo Traviata	Frank's car	Unlocked after "Kill Frank"
Bulworth Mohican	Enzo's off-road truck	Unlocked after "Find Enzo"

You can increase the inventory of weapons and items available through the Arms Dealer in two ways. First, any weapons you equip from fallen enemies will automatically be added to the store. Second, add high-end weapons and items by assigning Rackets and Districts to your Underbosses.

For each district you conquer, you get the option to assign that district to one of your Underbosses. Each Underboss will offer to unlock a weapon free of charge from the Weapon Delivery van. From that point forward, you're able to call in the weapon van and equip that weapon for free, as if you've already purchased it. The other two choices that you didn't pick will be available from that point forward for purchase from the weapons delivery van. In subsequent District sitdowns, a new selection of upgrades will be available to you.

POLICE DISPATCHER

The Police Dispatcher, Fiona Davidson is a Burke favor. Fiona Works for the New Bordeaux police as a radio operator. For the right price, she can instantly get the heat off you by paying off corrupt police officers. Use this feature before or after police have been alerted to your illegal activities. A great time to use this feature, for example, is when you try to wiretap a junction box on a police station in forbidden territory. Call the dispatcher when suspicion arises and continue your crime while the cops turn a blind eye. This feature has five levels of increasing the time the police ignore crimes (from 30 sec. to 10 min.). This service costs $6000 or 1 Marker.

Vehicle upgrades work the same way. Weapons will be presented as choices for the first, third, and fifth districts. Vehicle upgrades are presented for the second and fourth districts. The sixth district unlocks a special or heavy weapon. Also available at the weapons van are Lincoln upgrades (Mob Doc), which are unlocked to upgrade stamina and the speed at which your health recovers.

ARMS DEALER

Cassandra's Associate, Mr. DuVernay, sells surplus weapons and supplies out of his van. To see what he has to offer, call him using the Associates Wheel, and then approach the back of the van and hold ✕ or ⬤. Use the Weapon Wheel to find and purchase weapons. Press ✕ or ⬤ to refill all of your currently held weapons' ammo supply.

THE MINIMAP

In addition to showing an overhead view of Lincoln's immediate surroundings, your Minimap also highlights nearby friends, enemies, objectives, and any other points of interest. A white route will indicate the most efficient path to your next objective while in a vehicle.

INTEL VIEW

Exploit your situational awareness by using Intel View. Pressing **VIEW** or **Touchpad** highlights every enemy you've spotted in red, even when they're behind walls. If you've wiretapped the local junction box, doing so will highlight all nearby enemies regardless if you've already spotted them or not. You will also receive vital information, such as locations of health, armor, collectibles, entry points, and good sniper spots. A wiretapped Intel View also labels enemy targets if they are Sentries or a special target.

ITEMS

ADRENALINE SHOTS

Your health is represented by green bars positioned on top of the Minimap. Your health decreases as you receive damage. By obtaining certain upgrades, you can increase the number of Lincoln's health bars. When you run out of health, you die and respawn at the nearest Safe House, losing about half of the money you were holding. Adrenaline Shots replenish lost health and can be found in first aid cabinets. You start out with the ability to carry three Adrenaline Shots, but can expand this ability by completing some of Vito's favors. To use an Adrenaline Shot, press up on the D-Pad when your health is low.

ARMOR

Tac-Vests add a layer of protection to your health bar. It appears as a blue line over the green health bar. When armor is worn, it takes the beating before your health does. Tac-Vests are found in armor cabinets, which look just like weapon lockers. These are highlighted yellow in the environment when the local junction box has been tapped and Intel View is used.

FUSES

TL-49 Fuses are scattered all over New Bordeaux. They are mostly found near trashcans, but they can also be found in underground passages or high on building rooftop ledges. Go out of your way to pick up as many of these as you can. It takes three fuses to wiretap one junction box; however, there are plenty more fuses than you will ever need to wiretap all the junction boxes. The amount of fuses you are holding appears in the display at the screen's bottom-left corner. Wiretapping junction boxes reveals fuses on the map. They appear as green blips. As you approach a fuse in the environment, you can easily spot it; a small, bright-green circle will hover over it.

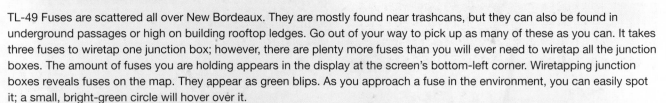

AMMO

Dropped weapons contain ammo. Walking over a dropped weapon automatically adds its ammo to your inventory (but only if you are carrying the identical weapon). If the dropped weapon is not the same as the one you are holding, you can opt to exchange it for your weapon by pressing ✗ or I while standing over it. You can also replenish your ammo at the Arms Dealer's weapon van.

MONEY

The value next to the wallet icon indicated in the bottom-left corner corresponds to the money Lincoln holds. This can be lost if he dies. The money shown to

the right of the wallet is stored in your safe and is not affected by life or death. Call the Consigliere from the Associates Menu to secure any money Lincoln has on hand. Money dropped by enemies can be walked over to be collected. You can also find money in stacks or in leather money bags. These must be picked up using ❌ or ⬛.

ROBBING BUSINESSES

Some businesses in town remain segregated. The owners will hassle you until you leave, and they'll immediately call the cops if they see you committing a crime. Many stores contain first aid kits with Adrenaline Shots inside, and a cash register that can be robbed (approach it

and hold ❌ or ⬛). A blue cash box can often be found in a backroom or kitchen; break into these to collect the money. The cash box in bars can sometimes be found behind the bar counter. Try to rob stores quickly and quietly; otherwise, you may have to take out witnesses that try to call the cops from a nearby phone. This is a good time to use the Associates' Operator feature to shut down phone service.

POLICE AWARENESS

The Police Awareness Indicator appears in the screen's center when you're near a cop. Police bring the hammer down if you commit crimes, act suspiciously, or break traffic laws within range of their attention.

WITNESSES

Civilians can also bring the heat if they see you committing a crime. When this happens, the civilian becomes a "Witness" and a telephone icon

appears above the civilian as they make their way for the nearest phone or patrolling police officer.

Crimes and Offenses a Witness will respond to:

- ☑ Being seen in public with a weapon drawn
- ☑ Aiming at a civilian for a while
- ☑ Killing a civilian
- ☑ Killing a police officer
- ☑ Shooting a number of times
- ☑ Carjacking
- ☑ Hitting a few people with cars
- ☑ Carjacking a policeman
- ☑ Blowing up a vehicle
- ☑ Driving over a civilian
- ☑ Performing a takedown on an enemy

BLUE ZONE

A blue zone appears on the map and minimap after a crime is reported. This means the police are actively searching for you. To end the search, look at your map and head past the nearest edge of the blue zone and remain there until the search is over. You can also call the Police Dispatcher to stop the search immediately.

RED ZONE

Cops in a red zone are in a "shoot-first, ask-questions-later" state of mind. Open your map and check the boundary of the flashing Active Police Zone, then try to get outside of it while losing the pursuit. Or try hiding until the Police Awareness level drops to a blue zone.

Cops within a blue police zone (also displayed on your map) still search for you, but less aggressively. You can move stealthily, avoiding contact until you get outside the zone.

The following creates a red zone when police are watching (blue police indicator is on-screen, but your Associates' Police Dispatcher service is not active):

- ☑ Aiming at a civilian
- ☑ Killing a civilian
- ☑ Punching an enemy a few times
- ☑ Killing a police officer
- ☑ Shooting

- ☑ Driving on the sidewalk for a while
- ☑ Hitting a number of vehicles quickly
- ☑ Hitting a police car with a car
- ☑ Carrying a weapon for a while in public (unholstered)
- ☑ Shooting at a vehicle
- ☑ Carjacking
- ☑ Carjacking a police occupied car
- ☑ Hitting a police officer with a car
- ☑ Hitting a few pedestrians with cars
- ☑ Stealing a car
- ☑ Stealing a police car
- ☑ Aiming at a police officer
- ☑ Shooting at a police officer
- ☑ Shooting at a civilian
- ☑ Blowing up a vehicle
- ☑ Throwing a Grenade or Molotov
- ☑ Performing a takedown on an enemy
- ☑ Interrogating informant
- ☑ Placing explosive
- ☑ Carrying a body for a while

The following creates a red zone event even when the Police Dispatcher service is active (you used the Associates' Police Dispatcher service):

- ☑ Injuring a police officer
- ☑ Killing a police officer
- ☑ Shooting at police or their vehicles
- ☑ Hitting the police car with your car

OTHER POLICE BEHAVIOR

Police investigate gunshots and explosions they hear but cannot see. The time to investigate varies on location. This happens quicker in the city and slower in remote areas. Police watch you for a while, but when you get too close to them, they tell you to go away. Police also attack you if they see you in a police zone, which is around many police stations.

To escape from the police, stay out of their circle of attention displayed on your Minimap. Be careful: this circle will grow as you break more laws, making it even harder to lose their pursuit.

WEAPONS

SHOTGUNS

BARKER 390 (GATOR SKIN)

A little extra flash to go with the 390's bang, this custom job has all of the added ammo capacity of the standard model. This is a pre-order weapon.

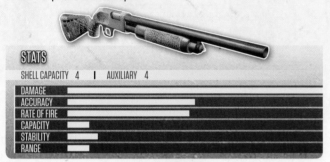

STATS						
SHELL CAPACITY	4		AUXILIARY	4		
DAMAGE						
ACCURACY						
RATE OF FIRE						
CAPACITY						
STABILITY						
RANGE						

BARKER 390

If you need something to hunt gators, you could do worse. Smaller ammo capacity might have you scrambling to reload.

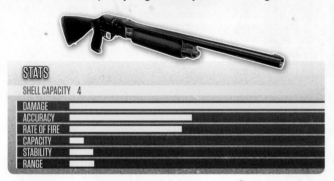

STATS				
SHELL CAPACITY	4			
DAMAGE				
ACCURACY				
RATE OF FIRE				
CAPACITY				
STABILITY				
RANGE				

LUPARA

Hit anybody with this double-barreled bad boy and they ain't getting back up again.

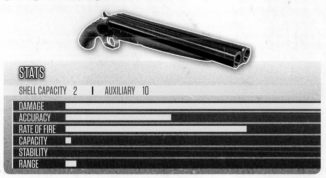

STATS					
SHELL CAPACITY	2		AUXILIARY	10	
DAMAGE					
ACCURACY					
RATE OF FIRE					
CAPACITY					
STABILITY					
RANGE					

CORNELL 40

An increased ammo capacity shotgun that cops call the "Hippie Kicker."

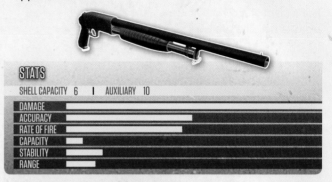

STATS					
SHELL CAPACITY	6		AUXILIARY	10	
DAMAGE					
ACCURACY					
RATE OF FIRE					
CAPACITY					
STABILITY					
RANGE					

BARKER 1500 TACTICAL

King of the semi-auto scatter shotguns, all that power comes at the expense of low ammo capacity and massive recoil.

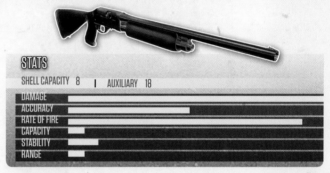

STATS					
SHELL CAPACITY	8		AUXILIARY	18	
DAMAGE					
ACCURACY					
RATE OF FIRE					
CAPACITY					
STABILITY					
RANGE					

RIOT 550

Added ammo capacity makes this a sought-after shotgun among collectors and weekend warrior types.

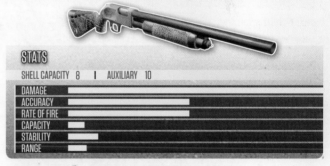

STATS					
SHELL CAPACITY	8		AUXILIARY	10	
DAMAGE					
ACCURACY					
RATE OF FIRE					
CAPACITY					
STABILITY					
RANGE					

ELMWOOD 1925

A bayou bootlegger wouldn't think of leaving home without at least one of these ultra-close-range, sawed-off shotguns.

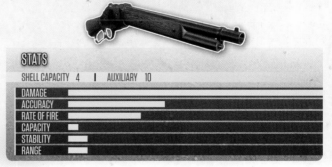

STATS					
SHELL CAPACITY	4		AUXILIARY	10	
DAMAGE					
ACCURACY					
RATE OF FIRE					
CAPACITY					
STABILITY					
RANGE					

HANDGUNS

ALFREDSON M419

Not a lot of firepower. The best you can say for this target pistol is that she's reliable.

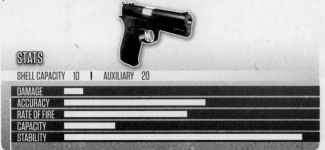

STATS

SHELL CAPACITY	10		AUXILIARY	20

DAMAGE	
ACCURACY	
RATE OF FIRE	
CAPACITY	
STABILITY	

MASTERSON SEMI-AUTO

Above-average damage is a solid trade-off for a below-average mag size.

STATS

SHELL CAPACITY	7		AUXILIARY	27

DAMAGE	
ACCURACY	
RATE OF FIRE	
CAPACITY	
STABILITY	

CLIPPER .44

Available as a Favor from Burke. This lightweight .44 only holds seven rounds, but its stopping power makes every shot count.

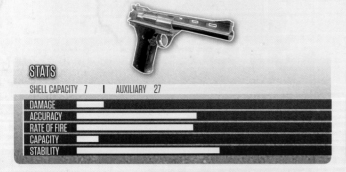

STATS

SHELL CAPACITY	7		AUXILIARY	27

DAMAGE	
ACCURACY	
RATE OF FIRE	
CAPACITY	
STABILITY	

ELLING 9MM

High mag capacity and better control than most pistols.

STATS

SHELL CAPACITY	13		AUXILIARY	26

DAMAGE	
ACCURACY	
RATE OF FIRE	
CAPACITY	
STABILITY	

SILENCED DEACON .22

Available as a Favor from Burke. Underpowered among pistols, it's still a solid silenced fire option with a mid-sized magazine. This is a useful handgun because you can take out enemies while retaining stealth.

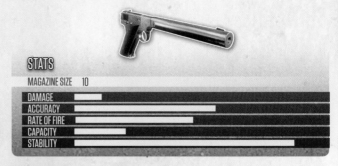

STATS

MAGAZINE SIZE	10

DAMAGE	
ACCURACY	
RATE OF FIRE	
CAPACITY	
STABILITY	

SILENCED MASTERSON

Available as a Favor from Vito. This suppressed semi-auto goes stealth with only a minimal drop-off in damage. This is our favorite handgun because you can take out enemies while retaining stealth. And it's more powerful than the Silenced Deacon .22.

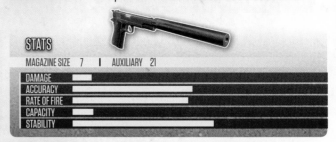

STATS

MAGAZINE SIZE	7		AUXILIARY	21

DAMAGE	
ACCURACY	
RATE OF FIRE	
CAPACITY	
STABILITY	

BLACKBURN FAF-33

Best ammo capacity among pistols, thanks to a double-stack high-capacity magazine.

STATS

MAGAZINE SIZE	15		AUXILIARY	30

DAMAGE	
ACCURACY	
RATE OF FIRE	
CAPACITY	
STABILITY	

ALFREDSON M200

Police-issued, the M200's found a second life as home defense. At least you can hit the broad side of a barn with it.

STATS

MAGAZINE SIZE	6		AUXILIARY	12

DAMAGE	
ACCURACY	
RATE OF FIRE	
CAPACITY	
STABILITY	

MASTERSON PHOENIX

It'll punch a fist-sized hole in your target. The smooth action on this revolver means added accuracy.

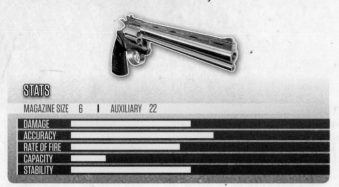

STATS

MAGAZINE SIZE 6 | AUXILIARY 22

DAMAGE	
ACCURACY	
RATE OF FIRE	
CAPACITY	
STABILITY	

SCOPED PHOENIX

Available as a Favor from Vito. All the impact of Masterson's hand cannon with an attached scope to line up your shots.

STATS

MAGAZINE SIZE 6 | AUXILIARY 22

DAMAGE	
ACCURACY	
RATE OF FIRE	
CAPACITY	
STABILITY	

SUBMACHINE GUNS

CZECH VER. B-65

(One-handed) It's got reduced stopping power and high recoil so use short controlled bursts.

STATS

MAGAZINE SIZE 20 | AUXILIARY 40

DAMAGE	
ACCURACY	
RATE OF FIRE	
CAPACITY	
STABILITY	

TRENCH 1938

Moderately powerful, this WWII-era SMG offers solid rate of fire with durable construction.

STATS

MAGAZINE SIZE 30 | AUXILIARY 60

DAMAGE	
ACCURACY	
RATE OF FIRE	
CAPACITY	
STABILITY	

TRENCH 1938 DRUM

Low accuracy, but it's got the largest magazine among all SMGs. Consider that a bigger margin for error when pulling the trigger. This is a pre-order weapon.

STATS

DRUM SIZE 50

DAMAGE	
ACCURACY	
RATE OF FIRE	
CAPACITY	
STABILITY	

ALFREDSON M833

Military-issue, this light and surprisingly powerful SMG got love from infantry over in Nam for its reliability in bad weather.

STATS

MAGAZINE SIZE 24 | AUXILIARY 72

DAMAGE	
ACCURACY	
RATE OF FIRE	
CAPACITY	
STABILITY	

DEUTSCHE M11B

Available as a Favor from Cassandra. Its closed-bolt firing mechanism is the secret behind the best in field accuracy of the M11B.

STATS

MAGAZINE SIZE 30 | AUXILIARY 120

DAMAGE	
ACCURACY	
RATE OF FIRE	
CAPACITY	
STABILITY	

M1N8

A low rate of fire but that means tighter control, and you won't run through all your ammo as quickly.

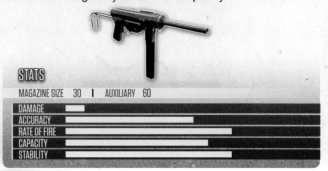

STATS

MAGAZINE SIZE 30 | AUXILIARY 60

DAMAGE	
ACCURACY	
RATE OF FIRE	
CAPACITY	
STABILITY	

SILENCED M1N8

Available as a Favor from Cassandra. The M1N8's suppressor reduces its recoil over the standard version. This is our favorite submachine gun because you can take out enemies while retaining your stealth.

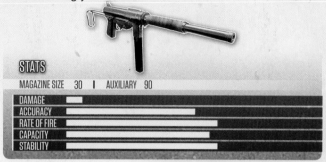

STATS
MAGAZINE SIZE 30 | AUXILIARY 90

DAMAGE	
ACCURACY	
RATE OF FIRE	
CAPACITY	
STABILITY	

CARTER M33-A

(One-handed) One of the smaller SMGs, but size hasn't hurt the Carter's punch any.

STATS
MAGAZINE SIZE 20 | AUXILIARY 40

DAMAGE	
ACCURACY	
RATE OF FIRE	
CAPACITY	
STABILITY	

BINYA

(One-handed) All the compactness of a smaller machine pistol and the power and ammo capacity of an SMG.

STATS
MAGAZINE SIZE 25 | AUXILIARY 50

DAMAGE	
ACCURACY	
RATE OF FIRE	
CAPACITY	
STABILITY	

RIFLES

HARTMANN .30

Even with a larger mag, this lightweight rifle has above-average control.

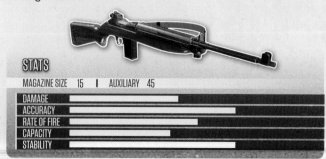

STATS
MAGAZINE SIZE 15 | AUXILIARY 45

DAMAGE	
ACCURACY	
RATE OF FIRE	
CAPACITY	
STABILITY	

MANITOU MODEL 67

Bolt-action civilian hunting rifle with limited magazine size. Make your shots count with this one.

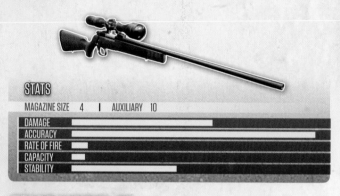

STATS
MAGAZINE SIZE 4 | AUXILIARY 10

DAMAGE	
ACCURACY	
RATE OF FIRE	
CAPACITY	
STABILITY	

CAMO MODEL 67

Keep a low-profile in the high grass with this military conversion of Manitou's bolt-action hunting rifle. This is a pre-order weapon.

STATS
MAGAZINE SIZE 4 | AUXILIARY 15

DAMAGE	
ACCURACY	
RATE OF FIRE	
CAPACITY	
STABILITY	

MAYWEATHER .30

With its smooth action and high effective range, no wonder this was a favorite rifle among grunts during WWII.

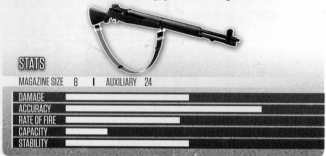

STATS
MAGAZINE SIZE 8 | AUXILIARY 24

DAMAGE	
ACCURACY	
RATE OF FIRE	
CAPACITY	
STABILITY	

PASADENA AR30

The AR30's got a factory defect in its bore dropping its accuracy, but it cuts through enemy personnel just the same.

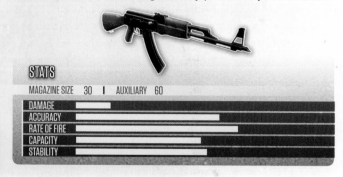

STATS
MAGAZINE SIZE 30 | AUXILIARY 60

DAMAGE	
ACCURACY	
RATE OF FIRE	
CAPACITY	
STABILITY	

STROMER .223

Available as a Favor from Burke. Thanks to the new .223 ammo and its straight-line layout, this baby produces much less recoil than other assault rifles.

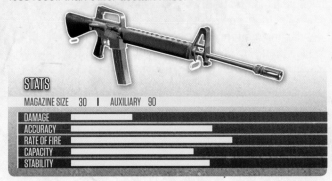

STATS

MAGAZINE SIZE 30 | AUXILIARY 90

| DAMAGE |
| ACCURACY |
| RATE OF FIRE |
| CAPACITY |
| STABILITY |

AUTOMAT SG

A full-power rifle cartridge has so much kick the U.S. Army retired it, thanks to grunts' complaints about the recoil.

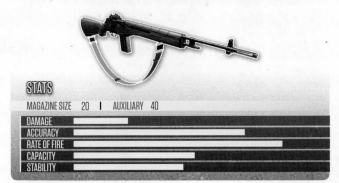

STATS

MAGAZINE SIZE 20 | AUXILIARY 40

| DAMAGE |
| ACCURACY |
| RATE OF FIRE |
| CAPACITY |
| STABILITY |

MAYWEATHER M04A3

With a stripper clip allowing faster reload times, this bolt-action rifle's seen duty since WWII.

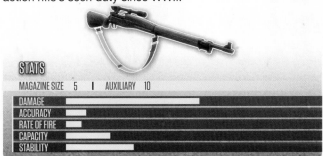

STATS

MAGAZINE SIZE 5 | AUXILIARY 10

| DAMAGE |
| ACCURACY |
| RATE OF FIRE |
| CAPACITY |
| STABILITY |

VIPER 55

"The Viper" on account of its rapid-fire mechanism. Great for quick-aim types who don't need to rely on the scope.

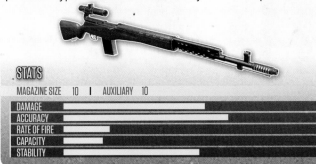

STATS

MAGAZINE SIZE 10 | AUXILIARY 10

| DAMAGE |
| ACCURACY |
| RATE OF FIRE |
| CAPACITY |
| STABILITY |

HAWK 4540 NIGHT VISION

Available as a Favor from Vito. This ain't no hunting rifle. Night vision on semi-auto makes for lethally efficient target acquisition.

STATS

MAGAZINE SIZE 20 | AUXILIARY 30

| DAMAGE |
| ACCURACY |
| RATE OF FIRE |
| CAPACITY |
| STABILITY |

SPECIAL WEAPONS

HARTMANN 7.62MM

Available as a Favor from Vito. Called "The Big Bad Wolf" during the war, this belt-fed MG's got a rep for blowing everything away.

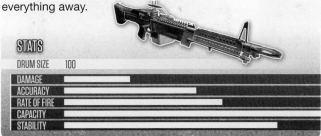

STATS

DRUM SIZE 100

| DAMAGE |
| ACCURACY |
| RATE OF FIRE |
| CAPACITY |
| STABILITY |

HARTMANN HLP

Available as a Favor from Burke. With better range than a rifle-mounted launcher, the HLP provides plenty of bang for your buck.

STATS

| DAMAGE |
| ACCURACY |
| RATE OF FIRE |
| CAPACITY |
| STABILITY |

HARTMANN AT-40

Available as a Favor from Cassandra. This single-use anti-tank weapon offers more range and damage than simply lobbing a grenade.

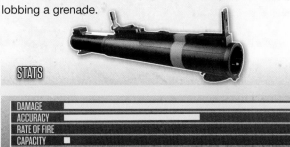

STATS

| DAMAGE |
| ACCURACY |
| RATE OF FIRE |
| CAPACITY |
| STABILITY |

SILENTIUM

This supressed semi-auto does both stealth and style with only a minimal drop off in damage.

STATS

MAGAZINE SIZE 7 | AUXILIARY 21

DAMAGE	
ACCURACY	
RATE OF FIRE	
CAPACITY	
STABILITY	

EXTERMINATORE

Some fools see this custom sawed-off and figure it's for show. It's usually the last mistake they make.

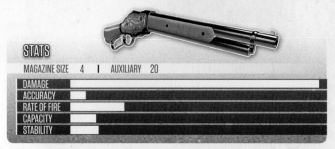

STATS

MAGAZINE SIZE 4 | AUXILIARY 20

DAMAGE	
ACCURACY	
RATE OF FIRE	
CAPACITY	
STABILITY	

PRAECISIONE

Even with the gold inlay, this custom WWII rifle's still lightweight with above average control and a larger mag.

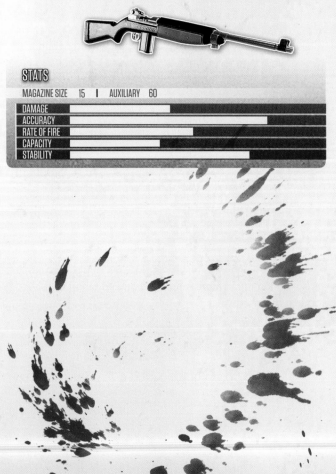

STATS

MAGAZINE SIZE 15 | AUXILIARY 60

DAMAGE	
ACCURACY	
RATE OF FIRE	
CAPACITY	
STABILITY	

EXPLOSIVES

FRAG GRENADE

Take out large groups of enemies with one toss of the grenade. Grenades can be found in the environment, but it's much easier to replenish your supply through the Arms Dealer. Try throwing a Screaming Zemi to create a crowd of enemies, and then finish them off with a grenade.

MOLOTOV

A crude bomb created with a bottle of gas with a rag wick inserted. Enemies don't have time to scramble away from a Molotov, as it explodes the second it hits the ground. The Screaming Zemi bomb trap is more effective with a Molotov since the enemies don't have a chance to run. You can find these in the environment, but it's much easier to replenish your supply through the Arms Dealer.

C4

Use a remote charge to blow up vehicles from a safe distance or set a trap for enemies. First plant the explosive on an object and then get to a safe distance and remotely detonate the bomb. You can only get C4 from the Arms Dealer.

SCREAMING ZEMI

The Screaming Zemi is used to distract groups of enemies. Throw the Screaming Zemi like any projectile (Hold **RB** to aim, then release to throw). The Screaming Zemi can later be upgraded to a smoking and explosive type through continued progress with an Associate. A good strategy is to use a Screaming Zemi to distract cops as you infiltrate their area to retrieve an item or hack a junction box. Or to use a Screaming Zemi as a prelude to destruction by gathering enemies around a Zemi and then throwing a Molotov or grenade in the middle of the group.

DEFEATING THE MOB:
HOW THIS WILL GO DOWN

New Bordeaux is the most corrupt place in America and it's teaming with Mafia Rackets, ranging from prostitution and gambling rings to drugs and human trafficking. Your job is to take over each racket. The best way to do this is to cripple each racket financially. Tear them down bit by bit before seizing the criminal enterprise for yourself.

Each racket is made up of several Targets of Opportunity, which can consist of supply caches, money stashes, or mobsters driving around the city. Destroy or capture as many as you can to downgrade the targeted enterprise to ruin; once its value hits $0, you can assassinate the leader or recruit them. Seizing every racket in a district will grant you total control over that area.

YOUR ALLIES

UNDERBOSSES

Lincoln is going to need assistance to take over New Bordeaux's criminal empire. Three Underbosses are here to help. Lincoln can assign one of his three Underbosses to manage and secure the newly captured rackets and districts.

Each Underboss gains income as they're assigned new territory—and as their wealth grows, so too will their loyalty toward you. Since each assignment favors one Lieutenant at the expense of the other two, choose wisely: your decisions will inevitably ruffle some feathers.

CASSANDRA

She's the leader of the Haitian gang and Lincoln's first major ally in New Bordeaux.

VITO SCALETTA

This former Empire Bay Mafioso was the protagonist of *Mafia II*. Now, as a resident of New Bordeaux, he operates out of an Italian restaurant.

THOMAS BURKE

Leader of the Irish Mob, this gangster has his own axe to grind with the Italians.

LIEUTENANTS

Each Underboss has a Lieutenant working for them.

EMMANUEL LAZARE

He manages the Haitian drug ring and is utterly devoted to his boss, Cassandra.

ALMA DIAZ

Saddled with unfinished business back in Cuba, Alma is confident that Vito can help her see things through.

NICKI BURKE

Nicki wants nothing more than to leave New Bordeaux, and Burke is her ticket out.

ASSOCIATES

The more territory your Underbosses control, the more Associates they can recruit to your cause. Some of these associates can provide special services—for a fee (or, if you've earned a Marker, use it for payment). For each assignment you make, consider which Underboss will offer the most useful Associates.

To access these Associates, hold **LB** or **L1** to open the Weapon Wheel. These Associates will arrive (or take effect) within seconds. For more information on associates, see the "Associates' Services" section also in the Basics.

CASSANDRA'S ASSOCIATES	VITO'S ASSOCIATES	BURKE'S ASSOCIATES
Arms Dealer: Jackie DuVernay	Hit Squad: Bobby "Ducks" Navarro	Police Dispatcher: Fiona Davidson
Switchboard Operator: Jennifer "Clicks" Moran	Consigliere: Betty Johnson	Valet: Hank McGahee

Increase the earnings of your Lieutenants to expand the services of their respective Associates. There's only so much money to go around, so invest the services that best suit your play style.

MAFIA RACKET STRUCTURE: THE ENEMY

The Mafia's army of foot soldiers consists of several different roles. Lincoln should keep each one in mind when approaching combat situations.

HEAVY
Carries a shotgun and can take a lot of punishment before going down.

MARKSMAN
Uses a sniper rifle to keep you at a distance.

GUNNER
Mid-range shooter who prefers automatic weapons.

TRIGGERMAN
Uses small arms and explosives to flush the player from cover.

SENTRY

Sentries are cunning criminals who call for reinforcements once they see you. When attacking a group of enemies, watch out for their Sentries. Sentries call in enemy reinforcements who will respond with lethal force. To stop Sentries from calling in reinforcements, neutralize them before they reach the nearest phone or disable the phones using your Operator Associate feature. When the area you're fighting in is wiretapped, Sentries are called out using Intel View.

ENFORCERS

A Racket Boss's heaviest hitter is his Enforcer. Killing Enforcers hurts the Racket Boss's cash and loosens his control over the racket. Keep in mind that any Enforcers left alive before you confront the Racket Boss will be waiting alongside their boss—and they'll be out for blood. For this reason, it's a good idea to take out a Racket Boss's Enforcers before you confront the boss himself.

VEHICLE
SHOWROOM

Mafia III offers you the amazing opportunity to drive a lot of vintage vehicles from 1968 and earlier. They may be lacking in speed and acceleration—compared to modern day vehicles—but what you lose in speed you make up for with style. And without seatbelts, anything over 35 mph is a life-threatening thrill ride.

BEHIND THE WHEEL CONTROLS

XBOX ONE	PLAYSTATION 4	ACTION
CLICK LEFT STICK	L3	HORN
Click Right Stick	R3	Look Behind
RB	R1	Drive-by Shoot
LT	L2	Brake/Reverse
RT	R2	Accelerate
✕	▢	Steal, Enter & Exit Vehicle
Left Stick	Left Analog	Steering
Right Stick	RIGHT ANALOG	Camera
B	◯	Emergency Brake
D-Pad Left & Right	D-Pad Left & Right	Change Radio Station
D-Pad Right (Hold)	D-Pad Right (Hold)	Turn Radio Off/On
LB	L1	Pull up targeting UI to take out opposing vehicles
A	✕	Ram Vehicle

VEHICLE UPGRADES

Vehicle upgrades are rewarded as part of completing districts. You get to pick a vehicle upgrade on the second and fourth district you take over, no matter which district it is. Vehicle upgrades are applied to the Associate Vehicle Delivery vehicles only. Vehicle upgrades are viewed and selected via the Arms Dealer van. By recruiting Cassandra, you gain access to this Associate. As you increase Earn for Underbosses, they will give you access to their Associates and upgrades to their Services. You can view future upgrades for the Arms Dealer in the Assets Menu under Associates & Upgrades.

AVAILABLE ASSOCIATE UPGRADES

UPGRADE NAME	UNLOCKING INFO
Suspension Upgrade	Available as a Favor from Cassandra
Vehicle Armor	Available as a Favor from Cassandra
Drivetrain Upgrade	Available as a Favor from Burke
Bulletproof Tires	Available as a Favor from Burke
Bodykit Upgrade	Available as a Favor from Vito
Supercharger	Available as a Favor from Vito

BOATS

SALMANDAR

CLASS	Swamp Boat	MAX SPEED	★ ☆ ☆ ☆ ☆

SAMSON RAIDER

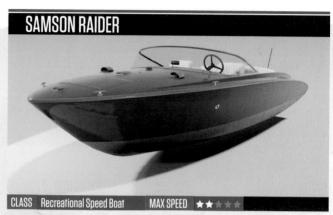

CLASS	Recreational Speed Boat	MAX SPEED	★ ★ ☆ ☆ ☆

NJORD KINGFISHER

CLASS	Swamp Boat	MAX SPEED	★ ☆ ☆ ☆ ☆

SAMSON RAIDER SMUGGLER VERSION

CLASS	Recreational Speed Boat	MAX SPEED	★ ★ ☆ ☆ ☆

NJORD SEAFARER

CLASS	Medium-sized Fishing Boat	MAX SPEED	★ ☆ ☆ ☆ ☆

CUTLER 50

CLASS	Large Recreational Boat	MAX SPEED	★ ☆ ☆ ☆ ☆

ECKHART COLUMBUS

CLASS	Small Recreational Boat	MAX SPEED	★ ★ ☆ ☆ ☆

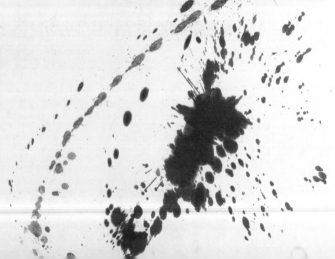

SPORTS

DE'LEO CAPULET

| CLASS | Sports | WEIGHT | ★★☆☆☆ | MAX SPEED | ★★★★★ |

ACCELERATION (SCALE 0 TO 3)

SAMSON OPUS

| CLASS | Sports | WEIGHT | ★★☆☆☆ | MAX SPEED | ★★★★★ |

ACCELERATION (SCALE 0 TO 3)

DELIZIA 58

| CLASS | Sports | WEIGHT | ★★☆☆☆ | MAX SPEED | ★★★★★ |

ACCELERATION (SCALE 0 TO 3)

SMITH MORAY

| CLASS | Sports/Convertible | WEIGHT | ★★★☆☆ | MAX SPEED | ★★★★★ |

ACCELERATION (SCALE 0 TO 3)

DE'LEO KASHMIR

| CLASS | Sports | WEIGHT | ★★☆☆☆ | MAX SPEED | ★★★★☆ |

ACCELERATION (SCALE 0 TO 3)

DE'LEO STILETTO

| CLASS | Sports | WEIGHT | ★★☆☆☆ | MAX SPEED | ★★★★★ |

ACCELERATION (SCALE 0 TO 3)

SAMSON DUKE

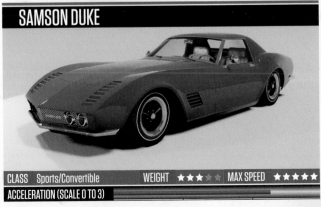

| CLASS | Sports/Convertible | WEIGHT | ★★★☆☆ | MAX SPEED | ★★★★★ |

ACCELERATION (SCALE 0 TO 3)

DE'LEO TRAVIATA

| CLASS | Sports | WEIGHT | ★★☆☆☆ | MAX SPEED | ★★★★★ |

ACCELERATION (SCALE 0 TO 3)

SMITH MORAY MX 100

CLASS	Sports/Convertible	WEIGHT	★★★☆☆	MAX SPEED	★★★★★

ACCELERATION (SCALE 0 TO 3)

MUSCLE

SAMSON DRIFTER

CLASS	Muscle	WEIGHT	★★★☆☆	MAX SPEED	★★★★☆

ACCELERATION (SCALE 0 TO 3)

2-DOOR

BERKLEY GYPSY

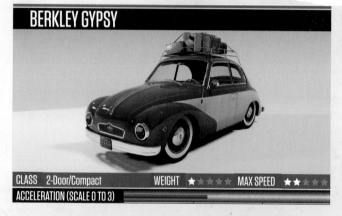

CLASS	2-Door/Compact	WEIGHT	★☆☆☆☆	MAX SPEED	★★☆☆☆

ACCELERATION (SCALE 0 TO 3)

LASSITER LEOPARD

CLASS	Muscle	WEIGHT	★★★☆☆	MAX SPEED	★★★★☆

ACCELERATION (SCALE 0 TO 3)

BERKLEY ALTAMONT

CLASS	2-Door	WEIGHT	★★★☆☆	MAX SPEED	★★★☆☆

ACCELERATION (SCALE 0 TO 3)

BERKLEY STALLION

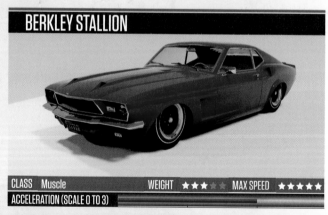

CLASS	Muscle	WEIGHT	★★★☆☆	MAX SPEED	★★★★★

ACCELERATION (SCALE 0 TO 3)

BERKLEY PIXA

CLASS	Compact	WEIGHT	★☆☆☆☆	MAX SPEED	★★☆☆☆

ACCELERATION (SCALE 0 TO 3)

POTOMAC ASCENT

CLASS	Muscle	WEIGHT	★★★☆☆	MAX SPEED	★★★★☆

ACCELERATION (SCALE 0 TO 3)

4-DOOR

POTOMAC GT

CLASS Muscle | WEIGHT ★★★☆☆ | MAX SPEED ★★★★★
ACCELERATION (SCALE 0 TO 3)

POTOMAC HERITAGE

CLASS 4-Door/Station Wagon | WEIGHT ★★★★☆ | MAX SPEED ★★★☆☆
ACCELERATION (SCALE 0 TO 3)

DE'LEO APOLLO

CLASS Muscle | WEIGHT ★★★☆☆ | MAX SPEED ★★★★★
ACCELERATION (SCALE 0 TO 3)

POTOMAC CROCKET

CLASS 4-Door/Station Wagon | WEIGHT ★★★★☆ | MAX SPEED ★★☆☆☆
ACCELERATION (SCALE 0 TO 3)

LASSITER MAMBA

CLASS Muscle | WEIGHT ★★★☆☆ | MAX SPEED ★★★★★
ACCELERATION (SCALE 0 TO 3)

POTOMAC GALLANT

CLASS 4-Door/Convertible | WEIGHT ★★★☆☆ | MAX SPEED ★★★★☆
ACCELERATION (SCALE 0 TO 3)

DE'LEO ANGELENO

CLASS 4-Door | WEIGHT ★★★★☆ | MAX SPEED ★★★★★
ACCELERATION (SCALE 0 TO 3)

POTOMAC INDIANA

| CLASS | 4-Door | WEIGHT | ★★★☆☆ | MAX SPEED | ★★★☆☆ |
| ACCELERATION (SCALE 0 TO 3) | | | | | |

LASSITER BISHOP

| CLASS | 4-Door | WEIGHT | ★★★★☆ | MAX SPEED | ★★★☆☆ |
| ACCELERATION (SCALE 0 TO 3) | | | | | |

POTOMAC UPTOWN

| CLASS | 4-Door/Compact Convertible | WEIGHT | ★★☆☆☆ | MAX SPEED | ★★★☆☆ |
| ACCELERATION (SCALE 0 TO 3) | | | | | |

BERKLEY EXECUTIVE

| CLASS | 4-Door | WEIGHT | ★★★☆☆ | MAX SPEED | ★★★★☆ |
| ACCELERATION (SCALE 0 TO 3) | | | | | |

SAMSON RICHMOND-LUX

| CLASS | 4-Door | WEIGHT | ★★★☆☆ | MAX SPEED | ★★★☆☆ |
| ACCELERATION (SCALE 0 TO 3) | | | | | |

BERKLEY COUNTRY SEDAN

| CLASS | 4-Door/Station Wagon | WEIGHT | ★★★★☆ | MAX SPEED | ★★★★☆ |
| ACCELERATION (SCALE 0 TO 3) | | | | | |

LUXURY

POTOMAC INDEPENDENT

CLASS	Luxury	WEIGHT	★★★★☆	MAX SPEED	★★★★☆

ACCELERATION (SCALE 0 TO 3)

SAMSON STORM

CLASS	Luxury	WEIGHT	★★★★☆	MAX SPEED	★★★★☆

ACCELERATION (SCALE 0 TO 3)

LASSITER PALATINE

CLASS	Luxury	WEIGHT	★★★★★	MAX SPEED	★★★★★

ACCELERATION (SCALE 0 TO 3)

POTOMAC VISCOUNT

CLASS	Luxury	WEIGHT	★★★★☆	MAX SPEED	★★★★☆

ACCELERATION (SCALE 0 TO 3)

LASSITER MAJESTY

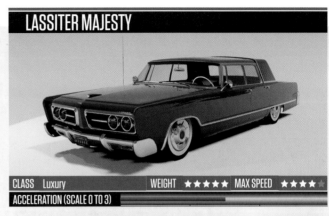

CLASS	Luxury	WEIGHT	★★★★★	MAX SPEED	★★★★☆

ACCELERATION (SCALE 0 TO 3)

LASSITER STERLING

CLASS	Luxury	WEIGHT	★★★★★	MAX SPEED	★★★★☆

ACCELERATION (SCALE 0 TO 3)

LASSITER COURANT

CLASS	Luxury	WEIGHT	★★★★★	MAX SPEED	★★★★★

ACCELERATION (SCALE 0 TO 3)

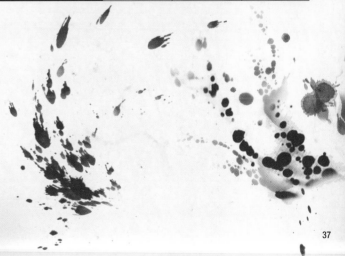

OFFROAD TRUCKS

BULWORTH ASPEN

| CLASS | Offroad | WEIGHT | ★★★☆☆ | MAX SPEED | ★★☆☆☆ |

ACCELERATION (SCALE 0 TO 3)

BULWORTH MOHICAN

| CLASS | Offroad | WEIGHT | ★★★☆☆ | MAX SPEED | ★★★☆☆ |

ACCELERATION (SCALE 0 TO 3)

ECKHART PIONEER

| CLASS | Offroad | WEIGHT | ★★★★☆ | MAX SPEED | ★★★☆☆ |

ACCELERATION (SCALE 0 TO 3)

SAMSON LOKATA

| CLASS | Offroad | WEIGHT | ★★☆☆☆ | MAX SPEED | ★★☆☆☆ |

ACCELERATION (SCALE 0 TO 3)

SAMSON ST 45 TANK TRUCK

| CLASS | Large Truck/Fuel Truck | WEIGHT | ★★★★★ | MAX SPEED | ★★☆☆☆ |

ACCELERATION (SCALE 0 TO 3)

SAMSON GARBAGE TRUCK

| CLASS | Large Truck/Garbage Truck | WEIGHT | ★★★★★ | MAX SPEED | ★☆☆☆☆ |

ACCELERATION (SCALE 0 TO 3)

BULWORTH BUCKLINER 500

| CLASS | Large Truck | WEIGHT | ★★★★★ | MAX SPEED | ★★☆☆☆ |

ACCELERATION (SCALE 0 TO 3)

POTOMAC 550

| CLASS | Truck/Compact | WEIGHT | ★★★★★ | MAX SPEED | ★★☆☆☆ |

ACCELERATION (SCALE 0 TO 3)

SAMSON KINGFISHER

CLASS	Truck	WEIGHT	★★★★★	MAX SPEED	★★☆☆☆
ACCELERATION (SCALE 0 TO 3)					

BULWORTH BANYAN

CLASS	Truck/Delivery	WEIGHT	★★★★★	MAX SPEED	★★☆☆☆
ACCELERATION (SCALE 0 TO 3)					

BULWORTH BUCKLINER 150

CLASS	Delivery/Pickup	WEIGHT	★★☆☆☆	MAX SPEED	★★☆☆☆
ACCELERATION (SCALE 0 TO 3)					

EMERGENCY

SAMSON PROTECTOR

CLASS	4-Door/Police	WEIGHT	★★★☆☆	MAX SPEED	★★★★☆
ACCELERATION (SCALE 0 TO 3)					

GRIFFIN RANCHO GT

CLASS	Delivery/Pickup	WEIGHT	★★★☆☆	MAX SPEED	★★★☆☆
ACCELERATION (SCALE 0 TO 3)					

ECKHART CHAMPION

CLASS	4-Door/Police	WEIGHT	★★★☆☆	MAX SPEED	★★★★☆
ACCELERATION (SCALE 0 TO 3)					

BULWORTH BUCKLINER 75

CLASS	Pickup/Delivery	WEIGHT	★★☆☆☆	MAX SPEED	★★☆☆☆
ACCELERATION (SCALE 0 TO 3)					

WRINKLER 353 MILITARY

CLASS	Truck/Compact/Military	WEIGHT	★★★★★	MAX SPEED	★★☆☆☆
ACCELERATION (SCALE 0 TO 3)					

SAMSON RHINO

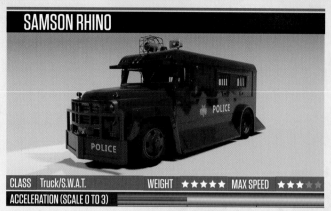

CLASS	Truck/S.W.A.T.	WEIGHT	★★★★★	MAX SPEED	★★★☆☆
ACCELERATION (SCALE 0 TO 3)					

SPECIAL

BULWORTH MOBILE STORE

CLASS	Delivery	WEIGHT	★★☆☆☆	MAX SPEED	★★★☆☆
ACCELERATION (SCALE 0 TO 3)					

PINKERTON TITAN

CLASS	Truck/Armored	WEIGHT	★★★★★	MAX SPEED	★★★☆☆
ACCELERATION (SCALE 0 TO 3)					

BULWORTH FREIGHT

CLASS	Delivery/Station Wagon	WEIGHT	★★★☆☆	MAX SPEED	★★☆☆☆
ACCELERATION (SCALE 0 TO 3)					

WRINKLER

CLASS	Utility	WEIGHT	★★★★★	MAX SPEED	★☆☆☆☆
ACCELERATION (SCALE 0 TO 3)					

ECKHART TAXI

CLASS	Taxi	WEIGHT	★★★☆☆	MAX SPEED	★★★☆☆
ACCELERATION (SCALE 0 TO 3)					

BULWORTH HEARSE

CLASS	Special	WEIGHT	★★★★★	MAX SPEED	★★★★☆
ACCELERATION (SCALE 0 TO 3)					

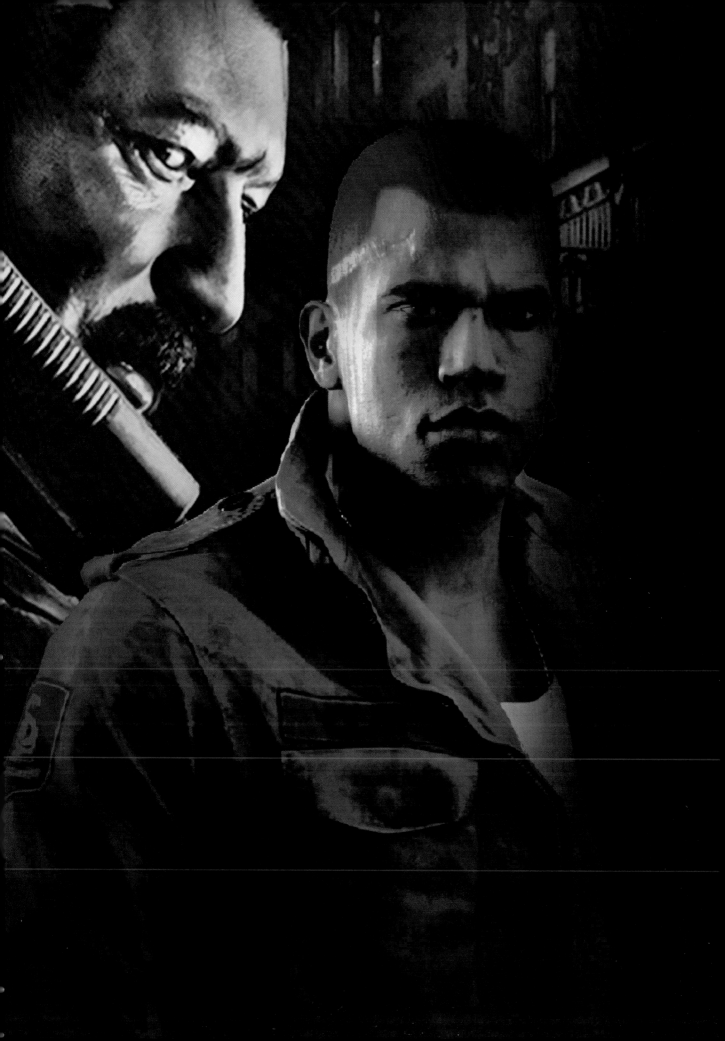

STORY
MISSIONS

As our story begins, Mafia III introduces its documentary-style frame and sets up the game's historical context: a 1960s America mired in an unpopular war, jolted by violent crime and political assassinations, and challenged by growing civil unrest. The cinematic opening mixes bright, tourist-friendly images of New Bordeaux, Louisiana with dark glimpses of the blood-soaked mob war at the heart of Mafia III.

The intro features snippets of interviews with Father James Ballard, retired priest at St. Jerome's Catholic Church in New Bordeaux's French Ward district, and with Jonathan Maguire, the FBI's former Assistant Director, Criminal Enterprise Branch from 1966-1999. It also includes recorded, on-the-record testimony from a former CIA agent, John Donovan, at a 1971 Senate Select Committee on Intelligence hearing in Washington. All speak of Lincoln Clay and his infamous vendetta against the Italian mob in New Bordeaux.

"This city survived the War of 1812, the Civil War, and God knows how many hurricanes. But when Lincoln Clay went after the mob, he inflicted more damage than all the wars and hurricanes combined."

Father James and Agent Donovan also provide some of Lincoln Clay's backstory: the abandoned boy who grew up in an orphanage then fell in with the local African-American mob led by Sammy Robinson. Lincoln eventually shipped off to Vietnam and became a highly decorated special forces soldier—two Purple Hearts, a Bronze Star, and the Distinguished Service Cross.

As the prologue ends, we learn that Lincoln Clay mustered out of the Army in 1968 and returned to Sammy's Bar in New Bordeaux's Delray Hollow district. There he discovered that Sammy was in trouble: he owed a lot of money to the powerful Italian crime syndicate that ran the city and took a cut from every racket.

NEW BORDEAUX:
THE HOME FIRES BURN

MISSION: "WHY TAKE THE CHANCE?"

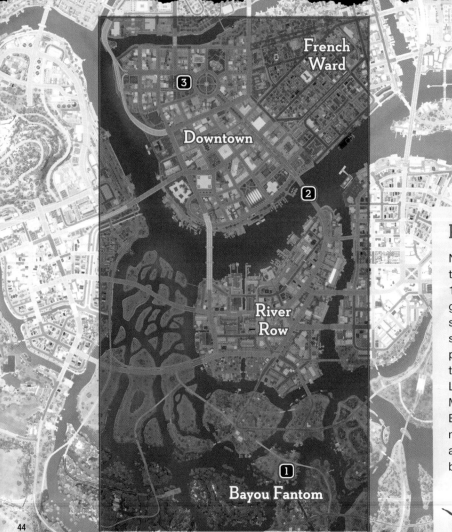

French
Ward

Downtown

River
Row

Bayou Fantom

LEGEND

1. Start
   (Warehouse)

2. Bridge Route to
   Downtown

3. Federal Reserve
   Bank

PREREQUISITE: START THE GAME

Now we jump into the action: a brazen heist of the Federal Reserve Bank. The date: February 12, 1968. From the outset, you control the game's protagonist, Lincoln Clay. Dressed as security guards, Lincoln and Giorgi Marcano—son of Sal Marcano, head of the Italian mob—plan to use a stolen armored delivery van to gain access to the Reserve's main vault. Lincoln and Giorgi form the heist's inside team. Meanwhile, two other co-conspirators, Danny Burke and Ellis Robinson (Sammy's son), will maneuver a big industrial drill via boat through a system of underground canals to a position beneath the vault's floor.

As in most games, the first handful of missions in Mafia III serve as a tutorial to introduce you to basic controls and tactics.

OBJECTIVE: Pick Up the Keys

You start out inside an abandoned warehouse **(1)** down in the Bayou Fantom. A Federal Reserve delivery van is parked at the open garage door; nearby, Giorgi counts bills from bags of cash provided by Vito Scaletta, an Italian mobster familiar to fans of *Mafia II*.

FINDING OBJECTIVES

As you move through New Bordeaux, the direction and distance (measured in meters) to your currently active objective appears onscreen as a white number inside a white diamond. This is your objective marker.

Walk across the room and climb the opposite staircase. Approach the door at the top and open it by pressing the control button that appears on the door.

Enter the room to find one bank guard bound with a bag over his head, and another "greased" on the floor. If you approach the bound guard, a control button prompt appears on his head.

Shoot the helpless guard? Or leave him be?

45

Here's your first moral decision: You can press that button to grease the bound guard too, or simply leave him alone. Then follow the onscreen objective diamond to find the keys to the armored delivery truck. Approach the keys and hold down the button indicated to pick them up. Your next objective appears onscreen.

OBJECTIVE: Get in the Armored Truck

Exit the room. You can't squeeze past the armored truck parked in the garage doorway, so exit via the door in the corner. Continue through the opening in the chain-link fence and approach the truck's driver-side door. Hold the Enter Vehicle button indicated to hop behind the wheel of the Pinkerton Titan. When Giorgi slides into the passenger seat, Lincoln automatically starts the engine.

CAR FACTS

Whenever you enter a vehicle, its make and model appear in the lower-left corner of the screen.

SETTING OBJECTIVES

This icon marks the map location of an inactive objective.

Open your Map view at any time to see Lincoln's current location marked by a black arrow icon. Scan across the map to find available objectives, marked as colored icons. If the objective icon is diamond-shaped and flashing, it is your currently active objective. If not flashing, it is an inactive objective. (These same icons also appear in the Minimap in the lower left corner of the game view screen.)

This flashing diamond icon marks the map location of an active objective.

If an objective is set to active, your map automatically creates a trip route, a white line that leads from your current location to the active objective's location. Note that in the game's early going, only one objective is available at a time. But later in the story, you may find many objectives available, sometimes in different districts of the city.

You can set objectives to active or inactive. On the Map screen, just move your cursor over an objective icon to open a popup window showing the chapter, mission, and a text description of that objective. If the objective is currently active, a white triangle appears in the upper-left corner of its

Your map automatically plots a trip route to the active objective.

description box. You can select to deactivate the objective, if you want.

While on the Map screen you can also press the Objectives button displayed at bottom left to open the Objectives Panel. This brings up detailed lists of chapters, missions and objectives. Later in the game, when multiple chapters are open at the same time, you can scroll across them to check for available objectives. To activate a different objective, just highlight and select it. Your map automatically creates a new trip route to the newly active objective. (Note that mission objectives you've already completed are checked off.)

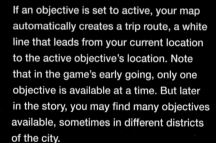

Open the Objectives Panel for a more detailed listing of chapters, missions, and objectives.

OBJECTIVE: Drive to the Federal Reserve

Vehicle operation instructions appear onscreen. (Be sure to check out the "Driving" section in our Basics chapter for some good driving tips.) Open the Map screen to see that a white trip route has appeared; it leads from your current location in Bayou Fantom to your next objective, the Federal Reserve Bank in the Downtown district of New Bordeaux. Use the driving controls to follow the white route that leads you over the bridge **(2)** connecting River Row to Downtown.

Follow the trip route and use the handy directional arrow signs (see Tip) to keep you on course.

ROAD ARROWS

Note that strategically placed road signs along the trip route include white directional arrows that point the way, corresponding to the map's route. Watch for them as you drive! Following these arrows helps keep you on track without constantly checking your maps.

As you travel, be sure to listen to the trip conversation between Lincoln and Giorgi. You learn details of the heist plan and pick up interesting bits of backstory—including Lincoln's harrowing tale of a special forces operation off the coast of Quang Ngai in Vietnam. Note his conclusion: "You put people up against the wall, they will do *anything* to survive."

DESTINATION MARKER

A green arrow sign always marks the endpoint of each map route.

Also note that the distance in meters displayed inside the onscreen objective marker steadily decreases as you follow the route. Shortly after you cross the Downtown bridge **(2)**, you arrive at your destination. Look for the sign with the green arrow pointing down **(3)** and pull into that spot. This triggers the mission-ending cutscene: the gate guard checks IDs then Lincoln backs up the truck to the bank's loading dock.

UNLOCKS: "This Changes Everything"

MISSION: "THIS CHANGES EVERYTHING"

PREREQUISITES:

COMPLETE "WHY TAKE THE CHANCE?"

As the delivery truck reaches the dock, the new mission title appears onscreen. Then your next objective appears too.

OBJECTIVE: Enter the Federal Reserve

Press the button indicated onscreen to exit the vehicle. Then follow Giorgi to the security door. When it opens, follow your partner inside the bank.

OBJECTIVE: Pick Up the Money

Turn left and walk to the back of the delivery van. Hold down the button indicated to grab the two bags of money.

OBJECTIVE: Follow the Guard

Haul the cash, following the guard and Giorgi to the security cage. After Giorgi checks his shotgun at the desk (the guard calls it a "scattergun"), the next gate opens. Follow the guard and Giorgi again as they head past the Break Room and then downstairs to the Vault area. Proceed into the "burn room."

OBJECTIVE: Place Money on the Table

Approach the table indicated by the destination diamond and hold down the indicated button to dump the money bags.

Giorgi starts tossing stacks of the old money piled on the table into the nearby oil-burning furnace.

OBJECTIVE: Kill the Burner Guard

Walk around the chattering racist guard and sneak up behind him. To perform a silent takedown, press and hold the button prompted onscreen. Lincoln slams the fool's head into the burner.

OBJECTIVE: Deal with the Guards

As Giorgi starts jimmying the side gate with a pry bar, he tells Lincoln to take care of the guards in the next room. Here the action freezes for a second. Press the Crouch control shown onscreen to crouch. When Giorgi finally pries open the gate, creep through the darkened next room and sneak up behind the first guard. Press the Cover button shown onscreen to duck down behind the big money stack.

Make sure the second guard across the room isn't looking, and then follow the onscreen instructions to execute a silent takedown on the first guard.

Creep out to pick up the Alfredsson M419 revolver that the first guard drops. Then sneak across the room behind the second guard. Take him down silently too and pick up his Trench 1938 assault rifle. Now you've got a sidearm and a long gun.

OBJECTIVE: Enter the Vault

Join Giorgi at the massive vault door and press the button prompt shown to trigger a cutscene: Giorgi enters the lock combination provided by Scaletta. It works! Inside, the pair starts gathering stacks of cash. Unfortunately, Giorgi opens a side cage and sets off an alarm!

OBJECTIVE: Defend Giorgi

FIRST WAVE

Now you have to fight off waves of bank guards until the drilling team down in the tunnel manages to bore up through the vault floor.

Three armed guards appear in the first wave. Hustle to take cover behind the gold stacks and target foes through the open gates. Try to gun down all three guards before they can deploy; once they do, they'll try to work around your flanks and attack from the side rooms on your left and right.

> **STOCK UP AFTER FIGHTS!**
>
> During lulls in fighting, reload both of your weapons then scavenge any dropped ammo from fallen foes. Do this whenever you clear an area of enemies, if possible. You can also swap your weapons for other models your foes have dropped, if you want.

SECOND WAVE

After a few seconds, the security doors slide open behind the green exit sign (circled in our screenshot) and a second wave of three guards emerges. Again, try to gun them down before they can scatter to the flanks. Once you eliminate this second wave, Lincoln tells Giorgi, "The only way we walk out of here is

with the weapons stored in that armory." Giorgi starts working on the armory door with his pry bar, but can't get it open. Now you get a new objective.

OBJECTIVE: Pry Open Armory Gate

Follow the objective marker to where Giorgi struggles with the pry bar on the armory gate's lock. Approach and press the prompted button to seize the bar. This brings up your next objective.

OBJECTIVE: Grab the Hartmann Machine Gun

The Hartmann Machine Gun is stashed in the armory, but you can't reach it until you pry open the gate's lock mechanism. See our "Lock Pulling"

sidebar for instructions on how to use the pry bar to open the gate. (You'll use this technique many times in the game, so learn it well.)

Enter the armory and pick up the fully loaded Hartmann 7.62mm machinegun from the table. You can also snag the Blackburn FAF-33 revolver sitting next to it. Be sure to grab an Adrenaline Shot from the Medicine Cabinet on the wall.

LOCK PULLING

Step 1: Expose the Lock

Use the control shown onscreen to move your pry bar in a circle and expose the lock mechanism. When the green "sweet spot" appears, keep rotating slowly until the green zone is smallest then press the button displayed to set the spot.

Step 2: Jimmy the Lock Loose

Setting the spot starts the meter, a line that moves back and forth across the arc. Hit the button shown again just as the line moves into the green zone. If you time it right, Lincoln jimmies the lock loose.

OBJECTIVE: Regroup with Giorgi

Move back into the main room. The moment you do, another wave of guards arrives through the security door. This time they toss smoke flares to reduce visibility. As you move to meet this new threat, the scene abruptly cuts to Assistant Director Maguire, who fills in more of the backstory.

UNLOCKS: "A Taste of the Action"

MISSION: "A TASTE OF THE ACTION"

Southdowns

Delray
Hollow

River
Row

LEGEND

1 **Start (Train Station)**

2 **Sammy's Bar**

PREREQUISITES:

COMPLETE "THIS CHANGES EVERYTHING"

Here you make a jump in time to one week earlier: February 20, 1968. Lincoln Clay, just back from Vietnam, sits on a bench outside the New Bordeaux train station **(1)** in the Southdowns district. His adoptive brother, Ellis Robinson, arrives in Lincoln's old Samson Drifter to pick him up.

OBJECTIVE: Drive to Sammy's Bar

After Lincoln and Ellis hop into the car, open your Map screen, then move your cursor westward (to the left) until it's over the yellow objective icon and select it. Activate the only available objective, "Drive to Sammy's Bar." The map auto-creates a white route from your current location to Sammy's bar.

Now close the map and follow that route, driving Lincoln's car from the Southdowns train station to Sammy's bar in Delray Hollow. Listen to the conversation en route to pick up backstory info. Ellis tries to get Lincoln to join in on his plans to sell heroin with Giorgi Marcano, but Lincoln demurs. When you arrive at the green destination marker **(2)**, hop out of the car and go to the front entrance of Sammy's.

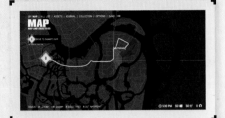

POLICE AWARENESS

When any cop (either on foot or in a squad car) is close enough to be aware of you, a blue indicator appears onscreen in the center. You also see a police icon appear on your Minimap. Avoid breaking laws when that blue indicator is visible. (For more detail, see the "Police Awareness" section of the Basics chapter.)

OBJECTIVE: Talk to Sammy

Open the door to trigger a long cinematic: watch Lincoln's joyous homecoming, and then listen to Father James try to describe what it's like coming home from a terrible war.

OBJECTIVE: Go to Bed

After the scene, Lincoln stands on the stairs leading down to Sammy's basement. Head downstairs and turn through the door on the left. Then approach the bed and press the prompted button to fade into the story's next day.

OBJECTIVE: Talk to Sammy and Ellis

Once Lincoln gets out of bed the next day, go pick up your first two collectible items, both in the basement room. Then head upstairs to the first floor.

FIRST COLLECTIBLES

In Sammy's basement, note that you can open your map and find blue icons marking the locations of nearby collectibles. First, follow the blue bunny icon to pick up the August 1964 issue of *Playboy* magazine sitting atop the desk directly across from Lincoln's bed. This is the first of four *Playboys* you can find in Delray Hollow.

In the same room, find the Alberto Vargas painting hanging on the brick support pillar (on the side facing away from the bed). It's the first of four Vargas paintings you can collect in Delray Hollow. Each Vargas painting in New Bordeaux was a gift from Sal Marcano, the city's mob boss.

This triggers another long cinematic: Lincoln interrupts a heated discussion between Sammy and Ellis and learns about trouble with the Haitian gang in Delray Hollow. Then Father James enters and asks for help in hauling a food donation from Sammy's Bar to the soup kitchen a few blocks away.

UNLOCKS: "Everyone Else Will Go Down"

MISSION: "EVERYONE ELSE WILL GO DOWN"

LEGEND

1 Sammy's Bar

2 Soup Kitchen

PREREQUISITES:

COMPLETE "A TASTE OF THE ACTION"

Lincoln and Father James park the delivery truck behind "Warm Hearts, Warm Souls," the neighborhood soup kitchen that serves poor folks in Delray Hollow. It's February 21, 1968—six days before Mardi Gras. As they approach the back entrance, Lincoln is telling Father James about his plans to train as an apprentice welder in California.

OBJECTIVE: Follow Father James

Your first task is easy: just walk through the open door into the soup kitchen. Father James asks you to start serving the folks lined up for food.

ALBUM COVER COLLECTIBLES

As the game points out, an entire generation found its rebellious voice in the music of the 1960s. Throughout New

Bordeaux you can find the classic covers of landmark albums recorded during that turbulent decade.

Step inside the soup kitchen, enter the office to the left, and pick up the album cover for *This Is Clarence Carter* sitting on the desk. It's one of four covers you can collect in Delray Hollow.

OBJECTIVE: Serve the Gumbo

Follow the objective marker to the service window then hold the prompted button to start serving gumbo to the guests. Hold the button again

as each guest steps up to the gumbo pot. Serve all five folks in line.

Watch as Lincoln chats with Raejeanne for a bit. As they banter, you can see a red convertible with three Haitian thugs pull up outside on the street. A moment later they burst through the front door, guns blazing!

OBJECTIVE: Kill the Haitians

Lincoln is unarmed, but he automatically tosses the hot gumbo pot into the face of the first approaching Haitian. Use the controls displayed onscreen to hop over the counter then launch a brawling melee attack on the gumbo-blinded fellow. Once you KO the hatted Haitian, punch out the second Haitian who approaches with raised fists to brawl.

The third Haitian is armed with a pistol. You can try to rush him, or else dive into cover at the left end of the nearby counter and wait until he approaches. Then pop up and knock him out too.

When the last Haitian falls, another cinematic plays. Lincoln finds a small pouch filled with odd trinkets on one of the thugs. Then Assistant Director Maguire fills in more of the backstory about the Haitian refugees who fled the regime of Papa Doc Duvalier, the brutal and superstitious president of Haiti from 1957 to 1971.

Led by a man named Baka, Haitian gangsters have been pushing aggressively into Delray Hollow, robbing folks and disrupting Sammy's lottery racket.

As a result, Sammy is three months behind in his payments to Sal Marcano—a predicament that could have lethal consequences. Sammy asks Lincoln and Ellis to eliminate the Haitian problem; he says Baka's hideout is likely an old salt-mining shantytown in the Bayou Fantom.

UNLOCKS: "NEVER GOING TO BE OVER"

MISSION: "NEVER GOING TO BE OVER"

LEGEND

1 Start
2 Shantytown Dock
3 Old Church
4 Getaway Car (Ellis)
5 Sammy's

PREREQUISITES:

COMPLETE "EVERYONE ELSE WILL GO DOWN"

As the mission opens (1), Ellis and Lincoln cross the Bayou Fantom in a Salamander airboat. Their primary target: Baka, leader of the Haitian gang. As you approach the shantytown dock, Lincoln tells Ellis to return to the car by the road and wait. Note the big church rising from the far side of the shantytown.

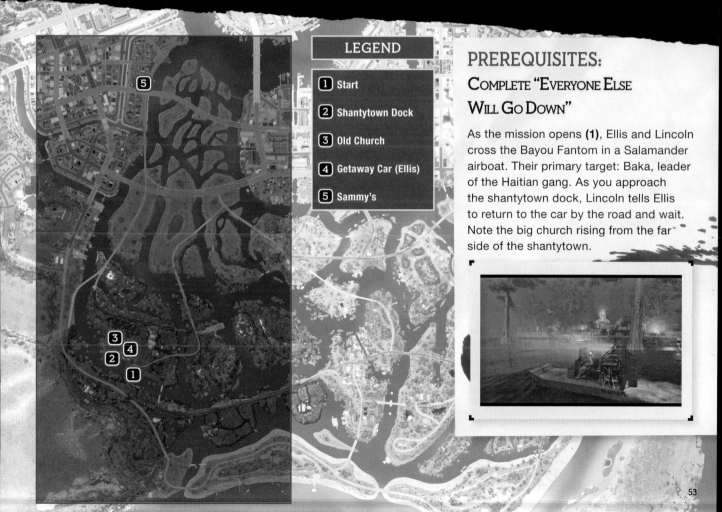

OBJECTIVE: Swim to the Dock

When you gain control, step off the boat and swim to the dock, following the objective marker. When you reach the dock, press the button displayed at lower-left to climb out of the water.

OBJECTIVE: Find Baka

Church

West Side

East Side

G

F

H

E

D

C

A

Dock

B

Shantytown: Overhead

CLEAR THE DOCK

Now you must work your way through the old shantytown to Baka. Your best bet is to take out the first few Haitian guards silently, one by one. (See our Tips in this mission, and check out the "Stalking" section in our Basics chapter.) Our walkthrough relies on such stealth tactics. But you are free to rush in with guns blazing and try to shoot your way across the town, if you want.

BAYOU STALKING

Stealth tactics are fun, and can make progress through well-defended areas considerably easier.

First, sneak up the dock stairs, turn left and take cover at the end of the makeshift fence **(A)**. Listen to the two guards converse by the gate. Once they split up, one heads off to the right, and the other descends the stairs toward you. When he stops and turns away from you to light a cigarette, stalk up behind him until you see the Melee attack button prompt. Press it to execute a silent takedown!

THE ENEMY'S AWARENESS INDICATOR

When an enemy sees or hears you, a white exclamation point icon appears over his head and a white Enemy Awareness Indicator (an arc with an arrow pointing toward the enemy) appears onscreen. The more the enemy sees and hears you, the more his white indicator arc expands.

If the arc gets too big, the enemy comes to investigate, raising the chance you'll get identified as a threat that triggers a full alert in the area. Take cover and keep low until he stops looking for you and the white indicator arc disappears. Alternatively: if no witnesses are nearby, wait until the enemy approaches your hiding spot and the Melee button prompt appears. Then execute a silent takedown.

Next, sneak to the far right end of the dock where another guard warms himself at a barrel fire **(B)**. Take him down from behind! Then double back to the

After you clear the docks, head through the boathouse.

same spot before you took down the first guard **(A)**. When the pacing guard moves to the right, follow him until he turns to go around the boat. Sneak up behind him for another silent takedown.

The immediate area is now clear. From here, the only way into the shantytown is through the boathouse to the right of the covered boat.

CLEAR THE TOWN CENTER

Enter the boathouse. (If you head downstairs you can find a nice Automat SG assault rifle.) Upstairs, take cover at the far

doorway (next to the wall mask) and observe the two guards out in the yard by a campfire. When one patrols away, hustle out to take cover behind either the table or the woodpile and whistle to draw the remaining guard. Take him down silently!

WHISTLING

Whistling lets you lure foes individually to where you're hiding so you can perform silent takedowns without triggering a general alert. It's also a great way to draw clumps of enemies apart. Just position yourself behind cover a good distance away from your targets. Whistle until one foe wanders over to investigate, and then take him down. (If no enemies register awareness when you whistle, move closer.) Repeat if more goons are in the area.

Now head across the clearing past the campfire then sneak around the corner of the hut to find the other guard. He stands on the other side of a low wall with his back to you. Sneak up behind and knock him out.

Now hustle from the low wall across the yard into the next hut **(F)**. Take cover under the far window and observe the cluster of four guards **(G)** out in the next yard.

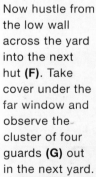

Then slide to cover at the open doorway to the left and start whistling to draw guards away from the crowd, one by one.

When each comes to investigate, take them down in the doorway. You can eliminate three of the four clustered guards this way. To get the fourth guard's attention, you'll have to get closer; sneak across the yard to the old leather sofa then whistle.

CLEAR THE WEST SIDE

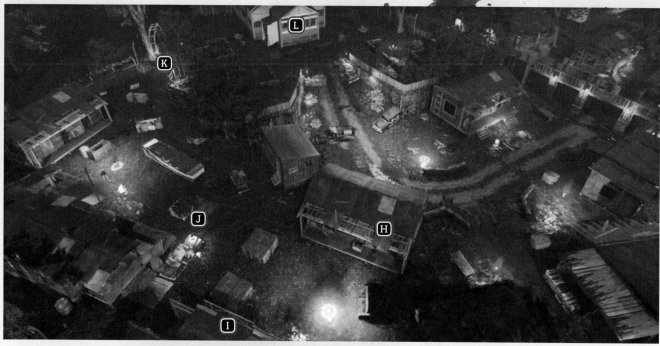

Shantytown: West Side

Check the map to see a yellow circle that surrounds the old church; Baka is somewhere within that zone. But another goon platoon is deployed across the western edge of the shantytown. Before you assault the church, move across the yard into the house **(H)** where you find a Medicine Cabinet inside. Snag the Adrenaline Shot from the cabinet then take cover at the open doorway next to it. Whistle to lure the guard posted by the fire and take him down.

Observe the next guard pacing through the hut on the opposite side of the yard **(I)**. Wait until he can't see you then hustle across to the doorway. When he paces past, take him down! Move down the yard, dashing from cover to cover **(J)**, until you can lure each of the remaining guards for silent takedowns. Then move through the reddish metal arch **(K)** to enter the churchyard.

Reach the churchyard through this metal arch.

Gun down the two guards posted just outside the church and climb onto the church's entry porch **(L)**, where you can plunder another Medicine Cabinet on the wall. (Be sure to open it for the Adrenaline Shot inside.) Then approach the doors and press the Kick Door control displayed at lower-left on your screen.

OBJECTIVE: Confront Baka

Immediately open fire on Baka, who stands just 13 meters away at the altar across the floor. He's tough, but after a few good hits he drops to a knee, wounded, with a skull icon over his head. Approach and hold down the button indicated to trigger a cutscene: Lincoln confronts Baka and sets a haunted captive free.

OBJECTIVE: Get to Ellis

Shantytown: East Side

CLEAR THE CHURCHYARD

Time to flee this deadly shantytown. Ellis is waiting for you in the car by the exit road. But a tossed Molotov cocktail (a bottle of gasoline with a lit rag as a fuse) explodes in a deadly fireball at the church entrance. Outside, a big squad of vengeful Haitians seeks to block your escape.

One option is to just rush out onto the porch **(L)**, take cover, and start shooting attackers in the yard below **(M)**. But another effective option is to fight fire with fire! Before you exit the church, grab the Molotov bottle on the floor right in front of you then hustle to the low open compartment underneath the cow skull hanging on the wall to grab another Molotov.

Now you've got two Molotov cocktails in your weapon inventory.

Step out onto the church porch, take cover, select Molotov cocktail in your inventory wheel, and toss the two firebombs into groups of enemies.

MOLOTOV TOSSING

Molotov cocktails can be very effective against clustered groups of enemies. You can nail foes even when they're in cover, and take out multiple enemies with one throw!

After you toss the first two Molotovs, you can reenter the church and hustle through the closed door at the back of the room to find two more Molotov bottles on a table. (Find the Medicine Cabinet on the wall as well.) Grab them and go toss them at the hostile gangsters in the yard below the church. Try to nail the car that pulls up to trigger an explosion. When your Molotovs are gone, mop up any survivors using your guns.

CLEAR THE EAST SIDE

Descend through the churchyard, picking up dropped ammo and, if you want, swapping out weapons. At the bottom, turn left and take cover behind the junked car as more Haitian thugs open fire from a raised walkway **(N)**. Target the red explosive barrel on the upper walkway (see our screenshot) to trigger a fearsome explosion that takes out the nearby gunman.

Target explosive red barrels when enemies are near them.

Push forward to the walkway structure and take cover. More shooters open fire from the other side. Target the red gas can **(O)** sitting on a crate to the right to eliminate another gunman. Then fight your way down the road, dashing forward from cover to cover and picking up dropped ammo as you move past fallen foes. Be ready to dodge Molotovs tossed your way! You can find Medicine Cabinets inside the first hut on the right side of the lane, and in the last hut on the left side **(P)**. Look for more Molotov pickups in the huts too.

Keep pushing down the lane until you hear Ellis honking the horn of Lincoln's car. Watch out for one last gunman who may be posted at the exit gate (circled in our shot) then sprint to the car and hop in. Ellis automatically hops out of the driver's side and goes around to get in the passenger side as Lincoln slides behind the wheel.

OBJECTIVE: Drive to Sammy's

Now open your map and select the objective diamond up in Delray Hollow to map a route back to Sammy's Bar **(5)**. Drive that route, listening to the trip conversation on the way. When you arrive at the green-arrow destination marker, exit the vehicle and follow the objective marker inside the garage to trigger a cinematic: Lincoln learns that Sal Marcano wants to meet him at the country club up in Frisco Fields.

UNLOCKS: "...TIME TO MAKE A CHANGE"

MISSION: "...TIME TO MAKE A CHANGE"

LEGEND

1. Start (Sammy's)
2. Frisco Fields Country Club

PREREQUISITES:
COMPLETE "NEVER GOING TO BE OVER"

OBJECTIVE: Drive to the Retrousse Yacht Club

Exit Sammy's garage and hop in Lincoln's car parked on the street. Follow the trip route north to Frisco Fields and into the green-arrow destination marker in the entry drive of the Retrousse Yacht Club.

OBJECTIVE: Talk to Security

Follow the new short trip route to the next destination marker at the club's security gate. After Lincoln exchanges pleasantries with the gate guard, the gate opens.

OBJECTIVE: Meet Giorgi

Drive to the next destination marker in front of the club to trigger a long cinematic.

Giorgi greets Lincoln and escorts him to a meeting with his father, Sal Marcano, the don of New Bordeaux. Lincoln also meets Vito Scaletta, formerly of Empire Bay, now one of Marcano's local lieutenants.

Sal lays out his plan for the Federal Reserve heist; you learn that Vito is fronting the "burn money" for the job, and has also provided the bank vault's combination. Then Sal proposes another, more troubling proposition—one regarding the future of Delray Hollow.

UNLOCKS: "STILL PULL THIS OFF"

MISSION: "STILL PULL THIS OFF"

PREREQUISITES:

COMPLETE "...TIME TO MAKE A CHANGE"

Here you return to the point where you left off inside the U.S. Federal Reserve during the game-opening mission. It's February 27, 1968—Mardis Gras in New Bordeaux. Smoke grenades now obscure your vision in the vault, and a new wave of four guards arrives via the far doors.

OBJECTIVE: Kill the Guards

Take the game's advice and use Intel View to spot the red outlines of hostile guards through the smoke. Lincoln is still armed with the Hartmann 7.62mm machinegun, a powerful weapon that eviscerates targets quickly. You can push forward more aggressively through the room, taking down targets with the gun's quick bursts.

Intel View is very useful in low-visibility situations like darkness or smoke.

OBJECTIVE: Regroup with Giorgi

After the fourth guard drops, Giorgi calls out that the drill is through the floor! Before you rejoin him, go back to the Medicine Cabinet in the armory to grab another Adrenaline Shot. Then hustle back into the vault to watch the floor crack, sparks fly, and a hole open. From below, Ellis reports that they're making room for the money drop. But suddenly, the vault goes dark.

OBJECTIVE: Defend Giorgi

Once again, use your Intel View to spot the outlines of foes in the dark. Another wave of four guards arrives carrying flashlights. Once you take out these four, the emergency lights flicker on and a final assault begins: ten guards arriving in waves, this time emerging from the wing elevators on either side of the vault! Keep them away from Giorgi, who is busy dropping money through the drilled hole.

OBJECTIVE: Get to the Vault

When you finally clear the area, return to Giorgi in the vault. This triggers a scene: below, Danny Burke plants TNT, planning to blast a floor hole big enough for Lincoln and Giorgi to drop down. But the explosion destroys the floor supports and the entire vault drops into the canal tunnel!

OBJECTIVE: Get to the Boat

After the fall, exit via the vault door into the canal. You see Ellis Robinson and Danny Burke—looks like Danny got his leg smashed in the unexpectedly large blast. This triggers a quick documentary interlude: Assistant Director Maguire explains how Sal Marcano pulled control of the Pointe Verdun district from the Irish mob run by Thomas Burke and gave it to an enforcer named Roman "The Butcher" Barbieri… who promptly sent a message by shattering one of Burke's legs. Maguire also profiles Burke's son, Danny, a "gearhead" and part of the Federal Reserve heist crew.

Then the scene switches to Burke's Iron & Metal shop the day before the heist, February 26. As Thomas Burke tests the industrial drill for the heist, the team meets up for the first time. Listen to Thomas describe the logistics of the operation.

The sequence ends with a return to the documentary: a bitter, scathing testimonial from Thomas Burke's daughter, Nicole "Nicki" Burke. She explains how Burke knew of the old canals from his days of running moonshine, including the canal running directly under the Federal Reserve. And she blames him for how the heist turned out…

UNLOCKS: "DAMN IF THIS AIN'T A GAS"

MISSION: "DAMN IF THIS AIN'T A GAS"

PREREQUISITES: "Still Pull This Off"

Once the cinematic ends, you're dropped right into a hot mess. The full heist crew is now aboard their boat, the *Snatch & Dash*, but armed guards are swarming into the canal, and Danny is hurt.

OBJECTIVE: Escape

You control the boat, so accelerate hard and steer straight ahead. About 600 meters down the canal (when your objective marker reads 1275) a police launch dashes in from a channel on the left, and then a second police launch veers in from the right. Keep your throttle wide open; your boat is faster than theirs.

> **CHECK YOUR STERN**
>
> Press the Rearview control shown onscreen to look behind your boat and survey the pursuit.

When your objective marker reads 950 meters, a third police launch swerves across your path from the left. Ram it if you want, but if your boat takes too much damage you fail the mission! At 500 meters, a cave-in obstruction blocks the right-hand channel, so veer over to the left channel and punch it hard.

Police boats try to cut you off!

The left channel ends at 100 meters, but don't slow down! Steer directly onto the ramp-like section of corrugated metal and watch the boat catapult out of the canal. Then watch the cinematic as the team climbs up a ladder to street level.

UNLOCKS: "...A Friend in Jesus"

MISSION: "...A FRIEND IN JESUS"

PREREQUISITES: "DAMN IF THIS AIN'T A GAS"

Your ultimate goal now is to get back to Sammy's Bar in one piece without getting caught. Fortunately for the heist team, New Bordeaux's French Ward district is teeming with wild Mardis Gras revelers. This gives you plenty of cover as Lincoln carries the wounded Danny Burke past the police presence in the streets.

OBJECTIVE: Find a Payphone

When in doubt, follow Giorgi as he pushes through the crowd. Proceed past the first fountain and around the corner to the right. Follow that flagstone lane out to the wider walkway then turn left. Move down the right side of the walkway until you reach the payphone that Giorgi secures for you.

OBJECTIVE: Call Sammy

Approach the payphone and press the button prompted to call Sammy. He can't get a car to your location because the roads are closed off. Sammy sends you to a nearby grocery store on the back side of the cemetery; he'll stash a getaway car at the loading dock.

OBJECTIVE: Go to the Getaway Car

After you hang up, turn left and walk through the black archway with the Teach's Alley sign. Turn right and move down the street through the big parade floats. The street is blocked off, so turn right and enter the Deep Dive Bar & Lounge. Move through the bar and exit via the back door.

You emerge onto a small plaza. Keep an eye on your Minimap to see the objective marker, and keep working toward it. Veer left through the plaza and walk past the police car. On its radio you hear a report that the cops have found the heist team's abandoned boat and are closing in on the French Ward.

Follow the street to the right, through the green archway.

Then stroll past more parade floats and the striped barricades where a police van blocks the street.

Veer to the right of the barricades and follow the street until you trigger the cutscene: NBPD units are aggressively searching the crowd up ahead. Lincoln sends the other guys on to Sammy's getaway car while he diverts police attention. Giorgi slips him something to help the cause.

Now the going gets intense. As the crowd panics, sprint through the open passage in the street-front directly ahead. (To sprint, hold down the control shown onscreen.) It leads to a back alley.

RED & BLUE POLICE ZONES

As the game points out, cops in a red zone are "in a shoot-first, ask-questions-later state of mind." Open your map and check the boundary of the flashing Active Police Zone then try to get outside of it while losing the pursuit, or else try hiding until the Police Awareness level drops to a blue zone.

Cops within a Blue Police Zone (also displayed on your map) still search for you, but less aggressively. You can move stealthily, avoiding contact until you get outside the zone.

For more detail on how police zones work, see the "Police Awareness" section of our Basics chapter.

As you continue down the alley, police cruisers arrive at the far end. Duck left into the open doorway off the alley and follow the passage out onto the street.

Sprint across the street and veer leftward past the bandstand and the dolphin parade float then run through the brick pillars of the cemetery entrance. (Remember that Sammy said the getaway car is at a grocery store loading dock that backs up to the cemetery.)

Your goal is to reach the exit gate on the opposite end of this cemetery. Turn right and sprint down the aisle between rows of mausoleums toward the big angel statue. Continue to eye your Minimap to see where the cops (the blue radar blips) are searching, and avoid them. If an isolated cop blocks your route toward the objective marker, you can sneak up behind him for a silent takedown to elude detection.

The cemetery's back exit leads out onto a set of railroad tracks. The building directly across the tracks is the grocery store destination. Head for the doorway into the back enclosure—the loading dock where Ellis and Danny await your arrival in a red convertible. They report that Giorgi has gone on ahead on his own.

OBJECTIVE: Lose the Police

Drive down the dumpster-filled alley toward the closed gate. As a police vehicle pulls up outside, smash through the gate and head straight for the ramp at the corner, on the right side of the street. Hit it straight on to launch over the top of two more cop cars arriving up the street ahead!

Steer for the center of that ramp to vault over two cop cars.

Swerve through tight traffic spaces to cut off police pursuit.

Now it's time to ditch the other police vehicles that give chase. Head straight down the street to the stop sign and turn left. Then drive like a bat out of hell, zigzagging through the city streets while avoiding collisions with panicked motorists. A good escape tactic is to slalom as close as possible through oncoming traffic so that unnerved drivers swerve behind you and cut off pursuing police cruisers.

Once you finally get outside the Police Zone and shake off the pursuit, your car's occupants celebrate with some bad singing. This triggers a long, chapter-ending cutscene that sets up the central conflict in *Mafia III*. We won't spoil the full scene here, but suffice it to say that Lincoln loses almost everything that has given his life structure and meaning…and gains a dark new overriding purpose.

DELRAY HOLLOW:
THICKER THAN BLOOD

MISSION: "SOMETHIN' I'VE GOT TO DO"

Lincoln Clay has more than just revenge in mind. As he told Father James, simple revenge is not enough—he seeks more comprehensive satisfaction. His plan: target everything Sal Marcano has built in New Bordeaux, everything he holds dear...and then wrench it away slowly, relentlessly, district by district.

French Ward

1

LEGEND

1 St. Jerome's (Father James' Church)

2 Sammy's Bar

3 Blue Gulf Motel (Donovan's Tac-Ops Center)

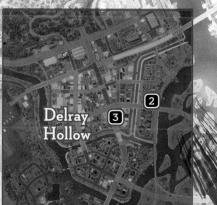

Delray Hollow

2

3

PREREQUISITE: COMPLETE "...A FRIEND IN JESUS"

But before Lincoln can set his terrible and ambitious agenda in motion, he knows he must first go back home and confront the nightmares that haunt him.

HEALTH PICKUP

Before you follow Donovan out to his car, explore Father James' residence attached to the church. You can grab an Adrenaline Shot from the Medicine Cabinet in the bathroom, and pick up a TL-49 Fuse from the glass coffee table in the living room. (You'll use these fuses later to install wiretaps.)

Get into Donovan's Car

Follow John Donovan out to his red Potomac Independent and hop in. Lincoln takes the wheel.

Drive to Sammy's

Drive the trip route from St. Jerome's **(1)** in the French Ward to the burned-out remains of Sammy's Bar **(2)** back in Delray Hollow.

On the way, listen to Lincoln lay out his thoughts and plans for Donovan. Donovan mentions "a tac-ops center and all this other [stuff] you asked me for." When you pull into the destination marker, Lincoln hops out and Donovan says he'll be at "the motel."

Enter Sammy's

Climb into the building via the front corner window using the controls displayed onscreen.

Retrieve Your Gear

Walk down the corridor toward the bar to trigger a disturbing flashback sequence. Keep veering left around the bar as the visions appear, one by one. Lincoln relives the terrible night of the Marcanos' betrayal.

Continue to the staircase and head down into the basement. This triggers a cutscene: Lincoln retrieves gear including his Combat Knife from his trunk, as more memories of Sammy flood in. (Your Combat Knife lets you perform brutally efficient Lethal Takedowns on foes.) Then he uses its blade to prep himself for war.

UNLOCKS: "THAT'S THE PLAN, PADRE"

MISSION: "THAT'S THE PLAN, PADRE"

PREREQUISITE: "SOMETHIN' I'VE GOT TO DO"

After the cutscene, approach the nearby safe and open it to get notification that this is your Stash House. (See the Tip on this page.) You automatically store all the cash you're carrying in the safe. You can access it anytime, anyplace.

> **STASH YOUR CASH SAFELY**
>
> Whenever Lincoln acquires cash out in the field, it gets stored automatically in his wallet. You can return to Sammy's basement at any time and stash the wallet cash in the safe. Do this regularly, because if Lincoln falls in battle, you lose half of the money in his wallet. Later, you'll be able to call a courier to your location and transfer your wallet cash to the safe.

Discuss Potential Assets with Donovan

Go back upstairs and exit the building. Then hop into the dark blue and white Berkley Executive parked in the alley driveway near the front entrance. Follow the short trip route down the street to the Blue Gulf Motel **(3)** and pull into the parking lot.

Climb the motel's stairs and enter the last door on the left to trigger a long cutscene: Lincoln marvels at Donovan's sophisticated tactical center, and learns that the Haitian mob is not only reconstituted but also a possible ally.

UNLOCKS: "OLD TIME'S SAKE"

LINCOLN'S KILL LIST

Open the Map screen and scroll to the Kill List page to see Lincoln's list of primary targets. For now, the only target unlocked is the don himself, Salvatore "Sal" Marcano. But before you can get to Sal, first you'll have to take out all of the targets listed below him on the chart: the capos and lieutenants of the Marcano criminal empire.

Highlight Sal's photo and select View Intel and then select "More" to read John Donovan's expanded dossier on the Kingpin of New Bordeaux. Scroll to see intel about his criminal rackets as well. As you progress through the game, the Kill List will add profiles of Marcano's minions as well.

DELRAY HOLLOW:
THE WAY OF FLESH

MISSION: "OLD TIME'S SAKE"

LEGEND

1. **Blue Gulf Motel (Donovan)**
2. **Haitian Hangout**
3. **Pierced Heart Vodou Shop**

Delray Hollow

PREREQUISITE: "That's the Plan, Padre"

The Marcanos have handed control of Delray Hollow to the hated Dixie Mafia, who are now running heroin into the district.

Donovan thinks Lincoln can recruit the local Haitians to his cause. But after killing Baka and decimating their bayou hideout, Lincoln Clay is not exactly on their buddy list. Some old-school persuasion may be needed.

Wait for the Haitians

Descend to the parking lot and get into your Executive. Drive the white trip route to the destination marker near the river and hop out. Walk across the street and sit on the park bench to wait for the Haitians.

Time passes with a scene fade. Lincoln sits on the bench facing the Louisiana Shipping Company warehouse across the street. Soon the Haitian's bright yellow Samson Richmond-Lux pulls into the warehouse garage, giving you a new objective.

Get Inside

Cross the street to the warehouse and take cover at the garage doorway. Your target is the Haitian marked with a crosshairs icon above his head, the first Informant you encounter in the game.

Interrogate the Haitian

Your target has two companions. To reach the targeted Haitian, you must neutralize his partners. Here's the easy way: see the crates hanging over their heads? Target the cable

When the crates crash down, they KO the two companions and stun the Informant. Approach the Informant and hold down the button prompted onscreen to trigger Lincoln's interrogation. The Informant reveals where the Haitian gang boss hangs out.

USING INFORMANTS IN MAFIA III

Informants provide key information about rackets in New Bordeaux. This info opens up new objectives in the district. Informants associated with rackets are marked with an "i" icon over their heads. To interrogate an Informant, attack until he collapses then approach and hold down the button prompted onscreen.

Go to the Pierced Heart Vodou Shop

Return to your car and follow the trip route to the peeling blue building that houses the Pierced Heart.

Find a Way Inside

Go around to the side with the garage. Use the dumpster to climb onto the garage and cross the roof. Then hop over the balcony railing and enter the Pierced Heart via the second floor balcony door.

Search Pierced Heart

Turn right and enter the sitting room.

Wait

Approach the leather couch and sit down. This triggers a cutscene: Lincoln meets Cassandra, a familiar face who has become the new Haitian boss. She tells Lincoln about the despicable practices of Sammy's replacement, Ritchie Doucet, the man Marcano put in charge of the Hollow. Doucet's Dixie Mafia operate out of the Community Church as well as the old community theater, once called Perla's—named after Sammy's late wife. Lincoln decides to take down the theater first.

MOBILE ARMS DEALER

Recruiting Cassandra gains Lincoln access to one of her "Criminal Associates": Mr. Jackie DuVernay, a seller of surplus weapons and explosives, supplies, vehicle modifications, and skill upgrades for Lincoln. Be sure to check out the wares he peddles out of his van. Just walk to the open doors in back and press the button prompted to view Jackie's stock.

CASSANDRA'S ASSETS

Open the Map screen and scroll to the Assets page then highlight Cassandra's photo and view her Bio and other information. Select "More" to read John Donovan's expanded dossier on the mysterious Haitian leader. Scroll to see intel about her associates and service upgrades that can become available if you increase Cassandra's "earn" by giving her control of rackets you seize.

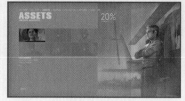

UNLOCKS: "PROSTITUTION" RACKET

RACKET: PROSTITUTION

Delray Hollow

PREREQUISITE:

COMPLETE "OLD TIME'S SAKE"

Now it's time to start putting the hurt on Sal Marcano. Your goal is to inflict damage on each racket until its revenue, called its "earn," is reduced to zero. When a racket's revenue hits zero, the Racket Boss is flushed out. Then you can either kill or recruit that boss to solidify Lincoln's takeover of the racket.

REDNECK INTEL

Open up the Kill List from your Map screen and check out Donovan's dossier on the Dixie Mafia. His expert conclusion: "They're hillbilly idiots, but they're smart enough to know that if they [screw] up, Sal will turn their asses into mulch."

LEGEND

1	Pierced Heart Vodou Shop	3	Doucet's (Perla's Nightclub)	5	"Rooster" Desaulniers
2	The Voice	4	Blue Gulf Motel	6	"Dirty" Gert Delong

Talk to The Voice

Your first task is to find out what kind of business Ritchie Doucet is transacting at the old Perla Theater. Cassandra has given you a preliminary

contact. Outside her vodou shop **(1)**, hop in your car (or steal any car) and follow the white trip route. It leads down a dirt lane to a destination marker next to an old, wheel-less trailer. Hop out and follow the objective marker down the alley to the green door of a garage right on the canal bank **(2)**.

Enter to trigger a meeting with Mr. Laveau, former bartender at Sammy's and a DJ known as "The Voice" on the local radio. Laveau tells you that a goon named Merle Jackson is running a forced prostitution racket out of the old Perla's Nightclub, now transformed into a strip club and renamed "Doucet's" after the district boss himself. Jackson has some girls strung-out on heroin and imprisoned on the second floor of the brothel.

UNLOCKS OBJECTIVE:
"FREE THE STRUNG-OUT GIRLS"

Free the Strung-Out Girls

TALK TO SHEILA

Exit the trailer and follow the trip route to Doucet's **(3)**. (Note that the Arms Dealer van is out front if you wish to purchase a new weapon or two.) Enter via the front doors and talk to Sheila the coat-check girl (the one wearing white lingerie) in the main lobby. Sheila tells Lincoln the girls are upstairs and Merle's goons are everywhere.

> **LOBBY COLLECTIBLE**
>
> Don't miss the Vargas painting hanging on the wall in the lobby near Sheila.

WORK YOUR WAY UPSTAIRS

Proceed past Sheila down the first hall and turn right through the doorway. A long corridor, patrolled by a Dixie Mafia thug, runs

alongside the bar area. Take cover behind the nearby cart and whistle to lure the thug to you then take him down silently.

Proceed to the end of the corridor and turn right to enter the backstage area. Take cover behind the table made of crates marked "Fragile" then grab the two stacks of cash next to the beer bottles on the nearby crate. Then use Intel View to scout the positions of other hostile guards across the backstage area.

> **SPOT CASH WITH INTEL VIEW**
>
> Use your Intel View to pinpoint the locations of money stashed in each area. Stacks of cash are highlighted in yellow.

Soon one Dixie thug patrols toward you, so stay in cover, whistle him over and take him down. Try to sneak up behind the other two guards for takedowns, including one guy standing just outside the door on the loading dock.

When the backstage area is clear, snag two more stacks of cash then explore the dressing room area. Here you can find a note on the table; $250 on the toilet tank in the bathroom; and a Tac-Vest in a locker.

Then carefully creep up the staircase behind the stage, checking with Intel View for other gunmen up above or approaching from below. Turn right at the top of the stairs and proceed past the three hospitality rooms to the open door. Step through the doorway into the narrow corridor.

THERESA MAYEUX

Approach the first closed door on the right and either use your Pry Bar to open it…or better yet, just kick it in. (We suggest the latter.) Poor Theresa is sitting on the floor. Enter and read the note on her bed if you want. Theresa runs out and escapes her hellish prison, inflicting damage to the racket.

DEBORAH ROUQUETTE

Kick in the next door to free Deborah and knock another couple grand off the racket's balance sheets. Then exit and move to the next closed door.

LUCY DOUSSAN

Get ready! When you kick in this door, you find an armed customer in Lucy's room. Gun him down quickly! After he drops, let Lucy escape for racket damage, and then scoop up more cash stacked on the corner table.

LEAVE DOUCET'S

Exit the room and find more cash in the bathroom at the end of the corridor on the left. Search the rest of the second floor for more money and items, then go back downstairs to find another nice wad of cash behind the main bar. Then exit the building to finally complete your "Free the Strung-Out Girls" objective.

OFFICE REWARDS

Before you leave Doucet's, be sure to check out the second floor office. You'll find a Vargas painting on the wall plus a $1500 pile of cash on the desk!

Talk to Donovan

PREREQUISITE: COMPLETE OBJECTIVE "FREE THE STRUNG-OUT GIRLS"

Your raid on Doucet's brothel puts a serious dent in the Prostitution racket's income, but you still need to inflict a bit more damage to lure out the racket boss, Merle Jackson. Drive back to the Blue Gulf Motel **(4)** and head upstairs to the tac-ops center. Donovan gives Lincoln a portable radio for calling in help from the Criminal Associates of his Underbosses.

RADIO YOUR ASSOCIATES

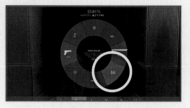

Once Donovan gives Lincoln the portable radio, you can open the Weapon Wheel and call any available associates for help. At this point in the story, the only one available is the Arms Dealer (circled in our shot). Now you can buy arms and equipment on the go!

Return to The Voice

Drive back to Laveau's garage studio **(2)** and enter. He tells Lincoln about Merle's pimps in Delray Hollow. If you eliminate them, Merle may be forced to return to the strip club where you can hit him. Icons marking the locations of both pimps, "Rooster" Desaulniers and "Dirty" Gert Delong, now appear on your map. Open the Map screen and activate the objective of the closer target, Rooster.

The locations of Merle's pimps appear on your map as skull-shaped "Kill" icons.

UNLOCKS OBJECTIVES:

"KILL MERLE'S PIMPS" AND "TRACK DOWN AND KILL DIXIE PATROLS"

Kill Merle's Pimps

PREREQUISITE: Complete "Free the Strung-Out Girls" AND "Return to the Voice" (First Time)

"ROOSTER" DESAULNIERS

Follow the trip route to the destination marker **(5)** and get out of the car. Rooster's house is the green one. From the street, use your Intel View to survey the situation. Rooster is posted alone behind his house. One guard stands with his back to you in the alley on the left side. Stalk that fool for a silent takedown.

> **HOSTILE TURF**
>
> When Lincoln Clay drives or walks into territory controlled by Marcano's racketeers, he's not a welcome guest. At first, goons will politely suggest you move along. If you continue to trespass, however, they'll resort to more forceful methods.
>
> Sometimes you can go into enemy turf with guns blazing, if their numbers are small and witnesses are few. Most times your best bet is to quietly infiltrate and stealthily thin out the enemy ranks one by one before you resort to gunplay.

Now use the nearby barrels to hop over Rooster's back fence. If Rooster is facing away from you, you can perform a silent kill then stealthily  search the house for cash and items, and return to your vehicle. However, if you're forced to shoot Rooster, get ready for his remaining men to retaliate. You may need to take them out before you can plunder the house.

> *RACKET EARN = $0*
>
> *If you inflicted maximum damage during your visit earlier to Doucet's strip club (when you freed the strung-out girls), then the racket damage you inflict by whacking Rooster should bring the Prostitution Racket's "earn" down to zero. Now you can choose to return to The Voice for advice on how to pursue the Racket Boss, Merle Jackson. But if you still need more damage to get to zero, or you just want to boost your bank account, you can continue to hit targets.*

"DIRTY" GERT DELONG

Follow the trip route to the destination marker **(6)** and get out of the car. Dirty Gert works his girls out of the low-rent Carousel Hotel (next door to Perfect Waffle), and he has a lot of muscle posted around the place. Work around the perimeter, using Intel View to pick out Dixie Mafia from the clientele. Whistle to lure individual thugs out to your hiding places for silent takedowns.

Dirty Gert is in an upstairs suite on the street side of the motel. Once you get a clear path to the balcony outside his room, go shoot him right  through the window for damage to the racket. Be sure to scour the room for cash, including a $500 bag under the bathroom sink.

Before you leave the area, work your way upstairs to the second floor of the motel's opposite building. You'll find a room with a lot of money stashed in nice stacks. Use your Intel View to find them all!

Track Down and Kill Dixie Patrols

PREREQUISITE: Complete "Free the Strung-Out Girls" AND "Return to the Voice (First Time)"

As you drive around Delray Hollow you occasionally pass white Eckhart Pioneer trucks with the Confederate flag emblazoned on the doors. Next to each truck, two Dixie Mafia goons are working to recruit some poor girl into the escort business. Stop and terminate them to inflict additional damage per goon eliminated. A total of 10 Dixie patrols can be found on the Hollow streets.

Return to The Voice (Second Time)

PREREQUISITE:

RACKET DAMAGE LOWERS EARN TO $0

Once your damage total hits $0, you can return to Laveau's garage studio. (Before you talk to him, see the "Final Contact" note.) Talk to

Laveau and select Accept. He reports that Merle Jackson is now holed up over at Perla's (the theater renamed Doucet's). This puts the star objective icon on the map, marking the location of a Racket Boss. Activate that objective to set a trip route.

RACKET WRAP-UP: FINAL CONTACT

When you return to your contact after you've slashed the Damage Remaining amount to $0 for a racket, you're given a choice. When you hold down the button to talk to your contact, a text prompt appears which says, "Continuing will cause any remaining racket objectives to be removed." You can either Accept or Decline.

If you choose Accept, all remaining racket objectives disappear from your Objectives Panel list except for the final "confront the boss" objective. So if you're a completionist who wants to finish everything available in each district, or you just want to pick up more of the objective-related cash stashes, select Decline then head back out into the district.

Kill Merle Jackson

Exit the garage and follow the trip route back to Doucet's club **(3)**. You can take a speed route up to Merle's office, avoiding most of his minions. Here's how: Stalk into the front lobby and veer left into the hallway, sneaking past the two guards with their backs to you. Continue down the long corridor that runs alongside the bar and stage, and then creep along the back wall in the backstage area until you reach the staircase. Climb the stairs to the first landing, then cross the landing and climb the opposite staircase to the second floor.

Turn left, take out the thug patrolling the next walkway, and then hustle past the two guards looking over the balcony with their backs to you. Continue around the corner and proceed to the open doorway on the right at the end of the walkway. If you duck into it fast enough you can elude detection!

Move down the hall past the rooms on the right where you previously freed the strung-out girls. Turn right at the corner and sneak into the upstairs bar where two more guards sit with their backs to you. You kill them quickly or try creeping past them to the right, moving down the next hall to the main office door. (Grab the Barker 390 shotgun from the weapon case on the way.)

Enter the office anteroom to see Merle "Trigger" Jackson, the racket boss, and one other henchman. Gun down the minion with a headshot then shoot Merle until he falls to his knees. Approach Merle and hold down the button displayed onscreen to subdue him and end his miserable, vicious criminal career.

Killing Merle breaks up the Prostitution Racket and gives control to Lincoln. Assign the new racket, now called "Perla's Nightclub," to Cassandra, your only Underboss at this point.

This bumps you up to the next Favor level with her, adding the valuable Screaming Zemi (a throwable distraction device) to the wares you can buy from the Arms Dealer van of Jackie DuVernay. You also get a starter set of two for free.

RACKET MANAGEMENT

Once Lincoln deals with the Racket Boss, he takes over the racket and assigns it to one of his Underbosses. At this point in Mafia III, the only Underboss available is Cassandra, so you give her Perla's Nightclub by default. The racket's headquarters also becomes a new Safehouse for Lincoln.

UNLOCKS: "SMACK" RACKET

RACKET: SMACK

Delray Hollow

PREREQUISITE:
"PROSTITUTION" RACKET SECURED

One district racket in your pocket, one to go. The other racket in Delray Hollow is a smack

operation. John Donovan has some intel on who's running it. Time to go meet him again.

LEGEND

1 Meet Donovan	**5** Enforcer (Doug "Hatchet" Marcheti)
2 Informants	**6** Enforcer (Deacon Caruso)
3 First Baptist Community Church	**W** Junction Boxes
4 Informants	

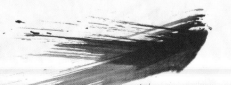

Wait for Donovan

Follow the trip route to the bus-stop bench **(1)** across from the First Baptist Community Church. Approach the bench and press the button prompted to wait for Donovan and trigger a cinematic: Donovan arrives to report that the Dixie Mafia is pushing its heroin out of the church. The racket is run by Charlie Kincaid, but he's hard to find. Donovan has identified a pair of Kincaid's street pushers for Lincoln to interrogate.

Donovan also explains how New Bordeaux is on a "standard communication grid" and thus easy to wiretap. He hands Lincoln three TL-49 fuses for wiretapping the Junction Box **(W1)** next to the nearby newsstand. Doing so will let Donovan construct an intelligence map of the area around the box and mark Targets of Opportunity for you. (See the "Donovan's Wiretap Network" sidebar for more.)

PINKO POSTERS

As their meeting ends, Donovan expresses a seething hatred for the Communist propaganda he tears off the nearby wall. This introduces a new category of collectible item. Grab every commie poster you find hanging in New Bordeaux!

DONOVAN'S WIRETAP NETWORK

Help John Donovan expand his wiretap network across the city to gain a lot of critical intelligence in *Mafia III*. Each New Bordeaux district is divided into a number of distinct sectors—five in Delray Hollow, ten in Barclay Mills, and so on. Each of these sectors has one Junction Box that you can wiretap to reveal key intel in that sector.

HOW TO WIRETAP A JUNCTION BOX

To wiretap a Junction Box, you need three TL-49 Fuses in your inventory. Approach the Junction Box and complete the Pry Bar minigame to

Dozens of TL-49 Fuses are scattered throughout the city. Collect them as you travel.

unlock it and automatically install the fuses. You can find plenty of fuses scattered around New Bordeaux, marked as green dots on your map.

WHAT THE WIRETAP REVEALS

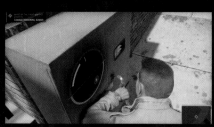

You need three fuses to wiretap each Junction Box.

Once you wiretap a sector's Junction Box, the in-game map reveals all of the collectibles, shops, Medicine Cabinets, TL-49 Fuses, and other key items and locations in that sector. Donovan marks each "Target of Opportunity" with an icon as well. These targets are the people, goods and operations that contribute to the racket's Earn total.

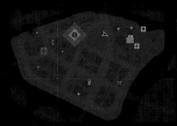

When you wiretap a sector's Junction Box, your map reveals key items and locations in that sector.

After wiretapping, your Minimap reveals all enemies (red blips) within its radius. In addition, your Intel View reveals all nearby foes (highlighted red)—even through walls and around corners, including those you haven't yet spotted directly.

USING WIRETAPS TO RECRUIT BOSSES

Each wiretapped node also reveals sensitive information about the rackets in the district. Lincoln Clay can leverage this information to convince certain bosses (though not all) to work for him when he takes over their rackets. Recruiting experienced bosses increases the Earn of your rackets.

Note that without wiretapped info, Lincoln has no choice but to kill racket bosses when he confronts them.

Wiretaps give you leverage with racket bosses so you can recruit them and increase your income.

Wiretap the First Baptist Church

Press the button indicated on the Junction Box to start the Pry Bar unlocking minigame. When Lincoln pries open the box, he automatically installs three of the TL-49 Fuses from your inventory. (Your current number of fuses is displayed in the lower left corner, next to your cash totals.) This gives you a new objective. Time to track down an Informant.

UNLOCKS: "INTERROGATE CHARLIE'S PUSHERS"

INFORMANTS FLEE!

Look for the "i" icon marking mob Informants for interrogation.

Unlike Enforcers, who stay and fight to the bitter end, an Informant hightails it to his vehicle and tries to escape as soon as Lincoln is detected on his turf.

One approach is to stalk the turf and take down the enemy crew silently, one by one, until you reach the Informant. Another approach is to find a sniper spot outside the hideout's detection perimeter with a clean line of fire to the Informant. Nail him with a headshot or a few body shots to incapacitate him, and then eliminate his associates.

If you get spotted before you reach the Informant, hustle straight for him and try to incapacitate him before he flees! An incapacitated Informant goes down on one knee and cannot move. This lets you deal with his associates then scour the hideout for cash and items before you go back to interrogate the downed fellow.

Interrogate each Informant to unlock new objectives, and then kill or recruit him.

If an Informant does manage to escape, you can still hop in your car and try to chase him down. If you catch up, you can hop into the driver's seat of the Informant's car, and then "Drive Like a Madman" to scare him into squealing. But if you can't catch him, don't worry: eventually, the fleeing Informant holes up in a new location.

Interrogate Charlie's Pushers (First Time)

For some objectives, *Mafia III* picks randomly from two or more possible targets on the map. The objective is the same for whichever target pops up—in this case, to interrogate an Informant to learn more about Charlie Kincaid's heroin operation in Delray Hollow. But here, the Target of Opportunity icon can spawn in one of two different spots on your map. You can get sent to interrogate either Big Al Turpin **(2a)** or Patrick O'Halloran **(2b)**.

WIRETAP EVERY SECTOR!

Before you try to infiltrate any enemy stronghold in a new sector, be sure to wiretap the Junction Box in that sector first. Wiretapping greatly enhances what your Intel View and maps reveal.

BIG AL TURPIN

If the objective map sends you to Big Al Turpin, follow the trip route to the small green house **(2a)** in the southern part of the district where he hangs out. You've already wiretapped this sector, so use Intel View from the street; you can see Big Al inside, marked with the Interrogate icon over his head. Remember, he spooks easily. Rush inside to incapacitate Al quickly—he drops to one knee when disabled—then turn your attention to his crew. Once the area is clear, return to Big Al and interrogate him to learn that Kincaid has a lot of product stashed at the church.

SPARING INFORMANTS

Like some Racket Bosses, Informants can be recruited instead of killed. Recruiting them increases the Earn of a racket over the long haul, once you take it over.

PATRICK O'HALLORAN

If the objective map sends you to Patrick O'Halloran instead, you want to wiretap his sector first. Make sure you have three TL-49 Fuses then break into the Junction Box **(W2)** located in the alley between the Everyday Laundromat and the Motor License & Insurance buildings. (It's just around the corner from the Blue Gulf Motel where Donovan has his tac-ops center.)

Then follow the trip route to the alley **(2b)** where O'Halloran (marked with an Interrogate icon) stands with two associates, one of whom is kicking  a customer. (Tip: Use Intel View to identify all of the bad guys.) Again, Informants spook easily, so approach carefully. One tactic: Toss a Screaming Zemi to draw the attention of the associates then rush to subdue O'Halloran and interrogate him. The pusher squeals that Kincaid has a lot of valuable dope at the church. After you either kill or recruit O'Halloran, dispatch his crew and move on to the next objective.

WITNESSES

When Lincoln Clay commits a crime in public, citizens who view the deed get scared and start running. One of them is likely to run for the nearest phone to call the cops. This person is then designated as a Witness.

When a Witness decides to report one of Lincoln's criminal acts, a phone icon pops up over his/her head and you get an onscreen notification: "Witness Is Calling Police." The Witness starts running to the nearest telephone. Hit the fool with a melee or weapon attack before he can place the call!

If a Witness manages to connect the distress call, the area around you becomes a Blue Police Zone and cops start rushing to the scene. Your best bet is to escape the zone then return when things calm down.

Destroy Charlie's Heroin

PREREQUISITE: COMPLETE "INTERROGATE CHARLIE'S PUSHERS" (FIRST TIME)

Follow the trip route to the First Baptist Community Church, the racket's main hideout. The complex includes a community center with a meeting hall behind the church where a number of drug shipments are being prepared; destroying them inflicts a lot of damage on Kincaid's Smack operations. As you might expect, though, the place is well-guarded.

Kincaid's drug processing center is in the big hall under construction behind the Community Church.

We recommend a covert approach, sneaking around the church grounds and stopping regularly to check your Intel View. Spot the red-highlighted Dixie Mafia goons and maneuver in behind them, or else hide and lure them with whistles, taking out as many as possible with silent takedowns. Be sure to neutralize any Sentry you encounter before they can call for help. (See our note on "Sentries.")

SENTRIES

Mob turf is well defended, with guards posted onsite plus mobile teams of Reinforcements ready to rush to district hotspots if contacted. Many mob hangouts have one or more designated Sentries who call in these Reinforcements if

they detect a threat on their turf. Each Sentry is marked with an overhead label in your Intel View.

When a Sentry is alerted, you get an onscreen notification, a phone icon pops up over his head, and he starts running to the nearest telephone. Take him down before he can place the call! If a Sentry manages to phone in a request for Reinforcements, a car full of mob hitmen arrives shortly thereafter, making your mission considerably more difficult.

Once the armed security team is significantly thinned out, use Intel View to locate the four red-highlighted heroin crates, which appear as boxlike figures. These are locked inside a big processing hall behind the church where a forced-labor crew prepares the shipments. Open the locked door with your Pry Bar and sneak across the hall to take down the lone Dixie gunman who is distracted by one of the workers. When he drops, the working girls scatter.

Now you must methodically destroy all four of the glowing crates marked with lightning icons. Shoot them! The first three crates you smash inflict damage to the Smack racket, but the fourth one knocks even more damage off the racket's net worth.

After the crates are destroyed, scour the buildings and grounds (including the garage) for piles of cash and items; you can inflict several more thousands of dollar damage to the racket this way. Use Intel View to find the yellow-highlighted stacks. Look for a Tac-Vest in the garage locker too!

BACK OFFICE STASH

Don't miss the $1500 stack of cash on the desk in the back office of the drug processing building. You'll also find a Vargas painting on the wall.

UNLOCKS: "INTERROGATE CHARLIE'S PUSHERS"

Interrogate Charlie's Pushers (Second Time)

PREREQUISITE: COMPLETE "DESTROY CHARLIE'S HEROIN"

Now the game makes another random choice, sending you to one of two other street pushers who report to "Four Fingers" Kincaid. Follow the map route to the new Target of Opportunity that appears: either Modine "Mo-Mo" Labranche (4a) or Natty Babin (4b).

MODINE "MO-MO" LABRANCHE

If your target is Mo-Mo, first find and wiretap the sector's Junction Box **(W3)** tucked in an alley behind a row of storefronts. (You can get there by cutting through Backwoods Lounge or R&R Liquor & Tobacco then using their back exits into the alley, or just go around the block.) Then follow the trip route to the Catfish Queen diner **(4a)** over on the west side of the district, where the pusher hangs out with one other Dixie Mafia partner. Wait at the diner entrance until Mo-Mo is turned away from you then sneak up behind him for a quick takedown.

Mo-Mo tells Lincoln that Charlie Kincaid protects his turf with Enforcers; those two tough guys now appear marked on the map. Eliminate Mo-Mo's partner and head for the nearest Enforcer location.

NATTY BABIN

If your Informant target is Natty Babin instead of Mo-Mo, follow the trip route to the Double Barrel Bar **(4b)** down in southern Delray Hollow, where Natty hangs out with one other Dixie Mafia partner. Before you enter the bar, continue south a short distance to the Perfect Waffle on the right side of the road and wiretap the Junction Box **(W4)** on the restaurant's outer wall. Then return to the Double Barrel Bar.

Natty tells Lincoln that Kincaid protects his turf with Enforcers who now appear marked on the map. Eliminate Natty's partner and head for the nearest Enforcer location.

> **DON'T FORGET TO WIRETAP!**
>
> Just another friendly reminder: Pick up those TL-49 Fuses (green map dots) and install them into the Junction Box in every sector of Delray Hollow.

Kill Charlie's Enforcers

PREREQUISITE: COMPLETE "INTERROGATE CHARLIE'S PUSHERS" (SECOND TIME)

This time you have to hunt down and kill both of Charlie Kincaid's special Enforcers, Doug "Hatchet" Marcheti **(5)** and Deacon Caruso **(6)**.

KILLING ENFORCERS

Each Racket Boss employs tough thugs known as Enforcers to protect mob assets and keep order in the district. Enforcers oversee well-defended turf and are clearly marked with an overhead "Kill" icon.

Taking out an Enforcer inflicts serious monetary damage to the racket. It also makes Lincoln's final confrontation with the Racket Boss easier. The reason: Enforcers who are not eliminated before you flush out the Racket Boss will join him in the final boss battle!

So we recommend that you hunt down and kill all Enforcers on the map before you flush out the boss. There's an added bonus to this approach: Enforcer hangouts typically feature some lucrative cash pickups.

DOUG "HATCHET" MARCHETI

If you haven't already wiretapped this sector's junction box **(W3)**, do so now! Then follow the trip route to the green house **(5)** where Doug "Hatchet" Marcheti hangs out in the backyard. Use Intel View to get the lay of the place. Next, stalk the perimeter and lure out a few of his clownish Dixie thugs for silent takedowns. Then rush in and dispatch Marcheti. You can also destroy a shipment of smack in the back room.

Chances are good that whacking the first Enforcer has knocked your damage total down to $0, and you can return to Donovan for an update on "Four Finger" Charlie. But if you still need to inflict more damage, or you just want to complete everything in the district, proceed to the next target, another Enforcer named Deacon Caruso.

DEACON CARUSO

If you haven't already wiretapped this sector's Junction Box **(W3)**, do so now! Then follow the trip route to the garage and junkyard enclosure **(6)** full of wrecked cars that Deacon Caruso and his crew of Dixie Mafia goons use as home base. Two different rooftops overlook the yard (see our overhead shot); use Intel View from these vantage points to survey the situation before you make your move. Note the Sentry posted at the open garage doors.

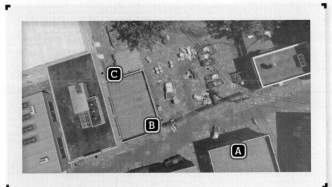
Here's an overhead shot of Dean Caruso's hangout.

One approach is to use the rooftop across the alley **(A)** from the junkyard as a sniper post. Wield a scoped rifle and take out the Sentry, and then target the red gas tanks and canisters scattered around the yard. This triggers violent explosions that can eliminate several more gunmen. Finally, pick off Caruso when he steps out the garage to return fire.

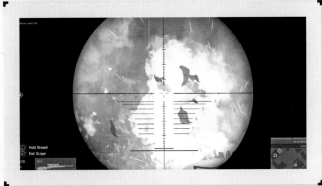
Target explosive canisters from the rooftop across the alley.

Another approach is to climb the stairs onto the roof **(B)** of Caruso's garage, directly overlooking the junkyard. Sneak across the roof to the ladder in the back corner and drop down into a storage alcove **(C)**, hidden from guards. Hide behind one of the equipment shelves and whistle to lure foes over one by one. The Sentry should be the first one over, followed eventually by the Enforcer himself!

GARAGE SALE!

Inside Dean Caruso's garage you can find a shipment of smack plus a collectible album cover on the shelf.

Talk to Donovan

PREREQUISITE:

RACKET DAMAGE LOWERS EARN TO $0

When your damage finally drops the racket's Earn to $0, you can go see Donovan again at the same bus stop (1) where you previously met. You get the option to remove all remaining racket objectives. If you select Accept, Donovan reports that Charlie Kincaid isn't quite as despicable as the rest of the Dixie Mafia crew, and might be a candidate for recruitment.

Confront "Four Fingers" Charlie Kincaid

Head across the street from the bus stop to the Community Church (3). You've already worked through this property once, so you should be familiar with it.

Charlie is holed up in the office at the back of the big meeting hall (the heroin processing center) behind the church. As before, stalk silently across the grounds, using Intel View to spot foes. Reduce their numbers by using silent takedowns, and be sure to eliminate Sentries when you find them. You don't want to face a wave of Reinforcements!

When you finally reach Charlie Kincaid in his office, your earlier wiretap of the Junction Box across the street has given you enough intel on Charlie's Smack Racket to recruit the boss, if you want. Subdue Charlie and make your selection: Kill or Recruit him, your choice!

Assign the New Weed Racket to Cassandra

Now that the Smack Racket is secured, press the button prompted in the Racket Assignment window to assign it to Cassandra. Note that for the benefit of the community, Lincoln turns it into a Weed Racket instead— no more heroin flowing into Delray Hollow. This also triggers a cutscene of John Donovan's testimony before the Senate Select Committee on Intelligence, and unlocks a brand new mission.

A NEW FAVOR

Handing over the former Smack Racket (now a Weed Racket) to Cassandra bumps you up to the next Favor level with her, adding a new Associate: Clifton Jean-Baptiste, AKA "The Gunsmith." His first weapon upgrade for you is improved accuracy of all firearms!

UNLOCKS: "KILL RITCHIE DOUCET"

DELRAY HOLLOW:
PRAY ON THE WAY UP

MISSION: "KILL RITCHIE DOUCET"

LEGEND

1	Pierced Heart Vodou Shop
2	Baron Saturday's Parking
3	Bone Rattler
4	Crawdaddy's Wild Ride
5	Curse of the Bayou Beast
W	Junction Box

Delray Hollow

PREREQUISITE: "SMACK RACKET" SECURED

Talk to Cassandra

Once you've secured both of the Delray Hollow rackets, you're ready to hit your first Marcano lieutenant, Ritchie Doucet. But to find him, you'll need help from Cassandra. Return to the Pierced Heart Vodou Shop **(1)** and enter to trigger the cinematic: Cassandra has found an informant of her own. He reveals that Doucet and his remaining Dixie Mafia have holed up at the nearby abandoned amusement park, Baron Saturday's Funpark.

WIRETAP THE PARK

You need your Minimap and Intel View fully active in the dark of this mission! So before you enter Baron Saturday's Funpark, be sure you've wiretapped the Junction Box **(W)** in this sector. (You may have done so already.) The box is on the wall of the Perfect Waffle restaurant down the road just south of the park entrance.

Get Inside

Veer left across the lot to find the access ladder (circled in our shot). Climb up two ladders onto the scaffolding then drop down onto the roof of the entry gate.

Find Ritchie

SECURE THE CATWALK

Walk the length of the roof. As you do this, the time of day transitions to nighttime (if it isn't dark already). Take cover at the far end and eavesdrop on the

two Dixie Mafia guards as they chat. When they finish their conversation, let them separate and take up positions facing away from you on the catwalk, looking down at the park's entry plaza below. Stalk up behind the nearest guard for a silent takedown, and then repeat on the second guard just down the catwalk.

Go to Baron Saturday's

Follow the new trip route down to Baron Saturday's flooded parking lot **(2)**.

CLEAR THE PLAZA

LEGEND

- **A** Catwalk
- **B** Park Entry Plaza
- **C** Crazy Gator Ride
- **D** Merry-Go-Round
- **E** Clown Mouth Exit

Take cover at the railing next to the Manitou Model 67 and grab the sniper rifle **(A)**. Use your Intel View to spot any glowing red targets in the plaza below then activate the rifle's scope view to nail them. After every kill shot, switch from the scope to Intel View, find the next target, and then bring up your rifle again to snipe them. Note that some guards across the plaza may be posted within your sniper rifle's range but outside of your Intel View range. So you may need to spot them using the rifle's scope.

SWAP GUNS FOR CLIMBERS

Be ready to switch weapons from the sniper rifle to your pistol if any foe manages to reach the ladder and climb up onto your catwalk.

When you see no more guards below, climb down and start stalking carefully across the plaza **(B)**, moving from cover to cover and using your Intel View to pick out any gunmen who may be hidden in the dark. Look for a guard patrolling the ramp of the Crazy Gator ride **(C)** to the left. Gun him down and hustle up the ramp to take cover as more Dixie gunmen move into position below near the merry-go-round **(D)**. Pick them off from your high position!

LOOK FOR MOLOTOVS

Keep an eye out for Molotov Cocktail bottles sitting on carts and stands as you move through the park.

When the immediate area is clear, proceed to the next section of the park by walking through the big toothy mouth-tunnel **(E)** of the clown with the crazy twirling eyes.

FIGHT THROUGH THE BONE RATTLER

Proceed past Papa Virgil's Shooting Gallery on the left to find a Medicine Cabinet by the restrooms. Then double back to the entrance to the Bone Rattler bumper car pavilion **(3)**. Just follow the glowing arrow that points the way!

Before you enter, take an Intel View scan of the area to see several pairs of Dixie gunmen inside the pavilion. Fight across the Bone Rattler and follow the walkway around its perimeter to the Exit sign.

Follow the arrow!

GET TO THE CURSE OF THE BAYOU BEAST

LEGEND

A	Exit from Bone Rattler
B	Crawdaddy's Wild Ride
C	Raised Walk-Bridge

Be ready when you exit the Bone Rattler **(A)**—two of Doucet's mob goons stand not far from the exit ramp. After you drop them, hustle to find cover because several more gunmen are deployed under the glowing arches of the Crawdaddy's Wild Ride platform **(B)** up ahead.

A good tactic: Head for the raised stone walk-bridge to the left **(C)** and neutralize the mob rifleman there. The post has a good view, provides good cover options, and you can find a sniper rifle on the cart. Clear the area, move past the Crawdaddy's platform, and fight your way to the entrance of the Curse of the Bayou Beast ride.

Chase Down Ritchie

The Curse of the Bayou Beast is a rail ride through the spooky recreation of a haunted bayou. The rail winds back and forth through a dark, misty interior as glowing characters and beasts suddenly burst to life. As you enter, Ritchie Doucet takes off running as one of his men rushes to engage you. Gun down the attacker and follow Doucet down the twisting tunnel.

When you reach the priest carrying the lantern and crucifix, follow that figure as it slides down the rail, and then take cover. A gunman opens fire at you from a high perch over the ride's waterway. Take him out and push forward. Soon another Dixie goon emerges from a hut on the right. Gun him down and continue around the next corner to trigger a new objective.

Confront Ritchie Doucet

Take cover behind a fake tree at the next bend and use your Intel View to spot more shooters up ahead. Here's where stealth tactics really pay off. Whistle to lure them one at a time for silent takedowns. Keep dashing ahead into cover then checking your Intel View to spot more of Ritchie's guards.

Stalk Doucet's men one by one!

Keep whistling them over, one by one, and pushing forward to the next pair. Eventually you reach the fanged mouth of a demon. Go through the open mouth and head up the stairs on the left. At the top, approach the double doors and kick them open to trigger your next objective.

Grab Ritchie Doucet

Immediately take cover at the doorway. Ritchie Doucet opens fire from behind a heavy desk piled with boxes. Two of his men are with him, so be patient until you can pick them off. Once Ritchie is isolated, attack until he's incapacitated and goes down on one knee. Then grab Ritchie to trigger the mission-ending cinematic: Lincoln offers Doucet a nice view from the ferris wheel. The scene ends with some more present-day perspective from Assistant Director Maguire.

UNLOCKS MISSION: "THAT GOES BOTH WAYS"

MISSION: "THAT GOES BOTH WAYS"

PREREQUISITE:

COMPLETE "KILL RITCHIE DOUCET"

Now that the district has finally been scrubbed clean of the Dixie Mafia infestation and wrested from Sal Marcano's hands, Lincoln and Cassandra need to have a serious chat about the future of Delray Hollow.

Talk to Cassandra

Descend the stairs to the dock where you see an Eckhart Columbus speedboat. Wade to the boat and climb aboard then take the helm. Use your map to chart a course toward the active objective icon. When you get close, hop out of the boat and climb up the riverbank.

Jog to the Pierced Heart and head upstairs to trigger a cinematic: Lincoln reports that Doucet is dead and the Hollow is now under Cassandra's control. Her Haitian crew is still uncomfortable with Lincoln, so Cassandra suggests that helping her friend Emmanuel Lazare would be a nice gesture.

This opens up an Optional Mission in Delray Hollow, "Are We Cool." When the District Assignment window appears, press the button indicated to assign Delray Hollow to Cassandra. She is now officially a district-level Underboss for Lincoln Clay.

OPTIONAL MISSION UNLOCKED

You can find coverage of "Are We Cool" in our Optional Missions chapter.

KICKBACK PICKUP

Lincoln gets a piece of the action from the racket income of every Underboss. Don't forget to pick up your kickback funds from the coffee table in front of Cassandra when they're available. Regularly check the Pierced Heart on your Map to see if Cassandra owes you any money.

UNLOCKS OPTIONAL MISSION:
"ARE WE COOL"

UNLOCKS STORY MISSION:
"FRIENDS LIKE THESE"

MISSION: "FRIENDS LIKE THESE"

Talk to Donovan

Exit the Pierced Heart and follow the trip route back to the Blue Gulf Motel. Climb upstairs and enter Donovan's room to trigger another cutscene: Donovan asks Lincoln if he's ready to see the other briefings.

Here, the game's open world starts to open up. Two dossiers sit on Donovan's desk: one for Vito Scaletta, and another for Thomas Burke. These two fellows will join Cassandra as your primary Underbosses. You can select either dossier…or better yet, just pick up both.

Pick Up Vito's Dossier

Pick Up Burke's Dossier

Viewing either dossier opens up the story chapter in the New Bordeaux district associated with that mobster. For this walkthrough, let's go check out Vito Scaletta in River Row first.

UNLOCKS STORY MISSION:
"CUT AND RUN"

UNLOCKS STORY MISSION:
"WE PARTNERS NOW?"

RIVER ROW: WORK THE MAN WHO BLEEDS

MISSION: "WE PARTNERS NOW?"

LEGEND

1. Blue Gulf Motel (Donovan's Tac-Ops)
2. Dock Entrance
3. Benny's Restaurant (Vito)

Delray Hollow

River Row

When Lincoln picks up Donovan's dossier on Vito Scaletta, he learns that the transplant from Empire City has a strained relationship with Sal Marcano. Vito oversees the two rackets in the River Row district, running black market goods and the local worker unions. But recently, Sal sent in his nephew, Michael Grecco, to engineer a slow takeover. Now Vito is struggling to keep his head above water.

Head to Vito's

Step outside of Donovan's motel **(1)**. Vito Scaletta's office is over in the River Row district, in a dockside restaurant called Benny's. Before you head there, explore any wiretapped sectors of Delray Hollow and collect TL-49 Fuses; you want to take at least three fuses with you to River Row, and preferably more. Then follow the trip route to the destination marker **(2)** at the entrance to a docks area.

Find Vito

Vito is somewhere inside the yellow circle that appears on your map. But something more than the Fishmonger smells fishy here—goons patrol the wharf while other mobsters lie dead on the ground. Turns out these guards are Michael Grecco's men, and this dock is now hostile turf! Take cover near the entrance and start whistling to lure thugs for silent takedowns.

Find and neutralize the mob gunmen who patrol the walkways along the waterfront edge of the dock. Then work your way down the center of the dock, including the big Shipping warehouse on the right and the Chum Grinder building on the left.

> ### HAVE A BLAST
>
> Note the red explosive canisters scattered around the area. If you have to resort to gunplay, target canisters when foes are near them.

Watch for thugs emerging from Benny's restaurant at the far end of the dock. Before you enter Benny's, consider

wiretapping the Junction Box right outside the front entrance. Then take cover at the doorway and nail the guards holed up inside the restaurant.

Free Vito

Follow your objective marker into the kitchen at the back of restaurant and approach the freezer door. Use your Pry Bar to jimmy the door lock and trigger a long cinematic: Lincoln rescues Vito from a chilly fate, and the two end up discussing partnership and Michael Grecco. Vito's new rival has a warehouse full of smuggled contraband, and he's muscled control of the dock union. This opens up both River Row rackets: Contraband and Union Extortion.

VITO'S ASSOCIATE

Recruiting Vito Scaletta gains Lincoln access to one of Vito's "Criminal Associates," his personal banker: Betty Johnson, the Consigliere. Radio the Consigliere anytime for mobile money deposit services.

Betty arrives to collect your wallet cash and store it safely so you don't lose it if you fall in battle.

> ### COLLECT VITO'S ART
>
>
>
> After the cinematic with Vito, go back into his office and snag the Vargas painting that sits on the cabinet next to his desk.
>
> Then head downstairs into the Benny's dining room and collect another Vargas sitting on the floor behind the reception desk near the front door.

UNLOCKS: "Union Extortion" Racket

UNLOCKS: "Contraband" Racket

RACKET: UNION EXTORTION

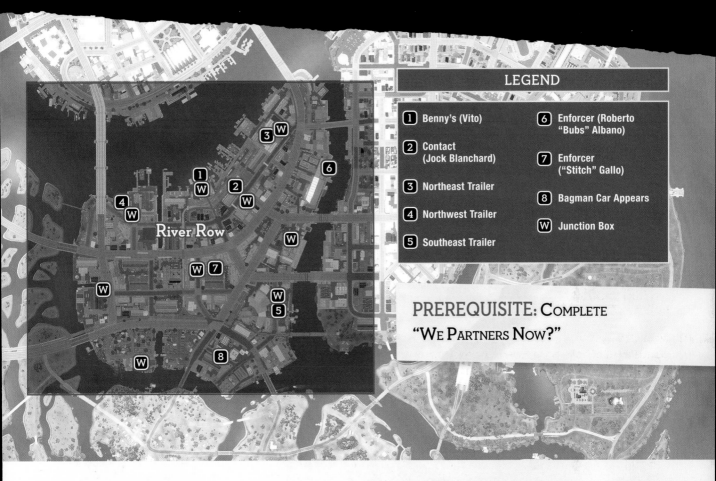

LEGEND

1	Benny's (Vito)	6	Enforcer (Roberto "Bubs" Albano)
2	Contact (Jock Blanchard)	7	Enforcer ("Stitch" Gallo)
3	Northeast Trailer	8	Bagman Car Appears
4	Northwest Trailer	W	Junction Box
5	Southeast Trailer		

PREREQUISITE: COMPLETE "WE PARTNERS NOW?"

Talk to Jock Blanchard (First Time)

First, find Vito's union contact man. Follow the trip route down the railroad tracks to the well-marked headquarters **(2)** of the United Dockworkers, Local 32. Enter the brick building via the door under the sign that reads "Support Your Local Dock Union." Approach

the man in overalls standing inside. This is Jock Blanchard, a dockworker union leader.

Talk to Jock to learn that a meathead named Andy Turetto is in charge of Grecco's efforts to extort union members. Turetto is taking steep payoffs to dispense union work permits. He's got permits locked away in trailers. His thugs are intimidating workers out at jobsites as well.

UNLOCKS: SABOTAGE UNION TRAILERS

UNLOCKS: KILL UNION ENFORCERS

UNLOCKS: TAIL BAGMEN TO UNION STASH

WIRETAPPING RIVER ROW

Remember to track down and wiretap the Junction Box in each new sector you enter; River Row has nine of them. Keep collecting TL-49 Fuses (three per box) so you have enough for the job.

Sabotage Union Trailers (3)

PREREQUISITE: TALK TO JOCK BLANCHARD (FIRST TIME)

Turetto has three mobile trailers in River Row that he uses for onsite control of union business. Each trailer is stuffed with work permits, so destroying them will inflict a real blow to his extortion scheme.

NORTHEAST TRAILER

Travel up to Rigolet's Canning Company **(3)**, a mob hideout. (Before you try to infiltrate, be sure you've wiretapped the Junction Box just around the corner.) The site features two union trailers—one up high on a platform, and the other one (your target) down on the ground. Enter the front gate and take cover at the metal container then check Intel View to find the guards. Whistle to lure them for a takedown.

If you want, check out the upper trailer first. Stalk around the container's left side, climb upstairs to the trailer, and take cover just outside the doorway. Lure the guard sitting on the couch inside and KO him, then enter and loot the trailer, including stacks of cash and a Tac-Vest in the Weapon Locker.

Now you can descend the stairs and sneak to the lower trailer, your target. Use Intel View to spot the guy inside and monitor his movement. Hide behind the trailer and wait for the mobster to step outside then creep up behind him for a silent takedown. Enter the trailer, approach the marked file drawers, and hold down the button prompted to plant explosives. Then exit to trigger the explosion that destroys the trailer and all the work permits.

NORTHWEST TRAILER

Travel to the lot next to Bayside Shipping **(4)** and scope out the union trailer in the yard. (Make sure you wiretap the Junction Box on the back side of the building first.) This area is teeming with union workers and Turetto's thugs.

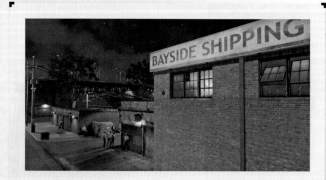

But if you work your way around to the largely deserted back entrance gate, you can take down a lone guard and sneak through the covered boats to the trailer door. Creep inside and plant the explosives. The two guards at the trailer's other door have their backs to you and don't notice! They get a warm surprise when you exit the trailer.

SOUTHEAST TRAILER

Travel to find the union trailers **(5)** in a parking lot next to the Tugboat Bar. Workers are lined up, waiting to pay extortion money for work permits. Go around behind the bar and wiretap the Junction Box (circled in our shot) to get better intel then take cover at the nearby opening in the fence.

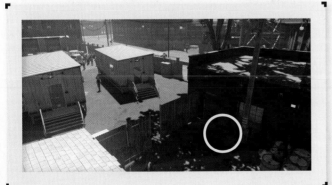

Lure armed thugs for takedowns. The open trailer on the right (closest to the street) has the file drawers stuffed with work permits. Plant explosives on the drawers and exit to destroy the trailer. Then break into the second trailer to find more cash and a TL-49 Fuse.

Kill Union Enforcers

PREREQUISITE: TALK TO JOCK BLANCHARD (FIRST TIME)

If you've destroyed all three union trailers and successfully tailed the bagman to grab the union stash (see the next objective), then you may have already inflicted enough racket damage to lower its Earn to $0 and go after its boss. But even if so, it's a good idea to hit both of Turetto's Enforcers before you go after Turetto himself. Otherwise, the Enforcers will be waiting for you alongside the boss, making that final battle extra tough.

ROBERTO "BUBS" ALBANO

Follow the trip route to the loading dock of the Padovano Pesce warehouse **(6)**. (Be sure you wiretap the sector's Junction Box first, located a good distance down the waterfront on the Dominik's Sugar building.) You can approach around either side of the building and take cover behind the trucks backed up to the dock. Scan the area in Intel View.

Lure over thugs including Bubs for silent takedowns; make sure you get the Sentry before you're detected so he can't call in Reinforcements.

93

"STITCH" GALLO

Travel to the work site in the lot behind The Original Lunette Billiard building **(7)**. Once again, you find an Enforcer and his mob goons beating up workers. The sector Junction Box is right on the building, not far from the action, so get it wiretapped (if you haven't already done so). Then sneak to take cover behind the tall stack of shipping pallets. Start thinning out the enemy crowd stealthily until you can get to Stitch.

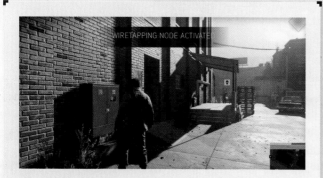

Tail Bagman to Union Stash

PREREQUISITE: TALK TO JOCK BLANCHARD (FIRST TIME)

Park on this street **(8)** in southwest River Row and watch for a cherry red De'Leo 58 sports car marked by an overhead "Follow" icon. The driver is one of Andy Turetto's bagmen ferrying a deposit of union dues to a secret safehouse in a local warehouse. Follow that car!

Two things: don't follow too close, and avoid drawing attention by making risky moves or hitting things. A Tailing Meter under your rearview mirror onscreen measures how suspicious the bagman is getting. If you trigger his panic, he speeds away and is very difficult to catch. If you lose him, you'll have to try again later.

If you manage to stay on the "Follow" car's tail without spooking the driver, he eventually leads you to a nondescript warehouse guarded by Turetto's goons. Gun down the bagman and goons then find the $9000 cash pile stashed on an office desk behind the cage in the back corner.

Talk to Jock Blanchard (Second Time)

PREREQUISITE: RACKET DAMAGE LOWERS EARN TO $0

Once you've inflicted enough damage on Andy Turetto's racket to lower its Earn to $0, you can visit Jock Blanchard **(2)** again. You get the option to remove all remaining racket objectives. If you select Accept, Jock reports that Turetto is down at the Dock Union trying to rectify the situation.

Confront Andy Turetto

Follow the new trip route back to Rigolet's Canning Company **(3)**. This time you need to infiltrate the building and confront the head man, Andy Turetto. The area is heavily guarded, so we recommend the southwest entrance—the gate is closed, but you can climb over the wall using the crate to the right (shown in our screenshot). You end up at the foot of a staircase.

Stealthily climb the stairs to the top and follow the catwalk behind the sign's big "COMPANY" letters and under the water tankuntil you reach the sniper rifle. Here you can grab the Manitou Model 67, move to the nearby spot designated a "Sniper Point" in your Intel View, and start picking off mobsters below, if you want.

But another great option is to continue through the door at the end of the catwalk and descend the interior staircase. Take cover next to the door at the bottom. Whistle to lure the two nearby guards from outside for silent takedowns.

Once the coast is clear, slip outside, turn hard right, and sneak past the dumpster to the next door that leads into an office. Enter and take cover next to the interior doorway. This is a great spot—use your Intel View to locate all the enemies nearby, including a pair of Sentries.

Now just start whistling. They come one by one to investigate, including Andy Turreto himself! Subdue and Kill/ Recruit him to secure the Union Extortion racket.

NEW ASSOCIATE & SERVICE: HIT SQUAD

Handing over the Union Extortion Racket to Vito Scaletta gives you the services of a new Associate: Bobby "Ducks" Navarro and his Hit Squad. When you radio Bobby, he promptly deploys his boys who give Lincoln aggressive armed support.

Assign the Extortion Racket to Vito

Now that the Union Extortion Racket is secured, press the button prompted to assign it to Vito Scaletta.

If you secured the Union Extortion racket first (as in this walkthrough), you add the Hit Squad to your Associates Menu. Whenever Lincoln is outnumbered badly, you can summon support from this three-man crew of armed associates.

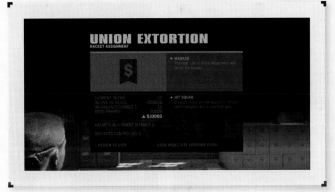

But if you secured the Contraband racket first, then assigning the Union Extortion racket to Vito is his second racket. This puts Lincoln in touch with Vito's associate, Dr. Gianni Bruno. The Mob Doctor 1 upgrade adds a third bar to your Health.

RACKET: CONTRABAND

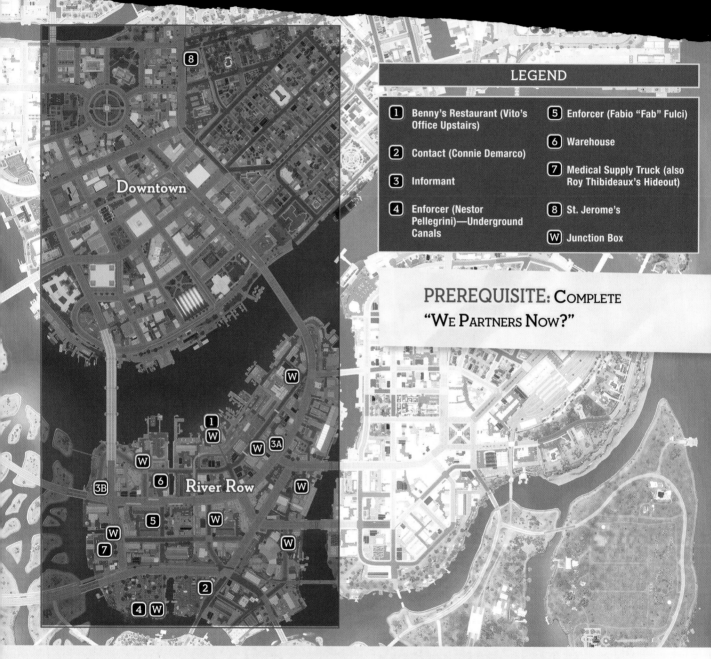

LEGEND

1 Benny's Restaurant (Vito's Office Upstairs)	5 Enforcer (Fabio "Fab" Fulci)
2 Contact (Connie Demarco)	6 Warehouse
3 Informant	7 Medical Supply Truck (also Roy Thibideaux's Hideout)
4 Enforcer (Nestor Pellegrini)—Underground Canals	8 St. Jerome's
	W Junction Box

PREREQUISITE: COMPLETE "WE PARTNERS NOW?"

Talk to Connie Demarco (First Visit)

Follow the trip route to a neighborhood of ramshackle huts and let your objective marker guide you to Vito's contact **(2)**, Connie Demarco. (Connie's house is the one with a big KEEP OUT sign on the front door; just enter through the side or back doors.) Talk to Connie to learn he's kept an eye on Roy Thibideaux's smuggling operation in River Row. Roy is bringing in rum and cigars from Cuba, and selling medical supplies back to Cuba—all of it illegally. His business front is called Skidaway Durables.

Interrogate Roy's Guards

PREREQUISITE: Talk to Connie Demarco

The Informant appears in one of two possible spots on your map (3a, 3b). If the Informant manages to escape, he soon reappears at the other spot.

BIFF AT JOEY'S

Follow the trip route to Joey's All American Diner (3a). (Make

sure the nearby Junction Box is wiretapped.) Biff is just inside the doorway, talking to a sidekick. Either hide just outside the front door and whistle them over one at a time, or else just rush in and incapacitate Biff first then KO his buddy. Grab Biff and learn about Roy's smuggling operation; he's trying to ship medical supplies to Cuba for extra cash.

UNLOCKS:

STEAL OR DESTROY MEDICAL SUPPLY TRUCK

ROSCOE AT BABY BEAR

Follow the trip route to Baby Bear B.B.Q. and Beer (3b) on the west side. (Wiretap that nearby Junction Box.) Roscoe is just inside the doorway, talking

to a sidekick. Hide just outside the front door and whistle them over one at a time, or just rush in and incapacitate Roscoe then KO his buddy. Grab Roscoe and learn about Roy's smuggling operation; he's trying to ship medical supplies to Cuba for extra cash.

UNLOCKS:

STEAL OR DESTROY MEDICAL SUPPLY TRUCK

Kill Roy's Enforcers

PREREQUISITE: Talk to Connie Demarco

NESTOR PELLEGRINI

One of Roy Thibideaux's tough guys runs a smuggling warehouse on the docks (4). First, be sure to wiretap the Junction Box (circled in our shot) on the back wall of the warehouse building, if you haven't done so already. Now you can see the whole layout through the walls.

Take cover behind a crate on the docks and whistle the Sentry to you. Once he's down, you can push forward to the contraband crates and start luring Pellegrini's other goons. Once you eliminate the Enforcer himself, use Intel View to find the two pallets of smuggled goods inside the warehouse. Don't miss the $500 pile of cash nearby!

FABIO "FAB" FULCI

Fab Fulci oversees the part of Roy's smuggling operation that ships out of the underground canals. Follow the trip route to

the parking lot outside the factory with the huge Big Break cigarette billboard on the roof. If you've wiretapped the sector's Junction Box, your Intel View reveals that enemies are down below you in the canals!

One entrance leading downstairs to the canals is across the street in the Bayside Shipping loading docks **(5)**. Find the green door that leads to a control valve room with a utility shaft that drops down into a tunnel.

Follow the tunnel to the end and take cover at the doorway to the canals. Use Intel View to see a *lot* of guys milling around out there, including a Sentry. Start whistling! You can draw every canal rat in the area to your position for a silent takedown, including Fab Fulci.

Rob the Warehouse

PREREQUISITE: TALK TO CONNIE DEMARCO

Follow the trip route to the Colonel Shipping warehouse **(6)**, home of the mob's regular card game. The safest route inside: use the wooden crates sitting outside the perimeter brick wall to climb over, and then ascend the back stairwell.

At the top of the stairs, use the Pry Bar to break in the back door. Open the next door and sneak up behind the guard with his back to you at the railing. Now move quietly along the railing. Your primary target is a huge stash of cash on the poker table down on the main floor. Three mob thugs stand around the table, so a nice move is to toss down a grenade or Molotov right on top of the table. You can nail all three at once!

Take out any remaining guards and then grab the three stacks of cash sitting on the poker table.

Steal or Destroy Medical Supply Truck

PREREQUISITE: Interrogate Roy's Guards

Once you interrogate the Informant, a new Target of Opportunity appears on your map. Follow the trip route to the big brick warehouse (7) on River Row's west side and wiretap the Junction Box on the building. Then step just around the corner and use your Pry Bar to open the door. Inside, you find a Weapon Locker with a rugged Tac-Vest inside, plus a stack of cash on the desk.

Move through the next room full of supplies and take cover at the door leading into the central storage area. Open the door and use Intel View to survey the area. Note that three Sentries are posted around the room. Start sneaking through the area, making stealth kills. Be sure to explore the upper levels of the warehouse to find offices filled with cash and collectibles.

WAREHOUSE OFFICE

The interior office on the second level of the warehouse holds two stacks of cash and a Vargas painting.

Downstairs on the main floor, look for the supply crates that you can destroy, plus several more stacks of cash. (As always, use your Intel View to spot all of these objects.) Then find the truck marked with the green cross. It is filled with medical supplies. You have two choices: you can destroy it or drive it to St. Jerome's (8), Father James' church in the French Ward.

Talk to Connie Demarco (Second Visit)

PREREQUISITE: Racket Damage Lowers Earn to $0

Head back to see Connie Demarco again (2). When you talk to him, you get the option to remove all remaining racket objectives. If you select Accept, Connie tells you that Roy Thibideaux is rattled and sleeping at his main warehouse.

CALL JACKIE D!

Before you make your move into the hideout of any Racket Boss, radio the mobile Arms Dealer to upgrade your weapons, stock up on ammo, and replenish your supply of explosives like Grenades, Molotovs, and Screaming Zemis.

Confront Roy Thibideaux

Follow the trip route to Roy's headquarters at Skidaway Durables, the big warehouse (7) where you dealt with the medical supply truck. This place is heavily guarded! A good infiltration route: go to the smaller building across the canal that connects to the warehouse via an enclosed skywalk. Climb the back stairs to the skywalk and sneak down its corridor. Then start whistling to lure a few of the guards for silent takedowns to even up the odds a bit.

When you reach the far end of the skywalk you can set up in the Sniper Point (seen in Intel View) overlooking the warehouse floor below and start picking off goons. If you try this tactic, target the Sentries first. But the easier path is to work your way stealthily across the warehouse's upper level, moving to the main office where Roy Thibideaux is holed up. Once you take down Roy, the racket is in your hands!

Assign the Contraband Racket to Vito

Now that the Contraband Racket is secured, press the button prompted to assign it to Vito Scaletta.

If you secured the Contraband racket before the Extortion racket, this adds the Hit Squad to your Associates Menu. Whenever Lincoln is outnumbered badly, you can summon support from this three-man crew of armed associates.

If you secured the Union Extortion racket before the Contraband racket (as we did in this walkthrough), assigning the second racket to Vito puts Lincoln in touch with Vito's associate, Dr. Gianni Bruno. The Mob Doctor 1 favor adds a third bar to your Health.

If You Control Both River Row Rackets...

Securing both rackets in River Row triggers a cutscene: Father James recalls his own military service as a medic in the 3rd Platoon, Company C of the Army's 614th Tank Destroyer Battalion during World War II. Because of their heroic actions in driving German troops from the heavily defended town of Climbach in France, this famous true-life battalion was the first African-American unit to receive a Distinguished Unit Citation during that war.

RIVER ROW:
FISH GOTTA EAT

MISSION: "GET MICHAEL GRECCO"

This chapter becomes available once you've secured both the Union Extortion and Contraband rackets in River Row. Now you're ready to hunt down the district boss, Marcano's lieutenant and nephew, Michael Grecco.

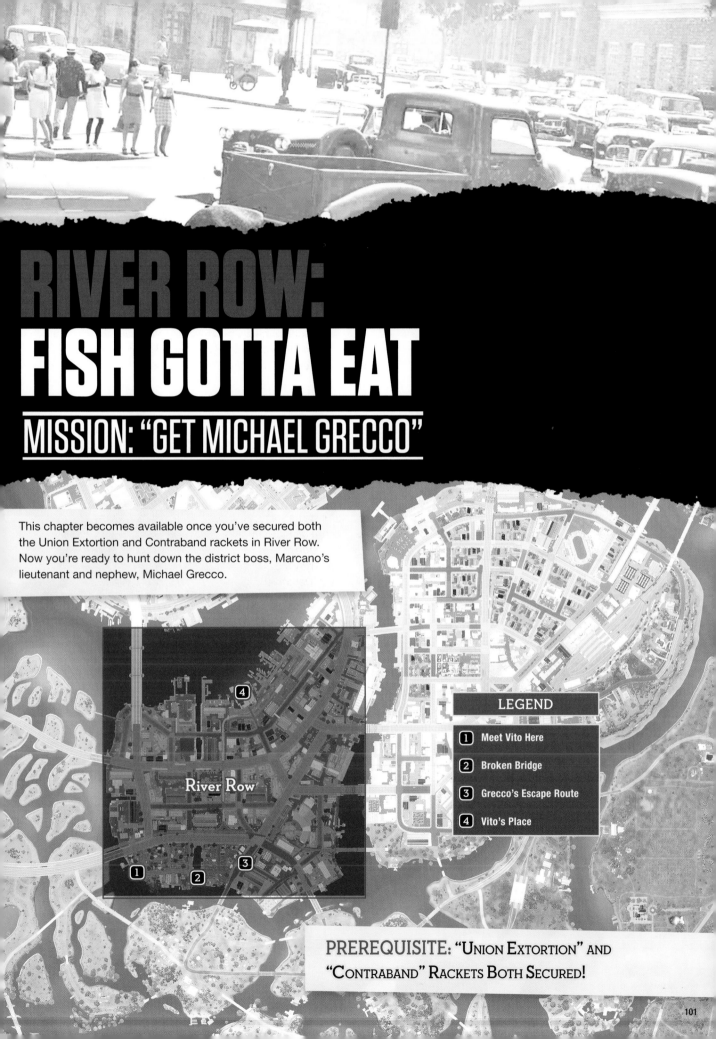

LEGEND

1. Meet Vito Here
2. Broken Bridge
3. Grecco's Escape Route
4. Vito's Place

PREREQUISITE: "UNION EXTORTION" AND "CONTRABAND" RACKETS BOTH SECURED!

Meet Vito

Find Vito Scaletta sitting in his car **(1)** down in southwest River Row. Talk to him to learn that Michael Grecco is holed up in a shack just down the road. But just as Vito and Lincoln make their move, a carload of Marcano's men beats them to the punch. Grecco escapes through a window and starts driving away!

Get Grecco

Follow Grecco's car as it makes the jump over a broken bridge **(2)** then turns left onto the main street and speeds north. Unfortunately, two carloads of Marcano's goons take up the pursuit too, and they consider you part of the problem. Your best bet is to focus on Grecco up ahead. Stay close, and try to shoot his tires to disable his car quickly. When Grecco hops out of the car to run, shoot and incapacitate him so he drops to one knee.

SHOOTING FROM CARS

Shooting while driving a vehicle uses different controls than shooting while on foot. Tap the Cycle Target button shown onscreen to select your target (such as the car's tires). To fire your weapon, press the Shooting button shown onscreen. Remember that you can click the Reverse Camera control to view targets behind you.

Kill Marcano's Men

Now you can focus on the other pursuers. Eliminate both carloads of Marcano's thugs as they pull up, if you can. Try to toss grenades at their cars before the occupants hop out and deploy. You can take out multiple targets in a wide radius when a car explodes. Remember that Vito is helping you in this gun battle.

Confront Grecco

Approach the fallen Grecco and hold the button shown to trigger a quick cutscene: Vito points out that the police are closing in, and Lincoln hauls Grecco into the car.

Lose the Police

Cut tight corners, swerve through oncoming traffic, and shoot narrow gaps to cut off pursuing cruisers. Accelerate hard when you hit long straightaways. Keep an eye on the Minimap—use it to avoid approaching blue cop blips, and keep steering away from the center of the Police Awareness radius.

Head Back to Vito's

When you finally ditch the cops, follow the trip route back to Vito's waterfront hideout **(4)**. Your arrival triggers a cinematic: under some duress, Grecco spills the beans about Sal Marcano's casino plans. Then Vito suggests that Lincoln contact Alma Diaz, a Cuban smuggler, and work with her for extra money. This opens up the Optional Mission in River Row, "Seems Simple Enough."

OPTIONAL MISSION UNLOCKED

You can find coverage of "Seems Simple Enough" in our Optional Missions chapter.

UNLOCKS OPTIONAL MISSION:
"SEEMS SIMPLE ENOUGH"

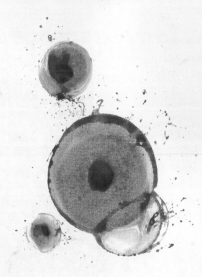

POINTE VERDUN:
THE BLADE STAINED RED
MISSION: "CUT AND RUN"

When Lincoln picks up Donovan's dossier on Thomas Burke, he learns that the disgruntled Irishman is bitter about his son Danny's death and the takeover of his Pointe Verdun turf by Roman "The Butcher" Barbieri. Burke feels betrayed, with no love lost for Sal Marcano. He's the perfect candidate for an alliance.

Pointe Verdun

Delray Hollow

LEGEND

1	**Blue Gulf Motel (Donovan's Tac-Ops Center)**
2	**Duffy's Irish Pub (Burke)**
3	**Ramp in Street**
4	**Burke's Iron & Metal**

Talk to Burke

Follow the trip route to Duffy's Irish Pub **(2)** in Pointe Verdun and try to enter the front door. You get a new directive.

Try the Back Door

Walk down the alley to the back of the building. (On the way, note the amusing antiwar wall graffiti that includes a commentary on Roman Barbieri,

AKA The Butcher.) Approach the back door to trigger a cinematic: Lincoln encounters Thomas Burke and makes a business proposition. But Burke suggests that Lincoln doesn't have the guts to challenge Sal Marcano, and gets behind the wheel of his blue Potomac Independent to drive away.

Get in Burke's Car

Enter the car on the driver's side; Lincoln pushes Burke over to the passenger seat. Your job now is to "Convince Burke."

Drive Like a Madman!

Your goal: Drive dangerously until you fill up the red meter onscreen (seen just under the rearview mirror). Exit the alley, turn left, speed through the intersection and steer straight toward the trailer **(3)** that forms a ramp in the street!

Every collision or near-miss with another car, object, or pedestrian builds the meter. Punch the accelerator hard, drift wildly around corners, run red lights, veer close to sideswipe oncoming traffic, and execute jumps that catch air with hard landings. Fun! When the meter finally fills up, Burke tells you to pull over.

Stop the Car and Get Out

Stop the car and get out. Burke says you have more to discuss, and then drives off.

UNLOCKS STORY MISSION:

"A Nation Once Again"

MISSION: "A NATION ONCE AGAIN"

PREREQUISITE: Complete "Cut and Run"

Talk to Burke

Follow the trip route to Burke's Iron & Metal **(4)** and enter the shop via the door under the blue awning. This triggers a scene: Lincoln learns about Roman "The Butcher" Barbieri and the racket he took away from Burke, the liquor distillery. Burke also speaks of the Roberdeau

Meat Packing Plant, where the Butcher makes mincemeat of any poor fool who refuses to pay his costly "protection" fee.

BURKE'S ASSOCIATE

Recruiting Thomas Burke gains Lincoln access to one of Burke's "Criminal Associates," Hank McGahee, who runs a vehicle delivery service. Radio Hank anytime for immediate delivery of a car from your garage direct to your current location.

BURKE'S LITERATURE

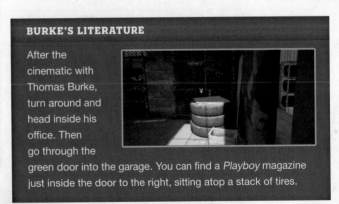

After the cinematic with Thomas Burke, turn around and head inside his office. Then go through the green door into the garage. You can find a *Playboy* magazine just inside the door to the right, sitting atop a stack of tires.

UNLOCKS: "Moonshine" Racket

RACKET: MOONSHINE

LEGEND

1. Nicki Burke
2. Informant
3. Enforcer (Dean "Dino" Barbaro)
4. Enforcer (Caesar De Angelis)
5. Sweetwater Distillery (Map to Moonshine Camps)
6. Swim Here
7. East Camp
8. West Camp
9. Alley Entrance Behind Duffy's
10. Duffy's Irish Pub (Cop Bar)
W. Junction Box

Pointe Verdun

Bayou Fantom

Talk to Nicki Burke (First Time)

Nicki is in the machine shop **(1)** just a short jog across the junkyard lot from the Burke Iron & Metal office. She tells Lincoln about Carl Bevers, the guy running moonshine out of the Sweetwater Distillery for Barbieri. She's heard that Bevers keeps moving his stills around, but he has a map for his drivers. She also mentions a guy named Bear who's been keeping an eye on the Butcher's Roberdeau meatpacking plant for the Burkes. This unlocks the other racket in the Pointe Verdun district.

UNLOCKS: "PROTECTION" RACKET

Interrogate Bootleggers

PREREQUISITE: TALK TO NICKI BURKE

Two Informants appear on the map **(2a, 2b)**, but as soon as you interrogate one, the other disappears. Take your pick. If the Informant escapes and you don't catch him, he ends up at the other Informant location.

RUDOLPHO CONTE

Follow the trip route to a residential neighborhood **(2a)** up in northwest Pointe Verdun. (Before you make your move, remember to wiretap the sector's Junction Box; it's on the wall of the Pearl Diver Motel just north of there.) Conte and his minions provided two stashes of moonshine for a crowded block party in an area of connected backyards, with houses arrayed in a circle around the party area. On top of that, beat cops are patrolling the street around the housing development. Getting to the Informant without triggering a panic with witnesses notifying police can be a tricky maneuver.

A good approach is to use the narrow alley between houses in the northwest corner of the development and then take cover at the doorway of the equipment shed where one batch of moonshine is stashed. (You can see it in Intel View.) Whistle to lure Conte's men one at a time through the shed to your doorway for silent takedowns. Eventually, Conte himself investigates; take him down and interrogate him to learn where all the hooch cash is being stashed: a bar that serves local police!

Don't leave the party without exploring the backyards to find several hefty piles of cash, including a bag holding $500, plus three stashes of moonshine barrels that you can destroy for more racket damage.

UNLOCKS OBJECTIVE: "ROB THE COP BAR"

NATALI BALBO

Travel to the east side to find Natali Balbo (2b) and his gang making a delivery behind Fareham Grocery. Your best approach: enter the store from the front, go through the Employees Only door in the back corner, and sneak out into the loading alley. Take cover behind the nearest crate and wait until one guard steps out of the storage room to the right; whistle him over for a takedown.

Now you can move behind the nearby barrels, closer to Balbo and the delivery truck. Again, whistle to lure his associates and then Natali himself for takedowns. Interrogate Balbo to learn what he knows about the cop bar stash. (Tip: Balbo's escape car is parked in front of the grocery; if he escapes the alley you can sprint back through the store, turn right, and meet him out on the sidewalk.)

Kill Bevers' Enforcers

PREREQUISITE: Talk to Nicki Burke

DEAN "DINO" BARBARO

Find Dino's crew unloading a moonshine shipment into the back door of R & R Liquor & Tobacco **(3)** in western Pointe Verdun. (Be sure to wiretap the sector Junction Box first; find it a block to the northwest, behind Frederic's Delicatessen.) A good approach is to enter the store via its front entrance, punch out the proprietor to silence him, then take cover at the exit door in the back and open it.

Now start whistling to lure in the goons from out back. You can get them all with silent takedowns, including the Sentry and Dino. Killing the Enforcer

inflicts racket damage. Then go nuts in the loading lot by blasting four pallets of moonshine barrels and the Sweetwater Distillery truck.

CAESAR DE ANGELIS

Head to the rail freight warehouse **(4)** over in southeast Pointe Verdun. The Junction Box in this sector (circled in our overhead shot) is tricky to reach because it's in a hostile zone, hanging on a wall in the warehouse loading area with mob guards posted near a distillery truck directly across the yard, facing the box. If you try to go straight for the box, the guards spot you and open fire! Instead, move stealthily to the crates near the box and then lure the guards for silent takedowns.

Climb the staircase next to the Junction Box and clear the upper level of the warehouse, where stacked crates provide good cover. Then lure Caesar upstairs and eliminate him. Taking out the Enforcer inflicts racket damage, but don't stop there. Downstairs, four destructible shipments of moonshine barrels are loaded inside the railcar, plus one more sitting outside the car. Then head outside into the loading yard and blow up the Sweetwater Distillery truck for even more damage!

Destroy the Moonshine Camps

PREREQUISITE: Talk to Nicki Burke

STEAL MAP TO MOONSHINE CAMPS

Nicki told you about rumors that Bevers has a map to his stills. Head to the Sweetwater Distillery **(5)** and take cover at the front entry gate. Slide around the corner to the right and work your way across the yard past the striped barriers and the delivery truck, taking out guards with stealth.

Climb the staircase behind the truck and turn left at the top. Go through the door into the office to find Bevers' moonshine camp map on the table next to a $500 cash pile. Grab the Tac-Vest from the Weapon Locker too, and then retrace your route out of the distillery.

WEST CAMP STILL

PREREQUISITE:

STEAL MAP TO MOONSHINE CAMPS

The west camp is on an island down in the Bayou Fantom. Follow the trip route south to the closest point to the island **(6)** then swim across the narrow waterway. Move down the dirt road to the camp **(7)** and take cover behind the stone ruin.

Work stealthily around the camp perimeter, taking down guards silently. Destroy the two stills to complete the objective, then head inside the cabin for some bonus cash. Tip: You can steal a boat from the camp dock to motor back across the water.

EAST CAMP STILL
PREREQUISITE:
STEAL MAP TO MOONSHINE CAMPS

Drive all the way to the perimeter of this camp **(8)** then approach on foot. Veer to the left side and target the big red propane tank (circled in our overhead shot) for a big explosion that takes out several nearby guards quickly. Then shoot to destroy the first still too.

Use cover and watch out for gunmen emerging from the dock shack. Clear the area and then destroy the second still to complete the objective. But don't leave until you blow up the stacks of moonshine barrels in the lean-to, and then enter the dock shack to find some generous cash prizes.

Locate and Destroy Moonshine Trucks (5)

PREREQUISITE: TALK TO NICKI BURKE

Five Sweetwater Distillery trucks are making regular deliveries around Pointe Verdun. Watch for their red rectangular blips to appear on your Minimap, then give chase and destroy them. A single grenade or Molotov does the trick, or several bursts of weapon fire.

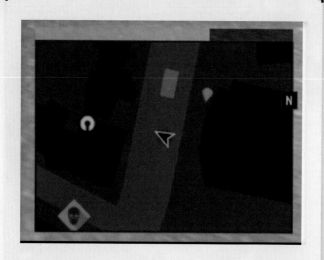

When the alley is clear, use your Pry Bar to jimmy open Duffy's back door. Enter the kitchen and find the $10,000 money stash waiting for  you on a silver platter (literally). Exit the back door.

Talk to Nicki Burke (Second Time)

Return to Nicki back at Burke's Iron & Metal (1). She tells Lincoln that Carl Bevers is at the Sweetwater Distillery. She also recommends keeping Carl alive, saying, "Nobody knows the bayou like he does."

Confront Carl Bevers

Head to the Sweetwater Distillery (5). The facility is huge and well-guarded, so we recommend breaking in the locked back door  on the east side. (You find a drunken worker sitting inside, near the big still.) Sneak rightward along the low wall and start whistling to bring a line of thugs for silent dispatch.

Rob the Cop Bar

PREREQUISITE: COMPLETE "INTERROGATE BOOTLEGGERS"

Head to Duffy's Irish Pub (10), which is crawling with not only cops but also local mob goons. (Make sure you've wiretapped the sector's Junction Box so you have full Intel View for this one!) A frontal assault would be very difficult, so circle around the block and approach via the alley (9) leading to the pub's back door. Approach stealthily, though—a few cops and thugs are posted on the back route. Lure them one by one with whistles to silent takedowns.

Exit outside via the side door and run across the alley into the big central distillery filled with massive rounded storage  tanks. When you get across to the far side, look upward with Intel View to spot Carl's location on the upper floor. (He's marked by the red icon with a star.) Keep working silently across the ground floor level until you reach the staircase.

Take cover at the first doorway at the top and peek in to see a reception office and another staircase, a fancier one with ornate wrought iron bannisters. But the "receptionist" is not very friendly. By now you've probably thinned the thug herd enough that you can just gun him down and fight your way up those stairs to the executive office where Carl Bevers is waiting. Take Bevers down and make your choice: kill or recruit? It's up to you.

Assign the Moonshine Racket to Burke

Now that the Moonshine Racket is secured, press the button prompted to assign it to Michael Burke.

> If you secured the Moonshine racket before the Protection racket (as we did in this walkthrough), this adds "Bribe the Cops 1" to your Associates Menu. Burke's associate, Fiona Davidson, is a police dispatcher who can call off police in your area. When Lincoln radios for her service, Blue Police Zones disappear and cops ignore your crimes for 30 seconds.

If you secured the Protection racket before the Moonshine racket, assigning a second racket to Burke bumps his racket income up higher. This unlocks the next Favor level from the police dispatcher, Fiona. With "Cops Nearby" added, Fiona can mark all nearby cops on your map.

The mission-ending cutscene brings more commentary from FBI Assistant Director Jonathan Maguire. He provides a quick biography of Thomas Burke.

RACKET: PROTECTION

Pointe Verdun

LEGEND

1. Bear Donnelly
2. Informants
3. Enforcer (Tito Leone)
4. Enforcer (Fede "Hats" Iocca)
5. Roberdeau Meat Packing Plant
6. Marquis' Fine Liquors
7. Marquis' Fine Liquors
8. Marquis' Fine Liquors
W. Junction Box
● Beat Down Crew

WIRETAPPING THE DISTRICT

Our map for the Protection Racket story mission includes all Junction Box locations. However, if you completed the Moonshine Racket mission first, you probably already wiretapped many if not all of the sector boxes. We include them in this map just in case.

Talk to Bear Donnelly

Follow the trip route to Mr. O'Connor's Irish Pub **(1)**, just a few blocks from Burke's shop. Enter and find Bear Donnelly by the pool table. He's been keeping an eye on the Roberdeau meatpacking plant where a fellow named Sonny Blue rents a room out to the Butcher's loan sharks and protection goons. He says one of Sonny's men, Ralph McNairy, got caught embezzling and is getting worked over in the meat packing plant right now. Setting Ralph free could cause considerable damage to the racket.

Interrogate Loan Sharks

PREREQUISITE: Talk to Bear Donnelly

Two Informants appear on the map **(2a, 2b)**, but as soon as you interrogate one, the other disappears. Take your pick. If the Informant escapes and you don't catch him, he ends up at the other Informant location.

"RED" GALLO

Travel to the Carousel Motel **(2a)** in northwest Pointe Verdun. (Wiretap the Junction Box at the site, if you haven't done so already.) Sneak along the right side of the leftmost building to the dumpster and then whistle to lure the nearby goon to a silent takedown. Take cover at the corner to see Red and another thug standing outside their room.

To make sure the Informant can't run (and to avoid gunplay with more guards inside the room), lure Red to the corner for a takedown. Red reveals the "protected" liquor store locations where the sharks also stash their collected cash.

LEONARDO RUGGERI

Leonardo Ruggeri and his crew are visiting The Butcher Block (2b) in west-central Pointe Verdun. Leonardo is inside the shop, but two of his goons stand guard out front near their parked car. Go around the corner to the right, turn into the alley, and slip past the Roberdeau delivery truck.

Approach the butcher shop's back entrance and use your Pry Bar to open the door. Then sneak down the back hall and take down Leonardo, who stands alone with a clipboard at the front counter. Interrogate him to learn about the protected liquor store stashes.

UNLOCKS: Trash Protected Liquor Stores

Kill Sonny's Enforcers

PREREQUISITE: TALK TO BEAR DONNELLY

TITO LEONE

Tito is watching two of his goons kick a beach cart vendor **(3)** next to Mama D's Creole Cajun Chicken shack near the lighthouse boardwalk. Sneak up to the restroom hut near the beating. (The sector's Junction Box is on the back

of that hut; be sure it's wiretapped.) Use Intel View to see a Sentry (circled in our shot) pacing back and forth past the hut, watching for trouble.

Go to the left to see a mob gunman facing away from you over by the bench. Make sure the Sentry isn't on that side then sneak up behind the gunman for a silent takedown. Hide his body behind the restroom hut then take cover and whistle over the Sentry for a takedown. Now you can work your way closer to Tito and take him out for racket damage. A nice trick is to toss a grenade or Molotov right into the midst of Tito and his two thugs who are working over the vendor. Afterwards, scour the area for cash pickups, including a $500 bag on the picnic table near the overturned cart.

> **LIGHTHOUSE POSTER**
>
> Don't miss the Communist Propaganda poster on the lighthouse door.

FEDE "HATS" IOCCA

Hats and his boys are working over a couple of debtors in a back parking lot **(4)** under a Black Suit billboard next to the freeway on-ramp. The approach is narrow and long, and a guard stands

at the entrance. Sneak up carefully to take cover then pounce for the quick takedown. Move down the lot and hide behind the old refrigerator on the left side. Start whistling to lure more gangsters. Or you can toss a grenade or Molotov to terminate Hats and both mugs doing the beating in a single blast, since they're clustered so closely together.

Take Out the Beat Down Crews (8)

PREREQUISITE: TALK TO BEAR DONNELLY

Sonny Blue has deployed teams of strong-arm thugs to send a strong message (i.e., beat up or shut down) late-paying customers around Pointe Verdun. Each "beat down crew" features two beefy guys (each wearing a cap and Roberdeau shirt, and marked with the "Kill" icon) who administer the beating or shut down the shop, plus a gunman nearby providing protection.

All eight of Sonny's crews are marked on our chapter map. Interrupt each beating by sneaking up to take down the gunman first, and then eliminate the two brawlers to inflict racket damage. (The location is listed as completed when you take out the first of the two "Kill"-marked meatheads, but might as well nail them both.) Look for bags of cash at each beat down spot too.

Rescue Ralph McNairy

PREREQUISITE: TALK TO BEAR DONNELLY

FIND RALPH INSIDE

Travel to the Roberdeau meatpacking plant **(5)**. (Make sure you wiretap the sector Junction Box for this one.) Ralph is held in an office on the second floor. A quick way up is to climb the chute that runs from the cattle pens up to the northeast corner of the plant (seen in our overhead screenshot).

Inside, use Intel View to work your way down the long room with the hanging cow carcass, hiding in cover and luring guards for takedowns. Work your way along the outside wall until you reach the metal catwalk with the red railings that leads to a door. Ralph is tied to a chair just on the other side.

Use Intel View to see that two goons guard Ralph. Open the door and surprise the nearest guard, who has his back to you. Then gun down the other guard. Cut Ralph loose to set him free.

If you want to explore further, you can find plenty of cash stashed around the plant, including $1750 piled on the desk in the office not far from where you found Ralph—just hop over the two low walls to reach it. (There's also a Vargas painting on the office wall.) Looting the plant inflicts a lot of damage on the Protection racket. But be prepared to face a lot of Sonny's thugs on the way.

Trash Protected Liquor Stores (3)

PREREQUISITE: INTERROGATE LOAN SHARKS

The Informant told Lincoln about three liquor stores that pay Sonny's hefty protection fees. You can steal the cash payments at each

store to really put the hurt to the racket's Earn. All three places **(6, 7, 8)** are part of the Marquis' Fine Liquors chain of stores.

At each store, you can simply run in the front door, hustle past the proprietor (or punch him to subdue him) and enter the back office. Or if you

want to avoid getting reported to the police, head around to the back entrance instead. You can pry it open and sneak into the office without being detected. Then grab the $2500 protection payment sitting on the desk.

Talk to Bear Donnelly (Second Time)

Return to Bear in Mr. O'Connor's Irish Pub **(1)**. He tells Lincoln that Sonny Blue is now at the Roberdeau plant.

Confront Sonny Blue

Head back to Roberdeau Meatpacking Plant **(5)**. (You should already have the sector wiretapped.) Check your Intel View

frequently in this well-defended meat packing plant. Sonny is in the upstairs office, so drive into the northwest entrance and use the same route up the chute from the cattle pens as you did when you rescued Ralph McNairy earlier. Unlock the door at the top and quickly take cover outside.

Two guards pace back and forth past the hanging cow carcass, so time your moves to take them both down without getting spotted. Work your way around the outside (right) wall until you reach the metal catwalk with red railings that leads to a closed door. You can see the star icon marking Sonny's location directly ahead.

Before you open the door, use Intel View to make sure the pacing Sentry in the next room is moving away from you. Move through the door to spot Sonny Blue across the room with his back to you—if you've arrived undetected, you can hear Sonny talk trash about Barbieri to an associate. Try to

sneak up behind him, vaulting the first low wall and then taking Sonny down from behind at the second low wall.

If you wait too long, though, Sonny enters the office at the far end of the room with his associate. You can try to follow directly, or else methodically work your way through the room with the cutting tables, taking down guards silently as they face away, or luring them with whistles…or just blasting your way through them. (If detected, you have a tough firefight on your hands, but know that Sonny won't leave the office.) Then slip into the office when Sonny has his back to you. If you've been detected, he hides behind his desk for cover.

Assign the Protection Racket to Burke

Now that the Protection Racket is secured, press the button prompted to assign it to Michael Burke.

If you secured the Protection racket before the Moonshine racket, this adds "Bribe the Cops 1" to your Associates Menu. Burke's associate, Fiona Davidson, is a police dispatcher who can call off police in your area. When Lincoln radios for her service, Blue Police Zones disappear and cops ignore your crimes for 30 seconds.

But if you secured the Protection racket *after* the Moonshine racket (as we did in this walkthrough), assigning it to Burke bumps his racket income up. This unlocks the next Favor level from the police dispatcher, Fiona. With "Cops Nearby" added, Fiona can mark the location of all nearby cops on your map.

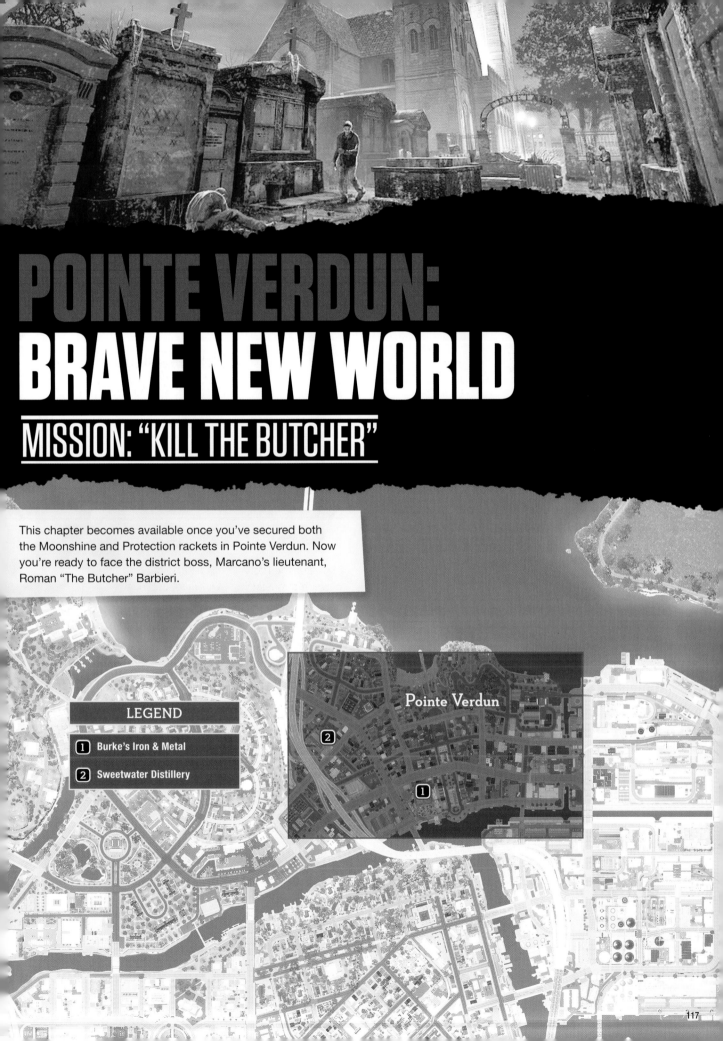

POINTE VERDUN: BRAVE NEW WORLD

MISSION: "KILL THE BUTCHER"

This chapter becomes available once you've secured both the Moonshine and Protection rackets in Pointe Verdun. Now you're ready to face the district boss, Marcano's lieutenant, Roman "The Butcher" Barbieri.

Pointe Verdun

LEGEND

1 Burke's Iron & Metal

2 Sweetwater Distillery

Return to Burke's Iron & Metal

Travel back to Burke's shop. Before you enter, this might be a good time to call the Arms Dealer to restock ammo, supplies, and explosives, and also upgrade your weapons if you can. Then open the shop door to trigger the cinematic: Burke prepares for the defense of his turf as Barbieri's crew approaches. Nicki arrives to man the spotlights; Burke heads off to the crane; and Lincoln sets up on the roof.

Defend Burke's Iron & Metal

The Butcher's crew arrives piecemeal, in waves of cars. Watch for their approaching headlights at the lot entrance at upper left. Some cars veer directly up the left side of the lot, but others steer across the back of the lot and turn up the right side. Use your sniper rifle's scope and target the explosive red barrels that Burke placed around the lot.

ROOFTOP COVER

Gunfire chews up the wooden slats that provide cover when you're on Burke's roof. If the wood breaks apart too much, just slide over behind the air conditioning unit.

The key is to detonate a barrel just as the arriving mob car is closest to it. If you time it right, the explosion destroys the car and takes out all of its occupants with a single shot. If you don't destroy the car, however, you'll have to pick off the mob gunmen individually as they deploy across the lot. Nicki helps by shining the spotlight on foes as they advance. Keep using the sniper rifle, but be ready to switch to your handgun if one of the goons makes it up the ladder to your rooftop.

FIGHT TO SUIT YOUR STYLE

You can drop to the ground at any time for a close-range battle in the lot, if you want. We recommend staying up on the rooftop sniper post as long as your ammo holds out, but fight the way you like best.

Kill the Butcher's Men

This objective appears only if you incapacitate Barbieri while any of his men are still alive in the junkyard. Hunt them all down then return to the fallen Butcher.

Get to the Butcher

Clearing out the first waves triggers a cutscene: up on the crane, Thomas Burke watches the arrival of an armored Pinkerton Titan that unloads more goons plus the Butcher himself, Roman Barbieri.

Approach the fallen Butcher and hold the button prompted to trigger a final cutscene: Barbieri remains defiant to the end, and then the FBI's Maguire reports on the aftermath.

Confront the Butcher

The objective marker indicates the Butcher's location and distance; he deploys over to the left side of the yard. Try to drop him with sniper shots, but don't ignore his men, who push forward aggressively and try to climb to the roof. Keep picking them off, targeting any remaining explosive barrels when shooters are near them. When the last of his men falls, Barbieri emerges and tries to rush your position. Nail him until he drops to a knee, incapacitated.

MISSION: "ONLY WAY'S FORWARD"

Talk to Burke at Distillery

Travel to the Sweetwater Distillery **(2)** and find Burke sitting outside in the north lot. This triggers the chapter-ending cinematic: a heartbroken Thomas Burke tells Lincoln that his daughter Nicki manages the moonshine runs, and they bring in good money. He suggests a partnership, which opens up a new optional mission for you: "The Righteously F***ed." You also unlock a pair of short optional "chapters" that call for nothing more than traveling to see Donovan and Father James for a single conversation with each.

OPTION MISSION UNLOCKED

You can find coverage of "The Righteously F***ed" in our Optional Missions chapter.

If You Control Delray Hollow, River Row, and Pointe Verdun...

Once you've secured all three districts, you trigger a cutscene from the 1971 Senate hearing with John Donovan, who explains to the Senators how Lincoln Clay called a sitdown meeting at an abandoned mansion in the bayou to make a plan with Cassandra, Vito, and Burke. Then you see the chapter-ending cinematic: Sal and Giorgi Marcano, father and son, discuss their casino project. Sal gets a phone call with some unsettling news: Lincoln Clay is still alive.

UNLOCKS OPTIONAL MISSION:
"The Righteously F***ed"

UNLOCKS OPTIONAL MISSION:
"Who We Shootin'?"

UNLOCKS OPTIONAL MISSION:
"How Things Really Work"

BAYOU FANTOM:
SITDOWN

MISSION: "AN EMOTIONAL ATTACHMENT"

PREREQUISITE:
GAIN CONTROL OF DELRAY HOLLOW, POINTE
VERDUN AND RIVER ROW DISTRICTS

Boyou Fantom

LEGEND

1 Bayou Mansion "Sitdown"

Call a Sitdown

Travel to the old mansion **(1)** in the Bayou Fantom and enter the front door to trigger a long cinematic. Lincoln's three new Underbosses meet for the first time, and it's not a happy gathering. Bad blood flows through the criminal underworld, and it takes a strong hand to keep troops in order. Fortunately, Lincoln Clay has everyone's attention and respect now.

Lincoln details his plan to lay waste to Marcano's organization from the bottom up. The first step is to take out the three remaining lieutenants who run the Barclay Mills, Tickfaw Harbor, and Downtown districts. Then hit the capos in Frisco Fields, French Ward, and Southdowns. Once all the Marcano soldiers

have been taken down, Sal and Giorgi will be isolated, defunded, and vulnerable. Finally, Lincoln reveals the news about Marcano's casino. Afterwards, he meets Donovan who monitored the meeting.

UNLOCKS STORY CHAPTERS:

"The Dead Stay Gone" (Barclay Mills)
"Compromised Corruption" (Downtown)
"Hot Rubber & Cold Blood" (Tickfaw Harbor)

UNLOCKS OPTIONAL CHAPTERS:

".45 In My Hand" (Cassandra)
"I Need a Favor" (Vito)
"I.R.A. Don't Ask" (Burke)
"How Things Really Work" (Father James)

What Now?

After the sit-down, your map suddenly explodes with possibilities. You can meet up with Donovan and continue plotting your takedown of the Marcano organization in New Bordeaux by hitting three new districts: Barclay Mills, Tickfaw Harbor, and Downtown.

Or you can pursue a number of optional side missions that bring in cash and keep your Underbosses happy. Check out our Optional Missions chapter for guidance through those opportunities.

Our Story walkthrough will stick to the plan devised by Lincoln and Donovan to bring down Sal Marcano. We'll work through districts in the order they're listed on your Objectives Panel. Each district takeover begins by meeting Donovan in his mobile tac-ops center, a blue Marquis' Fine Liquors delivery van.

BARCLAY MILLS:
THE DEAD STAY GONE

MISSION: "THE DEAD STAY GONE"

Barclay Mills

LEGEND

1 Meet Donovan (Bus Stop)

PREREQUISITE: COMPLETE "AN EMOTIONAL ATTACHMENT"

Meet with Donovan

Select the Barclay Mills chapter and activate the first objective, "Meet with Donovan." Follow the trip route to the bus stop **(1)** where Donovan pulls up in his van. He gives Lincoln his intel on Enzo Conti, the Marcano lieutenant who runs the rackets in Barclay Mills. Donovan calls him "old-school mob."

Lincoln suggests that because Marcano is a felon, somebody legit must be co-sponsoring the casino operation. But Donovan's had no luck finding out who. However, Enzo's train operation has been shipping all of the heavy construction equipment and supplies for the casino, so he most likely knows Marcano's silent partner. The goal is to flip Enzo and learn what he knows.

UNLOCKS: "Garbage" Racket

UNLOCKS: "Guns" Racket

RACKET: GARBAGE

LEGEND

1	Bus Stop
2	Maria Bava
3	Di Napoli Garbage Dump
4	Informants
5	Enforcer (Mister Honeysuckle)
6	Cleaner's Stash
W	Junction Box
●	Garbage Barge

Barclay Mills

PREREQUISITE: Meet with Donovan

Talk to Maria Bava (First Time)

From your bus stop meeting with Donovan **(1)**, travel south to the small two-garage auto shop **(2)** next to the freeway ramp and enter to talk to Maria Bava. She works at the Di Napoli Waste Removal site

and reports that her boss, "Puppy" Simmons, has been dumping waste in the bay, extorting drivers who work for competitors, and deploying a team of "cleaners"—hired killers who specialize in body disposal.

UNLOCKS: Sabotage Dump

Sabotage Dump

PREREQUISITE:

Talk to Maria Bava

Lincoln needs to open with a big play to shake up Puppy's garbage operation and flush out informants. His plan: blow up Puppy's heavy equipment at the Di Napoli dump **(3)**. Before you enter the dump, wiretap the Junction Box on the building just across the main road to the north.

PLANT EXPLOSIVE TO SABOTAGE GARBAGE DUMP

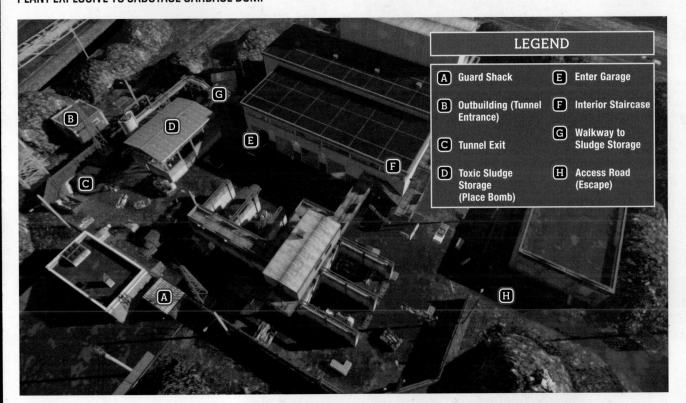

LEGEND	
A Guard Shack	**E** Enter Garage
B Outbuilding (Tunnel Entrance)	**F** Interior Staircase
C Tunnel Exit	**G** Walkway to Sludge Storage
D Toxic Sludge Storage (Place Bomb)	**H** Access Road (Escape)

Travel to the dump entrance on its north side where you see a guard shack **(A)**. Go around the building to the left (opposite side of guard shack) and kick in the door of the small outbuilding **(B)**. Inside, climb down the ladder into the lower level then exit via the door into a tunnel passage that leads out into the dump **(C)**.

Survey the area with Intel View then creep uphill to the left side of the structure on the left **(D)**. This structure is packed with barrels filled with explosive toxic sludge, so it's the perfect place to plant a bomb. However, the way inside is tricky. Proceed around its back side; above you, you can see the raised walkway **(G)** leading from the big main building into the structure. (You can also find a Weapon Locker with a nice Tac-Vest in the small hut behind the structure.) You need to reach that walkway.

Work your way to the main building and enter the first garage door **(E)** to find a nice $875 cash stash on the worktable against the left wall. Move past the garbage trucks and climb the stairs **(F)** on the far side of the room. Use stealth or fight your way around the interior walkway that leads through a control room into a big office space with plenty more cash (plus a Vargas hanging on the wall)

Exit the office's far door then turn right onto the walkway **(G)** leading over to the barrel-filled storage. Be ready! One of Puppy's tough Enforcers wearing a green haz-mat suit is posted here. Take him down for racket damage, then place your explosive on the generator motor.

GET AWAY FROM THE GARBAGE DUMP

Retrace your route back through the main building and descend the stairs. (Watch for another Enforcer in a green suit on the interior walkway.) Exit the Di Napoli Waste Removal dump via the access road **(H)** and watch the fireworks.

UNLOCKS: Interrogate the Extortionists

Interrogate the Extortionists

PREREQUISITE: Sabotage Dump

Two Informants appear on the map **(4a, 4b)**, but as soon as you interrogate one, the other one disappears. Take your pick. If the Informant escapes and you don't catch him, he ends up at the other Informant location.

WIRETAP THE EXTORTIONISTS

Be sure to wiretap the Junction Box in their sector before you visit either Informant.

HARRY "GIGI" JACKSON

Gigi and his crew are extorting some workers in the big, open garage of a truck repair shop **(4a)**. Head down the side alley and take cover at the back corner of the garage. Whistle Gigi's thugs one by one over to the alley for silent takedowns so you don't spook their boss. Eventually Gigi follows the parade of fools to your spot. After he tells Lincoln about Puppy's cleaners, kill or recruit him. Then find cash plus a *Playboy* collectible in the garage.

MISTER HONEYSUCKLE

Acquire a sniper rifle and travel to the toxic chemical dump site **(5)**. Take the Objective text's advice and climb the hilltop to the west, overlooking the cleaner's crew. From here you can pick off Mister Honeysuckle with a single headshot—he's the guy in the green haz-mat suit and the "Kill" icon overhead. Or you can try the low approach and sneak around the vehicles for silent kills. If you choose to clear out all goons, scour the area for stacks of cash.

Steal the Cleaner's Money Stash

PREREQUISITE:

INTERROGATE THE EXTORTIONISTS

Finish up your cleaner cleanup by traveling down to their grisly hazardous storage plant **(6)** where they stash their earnings…and chemically dissolve their victims. (The sector Junction Box is just down the road to the south; look in the parking lot underneath the towering "WBYU 620" roadside billboard.) Use Intel View to see a total of six "Kill" icons floating inside the facility! That's half a dozen tough cleaners in green haz-mat suits.

UNLOCKS: KILL THE CLEANERS

UNLOCKS: FIND AND DESTROY GARBAGE BARGES

UNLOCKS: STEAL THE CLEANER'S MONEY STASH

DALE "SUSIE" SUSANNAH

"Susie" Susannah and a partner loiter on the dock **(4b)** near a rusted out old tugboat on the eastern shoreline of Barclay Mills. Sneak up close along the low wall, gun down the partner, then incapacitate Susie and make him squeal.

Kill the Cleaners

PREREQUISITE:

INTERROGATE THE EXTORTIONISTS

Before you go after Puppy's Enforcer, the "cleaner" known as Mister Honeysuckle, wiretap the sector's nearby Junction Box. It's on the landward wall of the shipping warehouse down on the river dock.

Move around the left side to the entrance and take cover. Start whistling to lure over the killers. Each dead cleaner is worth racket damage, so hunt and kill all six of them! Find the blue strongbox sitting on the worktable in the back and pry it open to snag the $10,000 inside. Then get out of there.

Find and Destroy Garbage Barges (6)
PREREQUISITE:
INTERROGATE THE EXTORTIONISTS

Di Napoli Waste Removal gets rid of toxic sludge by dumping it from garbage barges into the scenic waterways of New Bordeaux. These barges are located

at six dock locations around the district (all marked on our district map). When you wiretap each sector's Junction Box in Barclay Mills, you reveal any barges in that sector. Destroy the barges to inflict serious racket damage to Puppy Simmons and his garbage organization. Careful, though—each dock is guarded by a handful of Puppy's thugs.

Talk to Maria Bava (Second Time)

When you've knocked the racket damage required down to $0, return to Maria (2) to learn that Puppy has emerged. He's at the Di Napoli dump, trying to shore up the operations that Lincoln has disrupted.

Confront Paul "Puppy" Simmons

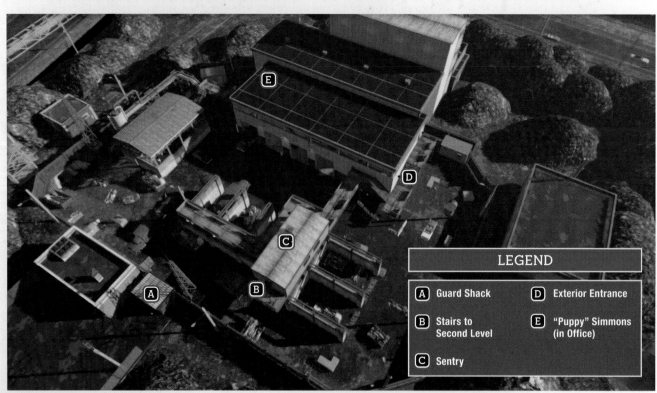

LEGEND
- **A** Guard Shack
- **B** Stairs to Second Level
- **C** Sentry
- **D** Exterior Entrance
- **E** "Puppy" Simmons (in Office)

Travel back to the Di Napoli garbage dump **(3)**. Go through the front entrance, sneak up to the guard shack **(A)**, and take down the lone guard from behind. Hustle to climb the nearby stairs **(B)**, stalk through the long room and take down the Sentry with his back to you at the other end. Wait for the pacing guard to return then take him down too.

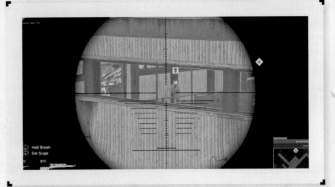

Note the sniper rifle on the desk here. This hints at one option: grab the rifle, go back outside **(B)** and climb the ladder onto the roof. Set up behind the air conditioner unit **(C)** and start picking off targets in the next building through the windows, including Puppy and his Enforcer, the cleaner. Find their overhead icons and slide around until you can get a shot angle at them.

Or you can simply advance along the walkway and stairs to the next building **(D)** where Puppy and a green-suited "cleaner" are in the long office **(E)** at the far end of the interior catwalk. If you choose this instead of the sniper option, you can fight your way down the center catwalk or try to work stealthily through the control room on the right. Either way, you end up facing Puppy in the office. Take him down to secure the Garbage racket.

Assign the Garbage Racket

Now that the Garbage racket is under control, you must assign it to one of your Underbosses. This is the first time you have a choice who gets to run the racket. Scroll through the assignment choices to see what Cassandra, Vito, and Burke have to offer in the way of Favors if you boost their income.

All three offer good options, so you can't really go wrong. Just remember that if any of your Underbosses feels repeatedly snubbed, he/she will rebel. (See "The Betrayal Missions" in our Optional Missions chapter.) Although some of the higher level Favors are very attractive, we think it's a good strategy to award rackets and districts equitably to keep all three Underbosses in the fold.

RACKET: GUNS

Barclay Mills

PREREQUISITE: MEET WITH DONOVAN

Bayou Fantom

LEGEND

1. Connie Demarco
2. Informants
3. Trainyard (Gun Map)
4. Santini's Money Stash
5. High-Grade Explosives Deal
6. Military-Grade Weapons Deal
W. Junction Box

Talk to Connie DeMarco (First Time)

Activate this objective and follow the trip route to the ramshackle shack **(1)** right in the center of the district. Enter for another meeting with Connie Demarco, Vito's man from River Row. Connie was recruited by John Donovan to help Lincoln scout out Pete Santini's illegal shipping operation. Pete is in charge of the train yard, and his gun-running business is booming…yes, literally. Rumor has it he keeps a map of all his high-volume deals.

Interrogate Train Robbers

PREREQUISITE: TALK TO CONNIE DEMARCO

Two Informants appear on the map **(2a, 2b)**, but as soon as you interrogate one, the other one disappears. Take your pick. If the Informant escapes and you don't catch him, he ends up at the other Informant location.

> **WIRETAP THE EXTORTIONISTS**
>
> Be sure to wiretap the Junction Box in their sector before you visit either Informant.

HOLLACE ETHERINGTON

Travel to the rail freight warehouse **(2a)** of the oddly-named Hangar Supply Company. (Note the building number: "013.") This is a gun smuggling depot run by Hollace Etherington, and he's got three large caches of weapons ready to roll. Examine the building from the road using Intel View to see the layout, noting the locations of the gun caches, the Sentry, and Hollace himself.

One good approach is to slip around the right side of the depot and take cover behind a crate or the portable toilets. Start whistling to lure over Hollace's crew until you get the Sentry neutralized, and maybe even incapacitate Hollace himself. Then you can rush the depot and gun down the others. When the area is clear, destroy all three star-marked gun caches for racket damage. (Remember, you can find them easily in Intel View, highlighted in red.)

Then scour the building for several nice stacks of cash. (Again, use Intel View to see them highlighted yellow.) When you finally interrogate Hollace, he reveals where Santini has been storing the money he's collecting from his gun sales.

UNLOCKS: STEAL SANTINI'S MONEY STASH

131

NESTOR "SPECS" ERMO

Specs and his boys are guarding a haul of stolen goods at a rail switching tower **(2b)** on the tracks running up the eastern edge of Barclay Mills. Be sure to wiretap the Junction Box just south of there, if you haven't already done so. Then approach from the south, moving along the tracks to take cover behind the black and white trailer. From there, stealthily eliminate the guard just around the right corner.

Whistle to lure the next guard who descends the control tower stairs and take him down too. Then sneak across the tracks under the trees and use the cover there to advance closer to Specs and the Sentry. Whistle them over for takedowns or just make a gun rush. Interrogate Specs to learn where Santini is stashing the proceeds from his gun business. Then break into the room on the tower's lower level to gun down the last guard and loot cash.

UNLOCKS: STEAL SANTINI'S MONEY STASH

Steal Santini's Gun Map

PREREQUISITE: TALK TO CONNIE DEMARCO

LEGEND

A	Jump Fence	**C**	Reception Office
B	Trailer	**D**	Map and Weapon Caches

Travel to the Barclay Railways train yard, marked **(3)** on our district map. (Be sure to wiretap this sector's Junction Box first, located a couple of blocks southeast on the building across from Joey's All American Diner.) Approach the train yard from the south and hop over the southwest entry gate **(A)**.

Move all the way to the security fence topped with barbed wire and proceed through the opening left by a fallen section. Then enter the nearby blue trailer **(B)** to find some cash and an Album Cover collectible inside.

Take cover at the trailer's side door and spot the Sentry out in the parking lot. Whistle to lure him over for a takedown inside the trailer. Then exit the trailer's side door into the parking lot and take cover at the next building's entry doorway **(C)** leading into a reception office with a black/white tiled floor.

Two guards stand inside, one room over. If you whistle, they hear and come investigate, one at a time. When both are neutralized, enter the office. Grab the $875 pile of money on the desk! Then enter the freight warehouse and follow the objective marker to the left until you reach a stack of white crates **(D)** next to a railcar.

Use your Intel View to see Santini's map, a guard, and some weapon caches on the other side. Climb over the crate stack to find a goon with his back to you. Take him down and grab the map. Then destroy the four star-marked weapon shipments to inflict damage to Santini's racket.

Now you can just retrace your route back out of the train yard. Or, if you want, you can work your way through the facilities where you can pick up a lot of cash to fill your wallet and inflict racket damage. But you'll also run into a lot of Santini's men in the process.

UNLOCKS: Bust Up Santini's Weapons Deals

Steal Santini's Money Stash

PREREQUISITE: Interrogate Train Robbers

Travel to the freight warehouse **(4)** next to the freeway ramp. Go to the end of the ramp and head down the stairs at the street corner. Climb over the fence into the warehouse lot and hustle over to take cover behind the ZAVI shipping containers. Use Intel View to survey the warehouse and then whistle to lure the guard by the truck.

Now take cover outside the big warehouse door. Again, whistle to lure over as many guards as possible for silent takedowns. (You can lure at least two, including the Sentry.) Then sneak inside, turn right, and creep up the stairs. Just before you reach the top, observe the guard's movements on this upper level. Wait until he's not looking so you can hustle to cover or even sneak up behind him for a takedown. When he is eliminated, pry open the blue strongbox on the wood table to steal Santini's money stash and inflict racket damage. (You can also find a note on the table.)

Here's a little trick before you go. Sneak over to take cover at the railing and spot the weapon cache below on the main floor. Toss a Screaming Zemi or two right next to it to draw over the ground floor guards. Then toss a Molotov into their midst to take out the guards *and* the gun cache! Gun down any remaining guards and destroy the other two gun caches for additional damage.

Sneak up to the railcar and climb up behind the fellow examining the weapons crate. Take him down and hide behind the crate. Toss a Screaming Zemi on the other side to draw all four guards (including a Sentry) to one spot; follow that with a Molotov once they've gathered to eliminate all of them at once.

Bust Up Santini's Weapons Deals

PREREQUISITE: STEAL SANTINI'S GUN MAP

Once you get Santini's map you can track down both of his gun sales sites and bust them up. Both mapped locations are down in the Fantom Bayou.

HIGH-GRADE EXPLOSIVES DEAL

Activate this objective and follow the trip route into the Fantom Bayou to the site **(5)** where Santini's customers are testing out his explosive wares. (Be sure to wiretap the Junction Box down the road to the east first. It's on the side of the brick garage next to the Trago gas station.) Approach the Bayou Explosives Testing site from the north and take cover behind the pickup truck to the right of the railcars. Then survey the area with Intel View.

This goon bonfire will scare all customers away. But to "bust the deal" you must destroy any one of the weapons crates—for example, the one sitting on the ground next to the table where the bag of cash sits. This inflicts damage to Santini's Guns racket. Take out any remaining guards, blow up the other weapon caches for racket damage, and scoop up all the cash lying around from various deals in progress.

MILITARY-GRADE WEAPONS DEAL

Travel to this Fantom Bayou site **(6)** where Santini's customers are testing out his guns before purchase. (Be sure to wiretap the Junction Box on the nearby rail switching tower by the tracks first.) Approach

the Bayou Firing Range from the east and sneak along its fence line to see the layout: a pair of railcars (a flatcar and a boxcar) sit behind a row of booths filled with customers shooting at targets. A handful of guards, including a Sentry up inside the boxcar, oversee the activity.

To "bust the deal" you must destroy one of the weapons crates. This inflicts damage to Santini's Guns racket. If you want to be stealthy, go around behind the boxcar and sneak in behind the Sentry for a silent takedown first; then work your way around the site, eliminating other guards before you blow up a crate. Or you can just shoot into the boxcar to complete the objective.

Whatever route you take, the moment gunplay begins the customers all flee. You can blow up the other gun caches for damage, and scoop up all the cash lying around from various deals in progress.

Talk to Connie Demarco (Second Time)

Head back to Connie Demarco's shack **(1)** and talk to him. He tells Lincoln that Pete Santini is now at the train yard.

Confront Pete Santini

Head back to the Barclay Railways train yard **(3)**. Start on the southern or eastern edge and head directly to the big circular turntable (where trains are rotated onto other tracks).

Climb down into the turntable's pit and find the tunnel directly underneath the spoke (the bridge-like track across the middle) that leads toward the Barclay Railways engine house. Pry open the tunnel's locked door and follow the long straight passage to its end.

Use Intel View to get a peek at numerous troops inside, posted on two levels. Turn right, go to the staircase on the left, and take cover at the bottom. Whistle to lure down three guards for takedowns, one by one. Then climb the stairs and take cover outside the big doorway directly ahead. Lure over the guard in the next room; then enter and grab the Tac-Vest sitting on the floor by the lockers. There's a Medicine Cabinet in this room, too.

Take cover at the next doorway and lure the nearby pacing Sentry to his doom. Then repeat with any other guards nearby. Enter the open warehouse, turn right, and climb the staircase to the upper level. At the top of the stairs, take cover and use Intel View to spot Santini beating up somebody in his office just ahead.

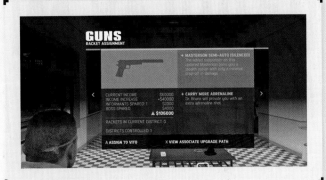

If You Control Both Rackets...

Securing both rackets triggers a quick cutscene: the FBI's Maguire bemoans the problems encountered in his investigation of New Bordeaux's mob war, including the theft of FBI files and surveillance equipment. Now who do you suppose was responsible for that?

Slip in the side office (left of Santini's office) and take down the minion with his back to you. At the next door, you can listen to the dialogue for a moment, then rush in and open fire on Santini and his thugs. Once Santini is incapacitated, clear out any other foes in the room. Then grab the racket boss and either kill or recruit him. Finally, award the Guns racket in Barclay Mills to one of your Underbosses.

UNLOCKS STORY MISSION:
GET ENZO CONTI

BARCLAY MILLS:
A LITTLE LATE FOR THAT

MISSION: "GET ENZO CONTI"

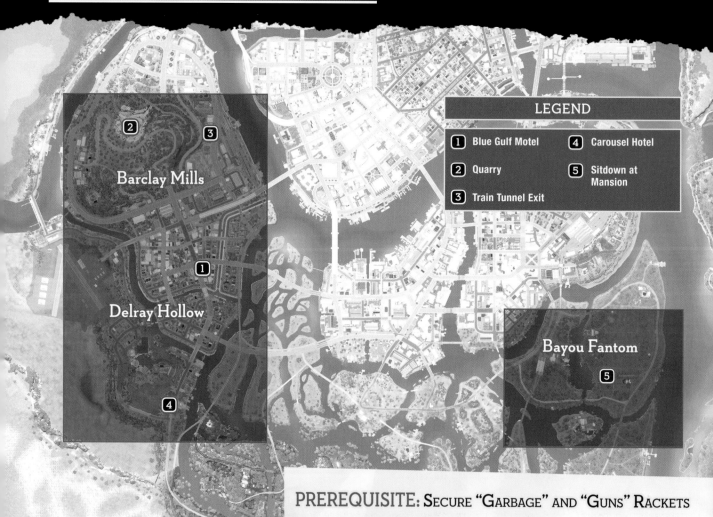

LEGEND

1. Blue Gulf Motel
2. Quarry
3. Train Tunnel Exit
4. Carousel Hotel
5. Sitdown at Mansion

Barclay Mills

Delray Hollow

Bayou Fantom

PREREQUISITE: SECURE "GARBAGE" AND "GUNS" RACKETS

See Donovan to Discuss Enzo Conti

Return to Donovan's tac-ops center in the Blue Gulf Motel **(1)** in Delray Hollow to trigger a scene: Lincoln is ready to make a deal with Enzo Conti, and Donovan puts them in touch. Enzo wants to meet in the quarry.

Talk to Enzo

LEGEND	
A Entry	**E** Rock Extraction Area
B Trailer (Vargas)	**F** Loading Depot
C Meet Enzo	**G** Train Tunnel
D Rock Crusher Building	

Follow the trip route to the main entrance of the Chitimacha Hill Mining Company (CHMC) quarry located **(2)** on our district map. Use your vehicle to smash right through the front entry gates **(A)**. Then follow the tire tracks past the trailer **(B)** (a Vargas painting hangs inside) up to the main building **(C)**.

Enter the building to trigger a cinematic: a tense initial meeting turns into a deeper understanding between Lincoln and Enzo. Enzo reveals the integral involvement of Remy Duvall in all aspects of Sal Marcano's casino. Remy is the front, the legit face of the project. He lives up in fancy Frisco Fields, but he's hard to find because Sal's sister-in-law Olivia Marcano is keeping him sequestered and safe.

As Lincoln and Enzo drink to their new partnership and prepare to move out, a squad of Sal's assassins arrives looking to short-circuit the deal.

Kill Marcano's Hit Crew

This is just an old-school gun battle. Take cover behind the wooden railing and start picking off the hitmen. Work fast because their gunfire tears

apart the railing chunk by chunk, eventually stripping away your cover. If that happens, hop over the railing and take cover behind the crate with the pizza box. A Pasadena AR30 assault rifle sits on the crate too.

When the first wave of hitmen is eliminated, get ready—an explosion tears open the building's left wall and more gunmen open fire from outside! This event triggers a new objective for you.

Plant Explosives in the Quarry

This is a three-step objective. Enzo wants to demolish the entire CHMC plant so Sal can't draw income from it. Three objective markers appear onscreen that lead you to TNT caches where you must plant bombs.

ROCK CRUSHER BUILDING

The nearest TNT cache is less than 30 meters away. First, gun down the multiple attackers outside the newly blasted hole. Then go climb the stairs to the big red building next door (D), which houses the industrial rock crusher. Watch out for a shooter on the exterior balcony!

Enter the building, turn left, and follow the objective marker to the crate of explosives. Plant a bomb here to complete the objective's first step. To reach the next bomb-plant location on an upper level of the quarry, continue through the white door next to the CHMC logo. Climb several flights of stairs, ready for more hostile gunmen at the top.

LOADING DEPOT

Descend the dirt ramp to the quarry's lower level and take cover at the staircase railing. Watch as more carloads of Marcano's men pull up and block your path to the loading depot **(F)** across the road. Shoot to draw their attention; when they rush forward to cover, target the two explosive red barrels to knock out several enemies. If they take cover behind their cars, toss grenades to detonate the vehicles!

Here you can hustle into the blue trailer on the right and use it for cover, moving from window to door as you clear out the remaining hostile goons. When you finally get inside the depot, plant your last bomb on the crates marked Explosives and exit via the side door into the garage.

ROCK EXTRACTION AREA

You emerge from the rock crusher building onto a high landing that overlooks a pair of construction trailers and a rock extraction area **(E)** just 60 meters ahead. Target the explosive red barrels (circled in our shot) in the distance to take out several foes then descend the exterior stairs.

Head inside either one of the trailers for cover and start gunning down the next wave of attackers. Once the immediate area is clear, exit

and climb the next staircase to a long, open storage shelter with a corrugated tin roof. Go inside the shelter and plant a bomb on the explosives crate indicated.

Escape the Quarry

A brawny Bulworth Mohican sits in the garage. Press the button indicated to open the garage door and then hop into the jeep and wait for Enzo to join you. Marcano's crew block the main gate, but you can drive straight for the train tunnel **(G)** directly across the quarry instead. Entering the tunnel triggers a quick glorious cutscene of the explosions behind you.

Lose Marcano's Men

Accelerate hard down the tunnel, veering toward each small team of shooters posted along the route in order to scatter them. You finally emerge in the Barclay Mills warehouse district **(3)**. Unfortunately, several more cars full of Marcano's killers are waiting for you. Now you need to lose them!

A nice move is to keep following the railroad tracks as they curve south between warehouse rows. The mob cars can't follow your Mohican as well over tracks or other rough terrain, so use that advantage for your escape. Keep an eye on the red blips on your Minimap, taking routes that avoid them as best you can.

Take Enzo to Henrietta's Hotel

When you finally shake the pursuit, take Enzo to the Carousel Hotel **(4)** in Delray Hollow. This triggers Lincoln's first interactive sitdown meeting with his three Underbosses at the old plantation mansion **(5)** down in Bayou Fantom.

Assign the District to an Underboss

You previously assigned the district's two rackets, Garbage and Guns, to your Underbosses. But now you must assign the entire district of Barclay Mills to an Underboss. When you assign the whole district, full control of its two rackets also goes to that Underboss. The other two Underbosses will resent this, especially if they lose a racket in the deal. But it's early enough that they'll grudgingly stick with Lincoln. Later, when more districts are available for assignment, you can redress the imbalance and keep everyone's loyalty, if you want.

Note that when a boss loses a racket, you lose any Favors you gained by assigning him/her that racket earlier. You can scroll through each boss to see what Favors are gained or lost before you make the assignment.

FRISCO FIELDS UNLOCKED

Completing your takeover of Barclay Mills unlocks the two rackets in the Frisco Fields district: PCP and Southern Union.

UNLOCKS: "Southern Union" and "PCP" Rackets (Frisco Fields)

UNLOCKS OPTIONAL MISSION: "Who We Shootin'?" (Donovan/CIA)

After the sitdown meeting, another scene plays: Lincoln reports Enzo's news about Remy Duvall and Olivia Marcano to Donovan. He learns that Duvall is head of the Southern Union, a KKK-like racist fraternity. And although Olivia comes from old Southern money, with all its power and high society connections, she's not above getting her hands dirty in the drug business. As a female capo, she makes a unique target.

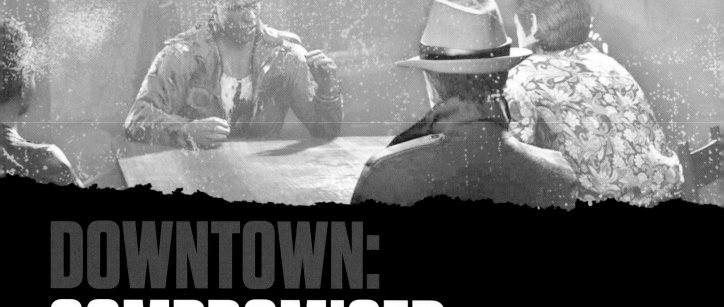

DOWNTOWN:
COMPROMISED
CORRUPTION

MISSION: "COMPROMISED CORRUPTION"

Downtown

LEGEND

1 Meet Donovan

PREREQUISITE: COMPLETE
"AN EMOTIONAL ATTACHMENT"

Meet with Donovan

Activate this objective and travel to the bus bench across the street from The Royal Hotel **(1)**. Sit on the bench to trigger Donovan's arrival. The partners discuss Tony Derazio, the lieutenant who runs the Downtown district for his capo, Sal's brother "Uncle Lou" Marcano. Derazio handles Lou's books, money-laundering, and bribery activity. Getting to Tony won't be easy. He lives in a fortress-like penthouse atop The Royal Hotel.

NEW COLLECTIBLE: REPENT MAGAZINE

Donovan's dossier on Tony Derazio is tucked into a copy of Repent magazine. After the meeting, pick up the magazine from the bus bench to start a new collectible category.

HOTEL JUNCTION BOX

Before you leave the area, wiretap the Junction Box on the back of The Royal Hotel.

UNLOCKS: "CONSTRUCTION" RACKET

UNLOCKS: "BLACKMAIL" RACKET

RACKET: CONSTRUCTION

LEGEND

1 Meet Lennie Davis		**6** Enter Site Here	
2 Informants		**7** Money Stash (in Trailer)	
3 Enforcer ("Geezer" Cruzat)		**8** Enter Site Here	
4 Enforcer (Marlon Boudreaux)		**W** Junction Box	
5 Construction Crane		● Construction Supplies	

PREREQUISITE:

COMPLETE "MEET WITH DONOVAN" (DOWNTOWN)

Talk to Lennie Davis

Find Lennie sitting at the bar in a Downtown dive called Swoosh (1). Lennie's a city clerk who made a mistake, and now a thug named Jimmy Cavar is making him pay. Cavar has blackmailed Lennie into approving phony building permits that benefit Jimmy's construction racket.

UNLOCKS: INTERROGATE CAVAR'S FOREMEN

UNLOCKS: FIND AND DESTROY CONSTRUCTION SUPPLIES

UNLOCKS: BRING DOWN CAVAR'S CONSTRUCTION CRANE

Interrogate Cavar's Foremen

PREREQUISITE: COMPLETE "TALK TO LENNIE DAVIS"

An Informant will appear on your map in one of these two locations (2a, 2b). If the Informant escapes and you don't catch him, he ends up at the other Informant location.

MAX ARDIZZI

Max and his crew are posted in an alley (2a) with two loads of stolen construction supplies. (First, wiretap the sector Junction Box a couple of blocks to the northeast, under the Cinema sign.) Sneak down the alley from the east and take cover at the striped girder on the right. Lure over thugs then sneak up to the crate behind Max and take him down.

Your interrogation reveals that Jimmy Cavar recently sold lots of stolen equipment and has a big money stash now. Before you leave, destroy both destructible piles of construction supplies (find them in Intel View) and blow up the Cavar delivery truck for more damage.

UNLOCKS: STEAL CAVAR'S MONEY STASH

VIRGIL GAUTHIER

Virgil and his boys infest an alley (2b) not far from where you met Lennie Davis at Swoosh. Approach down the alley from the west, moving past the Cavar truck to the brick wall. Duck into cover behind covered crates where the money bag sits and snag it. Then lure over Virgil and his men for takedowns.

Interrogate Virgil to learn that Jimmy Cavar has a big stash of cash from his illegal sales. Before you leave, destroy both destructible piles of construction supplies (find them in Intel View) and blow up the Cavar delivery truck for more damage.

UNLOCKS: STEAL CAVAR'S MONEY STASH

Find and Destroy Construction Supplies (8)

PREREQUISITE: COMPLETE "TALK TO LENNIE DAVIS"

Cavar has stockpiles of stolen city construction supplies stashed all around the Downtown district, stored in Cavar crates and ready for illegal resale. Once you wiretap a sector, any supply site in that sector appears on your map. Each site is guarded by a small handful of Cavar's goons including a Sentry. Take out these guards, and then destroy the multiple supply stashes and the Cavar delivery truck for more damage. Don't miss any stashes in each site! Use Intel View to find them all.

Destroy Cavar's Construction Vehicles

PREREQUISITE: COMPLETE "TALK TO LENNIE DAVIS"

Keep an eye out for Cavar trucks hauling illegal supplies around the Downtown district. Each is marked with a "Destroy" icon overhead. If you're driving, stay on its tail and keep a continuous stream of gunfire hitting the truck until it explodes. Or you can try to cut it off then hop out and toss a grenade under it.

Kill Cavar's Enforcers

PREREQUISITE: COMPLETE "TALK TO LENNIE DAVIS"

"GEEZER" CRUZAT

Geezer hangs out in a back alley lot **(3)** on the western side of the Downtown district. Wiretap the sector's Junction Box first. Then approach down the alley from the north and climb the exterior stairs to the roof overlooking the goons. From here you can toss a Screaming Zemi into their midst to gather them all together (including even Geezer), then follow with a Molotov or two.

Pick off any survivors with a gun. Geezer's death is worth racket damage. When the area is clear, you can descend from the roof to destroy supplies and the Cavar delivery truck for more racket damage. Be sure to scoop up any piles of cash too.

MARLON BOUDREAUX

Marlon Boudreaux is at a south-central Downtown construction site **(4)** behind the Red Bar. First, wiretap the sector's Junction Box; it's nearby, behind the Les Trois Pattes Bar (by a construction supply site you can destroy). Then approach Marlon down the alley between Steinberg Family Clothiers and the Red Bar. Sneak along the high fence topped with barbed wire on the right, and take cover at the end.

Whistle to lure the first guard for a silent takedown, and then move to the stacked pallets not far from the Cavar truck. Toss a Screaming Zemi next to the truck to draw Marlon and his boys to investigate. As they do this, toss a grenade under the truck. The truck's explosion should take out Marlon and his curious crew. You inflict racket damage for killing Marlon plus more for the truck! Be sure to scour the site for cash, and destroy any supply stacks for additional damage.

> ### PLAYBOY ON SITE
>
> Don't miss the *Playboy* magazine inside the trailer in Marlon's construction site.
>
>

Bring Down Cavar's Construction Crane

PREREQUISITE: COMPLETE "TALK TO LENNIE DAVIS"

Here's where you put the big hurt on Jimmy Cavar. Start by calling your Arms Dealer and selecting a high-power sniper rifle. Then travel to the high-rise construction site **(5)** that features two cranes. (Make sure you wiretap the sector first; Intel View really helps here.) Find the site entrance, take cover, and survey the area. Spot the Sentry and move to the stacks of wood by the ZAVI shipping container. Whistle for the Sentry and take him down.

Now if you move rightward, you can head up the stairs to the crane platform to find a great Sniper Point. Take cover here and wreak havoc on the mob muscle below. Pick off as many of the site goons as you can, but be ready for gunmen to rush your position up the stairs.

ATTACH DETONATOR

When the area is clear, head downstairs to ground level, following your objective marker around the shipping container to the big blue Cavar fuel tank at the base of the crane. Attach the detonator to get a new, fairly obvious objective.

CLEAR OUT. NOW.

Hustle around the ZAVI container and through the curving tunnel to the staircase. Run up the stairs to the top then veer rightward to the chain-link gate (marked as an Entrance in your Intel View) and hop over to exit the site. Then watch the spectacular show. If you want, you can explore the site after the crane falls and pick up any loose cash still lying around.

Steal Cavar's Money Stash

PREREQUISITE: INTERROGATE CAVAR'S FOREMEN

Jimmy Cavar has made some good scratch selling construction materials he's boosted from the city. Activate the objective and travel to the fenced-in Cavar construction site that runs under the River Row bridge. A quick route to the stash: start on the road under the bridge **(6)** and slip in via the gap between the fence and the bridge on the left (west) side.

Move along the bridge support to the opening where you can cross underneath the bridge. Take cover and spot the construction trailer **(7)** on the other side. Use Intel View to scout ahead: one guard moves away and another takes up a post with his back to you.

Sneak up and take down this guard. Now you can just step into the unguarded trailer and grab Jimmy's stash of $10,000!

Return to Lennie Davis

Travel back to Lennie **(1)** to learn that Jimmy Cavar has emerged at the big construction site where you destroyed his crane.

Confront Jimmy Cavar

Head to the site and go to the locked door **(8)** on the southwest perimeter. Jimmy is in a makeshift office on the third floor (circled in our shot) of his work-in-progress. It takes some work to get up there. But you can reach Jimmy fairly quickly and painlessly (for you, anyway) if you go stealth all the way.

Unlock the door, sneak downstairs to the first landing, ducking into cover at the railing. Listen to the thugs below you. When they turn to walk

away, hop over the railing and take them down silently from behind, one at a time. Sneak down the walkway to the stairs and climb to the next level.

At the top, turn right to see another guard pacing away from you. Take him down from behind silently, and grab the Tac-Vest from the nearby Weapon Locker. Continue across the floor, sticking to the brick wall on your left.

When the brick wall ends, circle around it to the left and sneak up behind the Sentry standing with his back to you at a low wall. Silence the fool, then climb the stairs just past him.

These stairs climb two levels. The top level leads to a Sniper Point with a scoped rifle that gives you an advantage if you want a shootout. But the easier route is to climb just one level and take cover. Use Intel View to survey the floor—again, a few mob goons are interspersed amongst harmless working men. Sneak forward along the left side of the floor to the big crate and take cover. Whistle to lure each successive mobster for silent takedowns. Work your way to the far end of the floor, using Intel View to make sure the way is clear.

Climb the stairs to the third level. Jimmy Cavar and an associate are up here facing away from you. Sneak up to take down the other guy first, then incapacitate Cavar. Grab him and kill or recruit him to take control of the Construction racket. Award the racket to an Underboss.

RACKET: BLACKMAIL

LEGEND

1	1Harold Cauley	5	Imperial Health Club
2	Informants	W	Junction Box
3	Enforcer (J.C. McCall)	●	Dead Drop
4	Follow Bagman to this Meeting		

PREREQUISITE:

COMPLETE "MEET WITH DONOVAN" (DOWNTOWN)

Talk to Harold Cauley

Activate this objective and follow the trip route into the underground Public Parking garage **(1)**. At the gate, get out and go through the nearby door. Talk to the fellow standing at the elevators, Harold Cauley, a reporter for *The Tattler* who says he's covering Tony Derazio's corruption racket. He points Lincoln toward Frankie Bernard, the man running Derazio's bribes and blackmail operation. Cauley also knows where Frankie's couriers make their "dead drops," and where Frankie stores his stash of blackmail cash.

UNLOCKS: INTERROGATE BLACKMAIL COURIERS

UNLOCKS: FIND AND STEAL THE DEAD DROPS

UNLOCKS: KILL FRANKIE'S ENFORCER

Interrogate Blackmail Couriers (2)

PREREQUISITE: Talk to Harold Cauley

Informants will appear on your Downtown map at four locations **(2a, 2b, 2c, 2d)**. After you visit two of them, you have what you need and the other two disappear from the map. From the first Informant, Lincoln learns that Frankie's mobile bagmen deliver cash to dirty officials; from the second Informant, he learns that Frankie is running his Blackmail racket out of the Imperial Health Club.

ESCAPED INFORMANTS

If an Informant escapes and you don't catch him, he ends up at one of the other Informant locations.

FIRST INTERROGATION UNLOCKS:

Find and Follow the Bagmen

SECOND INTERROGATION UNLOCKS:

Steal Frankie's Blackmail Stash

GLENN "DIMPLES" TANZI

"Dimples" Tanzi and his crew hang out in the alley behind the Backwoods Lounge **(2a)** in northwest Downtown. Use the front entrance of the lounge, take cover at the back exit, and open the door. Dimples and his guys are right there! Whistle them over one by one or toss a grenade or Molotov in their midst to incapacitate Tanzi and kill his crew. Interrogate Tanzi for information.

MANNY FORCELLA

Manny chats with an associate in an outdoor patio **(2b)**. A good approach is along the low wall on the waterfront side of the patio. Incapacitate Manny and eliminate his goons. Then interrogate him for information.

GIANNI AMICI

Gianni and his boys loiter next to their car at the head of an alley **(2c)** just off the main street. Their proximity to the vehicle makes this an easy mark; just toss a grenade under the car. The explosion incapacitates Gianni and wipes out his entourage. (If any survive, take them out quickly.) Interrogate Gianni for information about Frankie's racket.

WILLY JOVINO

Willy Jovino and his crew wait for a pickup in a loading lot **(2d)** behind a row of businesses in the southern sector of the Downtown district. Approach down the alley from the west (past the "Make Love Not War" wall graffiti).

Jovino's men are spread out, so lure a couple over for silent takedowns before you rush Willy and incapacitate him. Don't let him escape! Interrogate Willy to learn what he knows. Be sure to snag the $875 bag of cash next to the generator enclosure before you leave the lot.

Find and Steal the Dead Drops (15)

PREREQUISITE: Talk to Harold Cauley

Frankie Bernard pays off local politicians at 15 secret locations called "dead drops" where he leaves cash for pickup. These drop spots appear as icons on your in-game map, but only in sectors you've wiretapped. (We marked them as blue dots on our district map.) In the game world, Frankie marks each location with his maze-like stamp (see our shot).

> **WIRETAP FOR DROPS!**
>
> Frankie's dead drops appear on your map only in sectors where you've wiretapped the Junction Box.

Approach the mark carefully—a mob courier often lurks at the site guarding the drop until pickup. Take him out, find the cash bag, and snag it for racket damage. You also find a note for the intended recipient near the bag.

Kill Frankie's Enforcer

PREREQUISITE: Talk to Harold Cauley

J.C. MCCALL

J.C. McCall is a nasty brute. When you find him, J.C. is watching two of his gorillas dangle a poor snitch off the rooftop of a seedy building (3) in central Downtown. One tactic is to approach from the north with a sniper rifle and set up at the railing of the driveway directly across from the incident. Target McCall's head for a one-shot kill worth racket damage.

HALLWAY ALBUM

Look for an Album Cover collectible at the bottom of the stairs in the entry hallway, next to some bags of garbage.

Another approach is to work your way around the building, stealthily (or noisily) taking out the ground-level goons. Then you can go inside and use the stairs to the roof; or you can climb atop the air conditioner unit and climb a pair of ladders to the roof. If you use the doorway, watch out for a gunman just inside, and don't miss the Album Cover collectible in the hallway.

If J.C. knows you're coming, he may rush downstairs to meet you. If not, sneak upstairs to the roof and take him down from behind. Then grab the $875 bag of cash.

Find and Follow the Bagmen (3)

PREREQUISITE:

INTERROGATE BLACKMAIL COURIERS

As you learned from the Informants, Frankie has a crew of bagmen who deliver cash to dirty city officials. Each of the three bagmen drives a dark Potomac Gallant marked with an overhead "Follow" icon. When you see one, follow him to the meeting site **(4a, 4b, 4c)** to gun down the target (marked with a "Kill" icon overhead) and find a fat stack of cash.

FINDING BAGMEN

Check our map to see where a meeting site is located. Then patrol the streets around it until you spot the marked Potomac Gallant. Don't follow too close or drive erratically! If you call attention to yourself, the bagman flees.

Steal Frankie's Blackmail Stash

Travel to the Imperial Health Club **(5)**. Make sure the sector is wiretapped. The gleaming white Imperial has several rooms with lots of customers mixed with Frankie's men, so you want the full Intel View as you navigate through the club.

The stash you seek is upstairs off the executive office suite. Enter the Imperial via the back entrance and proceed into the room with two small pools. Exit that room to the main pool area and veer left to climb the stairs. At the first landing (where you see a steamy hot tub directly ahead),

take the left staircase up to the door marked "Personnel Only." Enter to see laundry baskets and more stairs.

Climb the stairs to the roof and use Intel View to scan around. As you move across the roof, try to avoid guards, or else maneuver with stealth for silent takedowns. Enter the doorway at the roof's back-right corner (it's around a corner) and drop down through the trap door.

You land in a secret darkroom. A camera is set up to take photos through a one-way mirror of some steamy hot tub activity in the next room. Illicit photos are hung over the counter. Grab the blackmail log book sitting there to inflict a hefty damage to the Blackmail racket.

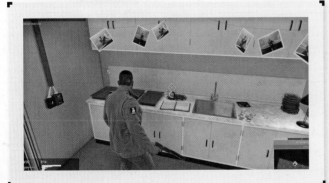

There's more good stuff to grab before you go. The door from the darkroom leads to an office suite. Scout ahead with Intel View then take cover at the door and open it. Whistle to lure as many of Frankie's men as you can for silent takedowns. Then move left past the gaming table and private bar to the well-appointed executive office and snag the $3000 pile of cash on the desk.

OFFICE PRIZE

Don't miss the Vargas painting on the bookshelf in the executive office.

Here you can retrace your route up to the roof and back down to the club's rear entrance to escape. Or you can work your way through the entire health club if you want, where you'll find a lot of cash and quite a few goons.

Talk to Harold Cauley

Return to Cauley in the underground parking garage **(1)**. He reports that an angry Tony Derazio has ordered Frankie Bernard to personally oversee the action at the Imperial Health Club.

Confront Frankie Bernard

Return to the Imperial Health Club **(4)**. Frankie is up in the executive office you visited earlier. So you can reprise the route via roof and darkroom that you used in your previous visit. (See the "Steal Frankie's Blackmail Stash" objective.) Guards will be deployed differently, but the route and basic approach remains the same. Just rely on Intel View to see what lies ahead, and react accordingly.

When you finally reach the office, Frankie will take cover behind his desk or palm planter. Incapacitate him and then seize him for a kill-or-recruit moment. Lincoln now takes control of the Downtown Blackmail racket. Assign it to one of your Underbosses. Time to go get Tony Derazio.

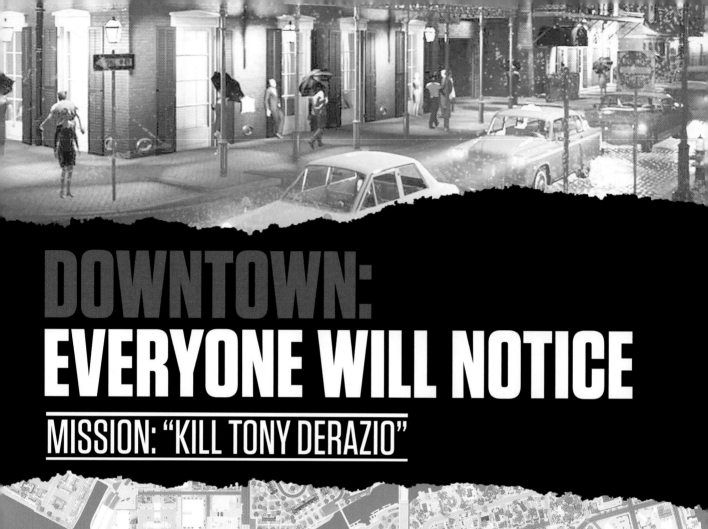

DOWNTOWN:
EVERYONE WILL NOTICE

MISSION: "KILL TONY DERAZIO"

LEGEND

1. Donovan's Van
2. Dominick's Car
3. The Royal Hotel

Talk to Donovan about Tony Derazio

Activate this objective and follow the trip route to Donovan's blue van parked in an alley **(1)**. Enter the van to trigger a cutscene: Donovan testifies at the Senate Committee hearing that he bugged a meeting between Derazio and one of his underlings. Then you see that meeting. When Derazio hands the keys to Dominick and gives him the hotel elevator access code, Lincoln has his way in. Donovan describes both entry options to the Senators.

Infiltrate the Royal Hotel: Option 1

STEAL DOMINICK'S CAR

We like this option because it gives you an armored vehicle for your eventual escape. Activate this objective and follow the trip route to Dominick's Armored Majesty **(2)**, not far from the hotel. Steal it and travel to The Royal Hotel **(3)**, using the garage entrance. Move through the utility area filled with circuit boxes then take the stairs up to the second floor, where you can use the elevator.

Infiltrate the Royal Hotel: Option 2

ENTER THE LOBBY

Travel directly to The Royal Hotel **(3)** and walk in the front lobby.

> **CHECK-IN AT THE DESK**
>
> Before you start killing folks, hop over the reception desk and grab the Vargas painting on the floor under the desk.

USE THE ELEVATOR

No use pussyfooting around—walk straight to the VIP elevator on the left side of the lobby and quickly gun down the two goons standing guard. Hustle into the elevator and use the keypad; Lincoln automatically enters the code and rides up to the top.

This triggers a cinematic: Tony Derazio calmly handles an agitated phone call from Lou Marcano as he prepares for Lincoln's arrival. We get a glimpse of his account ledger, with payments made to Lou and somebody called "US5CJ." Who could that be?

Find Tony

CLEAR FLOOR 13

The elevator stops on the 13th floor, which features a luxury room next to a secret blackmail post, with a camera and a one-way mirror. Use the kitchen carts for cover as you advance down the corridor and around the

corner to the emergency exit, picking off Tony's men. Use Intel View and your Minimap to spot them coming.

CLEAR FLOOR 14

Take the stairs up to the 14th floor where more gunmen await Lincoln's arrival. Fight to the laundry cart at the corner and use it to pick off attackers down the next hall. Again, be proactive with Intel View in these tight quarters so nobody gets the drop on you. You can also move through the two-bedroom connected suite to flank the bad guys who emerge from the elevator at the far end of the hall.

Move through the 14th floor laundry room to a service staircase that leads up to a supply room on the 15th floor. Continue up the next set of stairs to the penthouse area door.

CLEAR THE CAVAR OFFICE LEVEL

Open the door to reveal a Cavar Construction Company reception desk manned by "receptionists" who want to kill you. Quickly flip a grenade or Molotov just over the desk, check your Intel View to see other gunmen approaching, and pick them off. When the coast is clear, push forward past the desk and take cover at the next doorway as more shooters open fire from the next area, the Records room.

Another goon squad waits in the next room, a lounge area with a scale model of the Paradiso Hotel & Casino, Sal Marcano's pet project. Fight your way from here through two offices full of recording

equipment and film reels. Once you clear out this space, open the far door to another staircase. This leads to the lower level of Tony's luxurious penthouse suite.

CLEAR THE PENTHOUSE SUITE

The lower level of the luxury suite features a huge living room with a piano; a cavernous kitchen/dining area; a large bedroom/dressing area; a spectacular wraparound balcony; and a big squad of Tony's men. Use the doorways and furniture for cover, and use the balcony for flanking maneuvers. You can find lots of cash around plus a Tac-Vest stored in a closet in Tony's dressing area.

Climb the stairs to a terrace that features a library and small art gallery. Use your Pry Bar to unlock the security door that leads into a small antechamber outside Tony's office. Open the next door to trigger a quick sequence: Tony fires a rocket launcher at Lincoln!

Confront Tony Derazio

Make Tony pay for such audacious behavior. Shoot to incapacitate him, then approach and grab him to trigger a cutscene: Lincoln discovers Tony's ledger. As police units arrive on the street far below, Marcano's numbers boy spits out a few last insults. Lincoln makes sure his demise is a media sensation.

Lose the Cops

If Dominick's Armored Majesty is here because you stole it earlier, hop in. Otherwise, steal any vehicle and escape the garage. When you get to the street, start your usual evasive maneuvers to shake off the police pursuit. (Or you can radio your associate, the police dispatcher, to call off the cops if you've got that service available.)

Assign the District to an Underboss

When you finally get free, the scene automatically shifts to another sitdown meeting with your Underbosses at the bayou mansion. The Downtown district is now Lincoln's to assign. Give it to one of the three to trigger a chapter-ending cutscene: Lincoln delivers Derazio's ledger to Donovan, and together they figure out what "US5CJ" stands for.

Escape the Royal Hotel

You still have to get out. Mob gunmen swarm the premises, and now cops are arriving too; you're in the middle of a Blue Police Zone. Hustle to Tony's private elevator just off of the penthouse living room and ride down to the hotel's second floor. Exit and go left to the emergency exit. Careful, a cop is in the stairwell. You can sprint past him and down the stairs to the utility power room. Exit into the garage.

FRENCH WARD UNLOCKED

Completing your takeover of Downtown unlocks the two rackets in the French Ward district: Sex and Drugs. Now you can take down a capo, "Uncle" Lou Marcano.

UNLOCKS: "SEX" AND "DRUGS" RACKETS (FRENCH WARD)

TICKFAW HARBOR:
HOT RUBBER & COLD BLOOD

MISSION: "HOT RUBBER & COLD BLOOD"

Tickfaw Harbor

LEGEND

1 Meet Donovan (Bus Bench)

Meet with Donovan (Tickfaw Harbor)

PREREQUISITE: COMPLETE "AN EMOTIONAL ATTACHMENT"

Travel to the bus bench outside the Baby Bear BBQ & Beer restaurant **(1)** in the Tickfaw Harbor district. John Donovan pulls up in a surly mood; New Bordeaux's heat and smell remind him too much of the Mekong Delta.

He reports that Frank Pagani is the lieutenant who runs the district and reports directly to Tommy Marcano, Sal's brother and capo. Pagani has a cargo ship called the *Tanager* that smuggles illegal goods in and out of Cuba—in fact, he's in Cuba right now. Lincoln's plan: draw him back by hitting his businesses, all centered around stolen cars and freight.

UNLOCKS: "AUTO THEFT" AND "SMUGGLING" RACKETS (TICKFAW HARBOR)

RACKET: AUTO THEFT

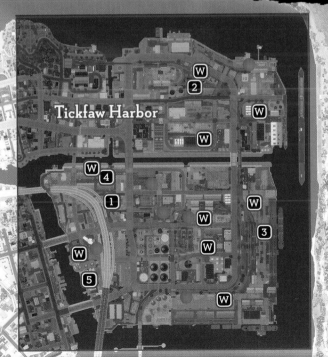

LEGEND

1. Gina Kowalski
2. Enforcer (Wayne Roussel)
3. Enforcer (Darrell Brand)
4. Boosted Car Shipment
5. Best Oil Lot
W. Junction Box
● Stashed Cars

Tickfaw Harbor

Talk to Gina Kowalski

PREREQUISITE: MEET WITH DONOVAN (TICKFAW HARBOR)

Activate this objective and follow the trip route to big auto garage **(1)**. Climb the stairs to the second-floor office and talk to Gina Kowalski. Gina tells you about Junior Holland, the man running Pagani's car theft operation. She says Junior works out of the nearby Best Oil station,

running high-end stolen cars locally and also shipping to customers out of town.

Destroy Stashed Cars (6)

Six valuable stolen cars are stashed around the district. They won't appear on your map, however, until you wiretap the sectors where they're located. (We've also marked their locations on our district map.) In most cases, you find the vehicle guarded by only two or three of Junior's goons, so securing the site isn't usually difficult.

Wiretap Tickfaw Harbor to reveal the locations of Junior's stashed cars.

The boosted cars are usually parked next to explosive barrels or tanks or gas cans that you can detonate with gunfire to destroy the vehicles.

Kill Junior's Pro Car Thieves

WAYNE ROUSSEL

Activate and follow the route to a car-filled lot next to a three-story freight office **(2)** by the railroad tracks in northern Tickfaw Harbor. The sector Junction Box (circled in our shot) is on the back wall of the building, so get it wiretapped first.

Climb the back stairs, pry open the locked door, and move through a waiting room with a sofa. Open the opposite door and sneak up behind the mobster on the porch when his back is to you for a silent takedown. Grab the rifle he drops and the $1500 sitting on the power box.

Wayne Roussel is down below in the lot, checking under the hood of a stolen car. He's got four thugs for backup, including a Sentry. Toss down a Screaming Zemi next to the car to draw them closer together. Then toss a grenade down to detonate the car and take them all out. If any survive, pick them off with your rifle. Taking down Wayne inflicts racket damage.

DARRELL BRAND

Darrell and his crew are inspecting stolen vehicles and loading them into cargo containers at Tickfaw Harbor's big commercial shipping dock **(3)**. Towering stacks of containers and crates are everywhere, so cover is plentiful.

Sneak to a spot where you have a clear line to the location and toss a couple of grenades and/ or Molotovs at the car nearest the thugs. Immediately follow up with gunfire to take down any survivors, especially if one is a Sentry. Be sure to take down Darrell for more racket damage.

Destroy Boosted Car Shipment

This is the motherlode of racket damage. Travel to a complex of four large warehouse buildings in west-central Tickfaw Harbor. The northeast building **(4)** houses a shipment of ten sleek, high-end stolen cars that Junior is prepping for sale to foreign buyers. Wiretap the Junction Box (circled in our shot) near the building's northwest corner for full Intel View. Then take cover at the stack of crates.

Whistle to lure the nearby pacing guard for a takedown then move to cover at the door. You can try to whistle over the remaining crew or just start tossing grenades at cars. The explosions not only cause racket damage per car, but they can also take out any remaining mobsters. Look for red explosive tanks to target too. Be sure to explore the warehouse after the destruction is wrought; you'll find several healthy stacks of cash.

Find and Kill Stolen Car Runners

A stolen car driven by a "car runner" will spawn periodically in front of you. The runner is marked with a "Kill" icon, visible above the car. To complete this objective, you must kill the runner (the driver), so you don't need to destroy the vehicle.

The stolen cars often appear in the oncoming lane, driving toward you. Try to swing your vehicle across its path, then hop out and either shoot the driver through the windshield or toss a grenade under the car. If the car gets past you, chase it down, shooting at its tires to disable it. Then hop out and gun down the driver. Taking out each "Kill"-marked car runner inflicts damage on Junior's Auto Theft racket.

Runners continue to spawn until you talk to Gina Kowalski the second time.

Talk to Gina Kowalski

Return to Gina **(1)** to learn that Junior is back at the Best Oil station making life hell for his underlings. Time to pay him a visit.

Confront Jack "Junior" Holland

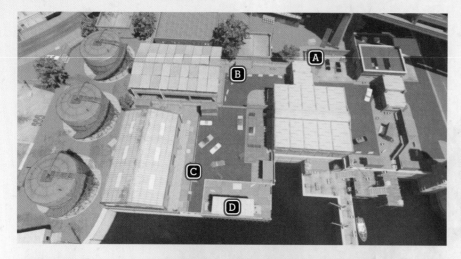

LEGEND

A Side Entrance   **B** Right Side Approach   **C** Open Container   **D** Trailer (Junior Inside)

Activate this objective and follow the trip route to the Best Oil auto service lot (at **(5)** on our district map) in southwest Tickfaw Harbor, Pagani's chop shop for high-end automobiles. (Be sure you've wiretapped the sector box first.) It's a big lot with several buildings surrounding it, so keep an eye out for emerging enemies using Intel View. Move along the east perimeter and find the side entrance **(A)**.

Keep checking your Minimap and Intel View—don't get surprised by Sentries. When you get to the trailer, rush in and incapacitate Junior. Then kill or recruit him to take control of the Auto Theft racket. Assign it to an Underboss.

Lure over the nearby guard for a takedown. Then move along the blue/white brick wall to take down the guard just around the corner, leaning on the wall.

Stick to the right wall, moving stealthily through the covered passage and along the striped road barriers around the right side of the lot **(B)**. Keep using Intel View to spot any guards posted ahead, and use the wrecked cars and for cover when you need to hide.

Securing the first racket in the district (whether Auto Theft or Smuggling) unlocks a new Tickfaw Harbor chapter called "The Connection to Cuba" with its new mission: "Kill Frank Pagani: The Setup." In this walkthrough, we'll complete that mission before we secure the district's other racket, Smuggling.

Once you work your way around the curve to the left, you see the blue trailer across the lot. Junior Holland is inside that trailer. Stick to the right side as you approach, using tire stacks and a shipping container open on both ends **(C)** for cover as you advance toward Junior in the trailer **(D)**.

UNLOCKS CHAPTER:
"THE CONNECTION TO CUBA"

UNLOCKS MISSION:
"KILL FRANK PAGANI: THE SETUP"

TICKFAW HARBOR:
THE CONNECTION TO CUBA

MISSION: "KILL FRANK PAGANI: THE SETUP"

Tickfaw Harbor

LEGEND

1 Meet Donovan

2 The *Tanager*

W Junction Box

By now you should have all of the Tickfaw Harbor Junction Boxes wiretapped. But just in case, we marked the two box locations in the sectors you visit in this mission.

Meet with Donovan to Discuss Frank Pagani

PREREQUISITE: COMPLETE
"AUTO THEFT" RACKET OR "SMUGGLING" RACKET

Find Donovan's blue van **(1)** parked behind a warehouse at the southwest tip of Tickfaw Harbor, and enter via the vehicle's back door.

Tommie Marcano

Donovan gives Lincoln a tracking device for the car. When planted, it can lead Lincoln to Frank's location when the car is delivered.

Inside, Donovan plays a wiretapped conversation between Frank Pagano and Tommy Marcano, Sal's other brother. Lincoln learns that the *Tanager* is arriving at port soon, and Pagano's beloved car is aboard, though Frank is not. Frank will fly back later.

Frank Pagano

Get to the *Tanager*

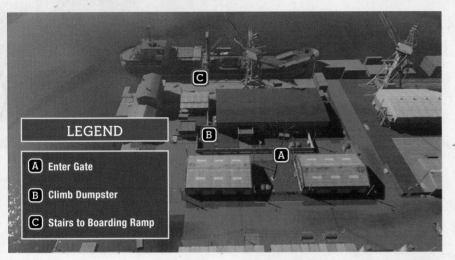

LEGEND

- **A** Enter Gate
- **B** Climb Dumpster
- **C** Stairs to Boarding Ramp

Start by making sure you have a full complement of grenades from your gun dealer. Activate the objective and follow the trip route to the pier where the *Tanager* **(2)** has now docked. Approach from the north along the waterfront and go through the fence opening **(A)** marked "A1" to enter the loading area. Spot the two guards in the enclosure to the left; take them out and use the dumpster **(B)** to climb over the next wall. Before you hop over, check your Intel View up ahead.

Proceed stealthily or guns blazing down the walkway between buildings to the open dock where you see the *Tanager* looming ahead. Veer leftward as you work across the dock to the staircase **(C)** using crates and stacks of pipes and bags for cover. Descend the stairs and hustle to the *Tanager's* boarding ramp.

Locate Pagani's Car

Now you need to find Frank's vehicle. Just follow the passage as it leads downstairs to the lower deck. Two guards face away from you in a room filled with gambling equipment like slot machines and blackjack tables—bound for Sal's casino, no doubt. Silently take down the guy on the right first; the other won't notice. Then KO the other guard from behind too.

Plant the Tracking Device

Go through the hatch into the cargo hold and approach Pagani's slick red sports car. No guards are posted in here! Plant the tracking device.

Escape

Retrace your route back up to the dock. The way will be clear until you hit the top of the stairs. Suddenly, two carloads of Marcano's men arrive, four gunmen per car. Quickly toss a grenade onto each car before the gunmen can deploy away from their vehicle. If you time it right, each carload is eliminated with one toss.

Sprint out the main gate (open now because the mob cars entered) and steal one of the cars in the lot. To complete your escape, you must drive out of the area marked by a yellow circle on your map.

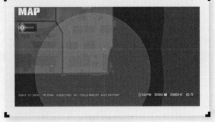

RACKET: SMUGGLING

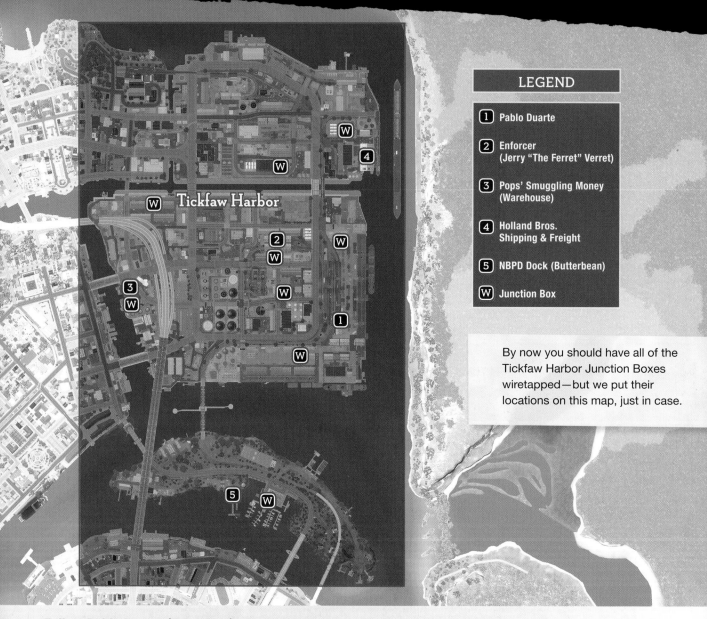

LEGEND

1. Pablo Duarte
2. Enforcer (Jerry "The Ferret" Verret)
3. Pops' Smuggling Money (Warehouse)
4. Holland Bros. Shipping & Freight
5. NBPD Dock (Butterbean)
W. Junction Box

By now you should have all of the Tickfaw Harbor Junction Boxes wiretapped—but we put their locations on this map, just in case.

Tickfaw Harbor

Talk to Pablo Duarte (First Time)

PREREQUISITE: Meet with Donovan (First Tickfaw Harbor Meeting)

Find the trailer (1) near the railroad siding in the Tickfaw Harbor commercial shipping dock and enter to speak to Pablo. "Pops" Holland, Junior's dad, is an old-time smuggler with a vast network of old-time connections, and he goes way back with Frank Pagani. Getting to him won't be easy.

Kill Pops' Enforcer

JERRY "THE FERRET" VERRET
PREREQUISITE: TALK TO PABLO DUARTE

Travel to this huge freight center **(2)** to find Jerry the Ferret and his boys intimidating the local warehouse crew. If you have Vito's Hit Squad available, this is a good place to call and let them lead the way. Otherwise, approach down the middle aisle between warehouses using the dumpster and power box for cover.

The Ferret won't run, so you can work methodically to reach him. After you take him out, be sure to shoot up the Holland Bros. cargo crates and grab the stacks of cash around the trucks and railcars of the loading area. Remember to use your Intel View to spot outlines of pickup (yellow) and destructible (red) items, even through walls.

Climb the exterior stairs, pry open the locked door, then quickly take cover—a goon with his back to you is just inside, studying info on a blackboard. Take him down and move through the next room to the doorway. Another guard out on the walkway looks away from you; make him pay for this mistake.

Two mobsters play dice downstairs, so a quick grenade or Molotov nails both with one toss. Clear out the last two gangsters then shoot all of the destructible equipment (highlighted red in Intel View). Finally, grab the big pile of $2500 cash sitting on the desk in the corner of the main floor.

Steal Pops' Smuggling Money

PREREQUISITE: TALK TO PABLO DUARTE

Travel to the two-story warehouse **(3)** over on the district's western waterfront. Use Intel View (after wiretapping) to see six goons spread over two levels inside, the money stash on the ground floor, and five crates of smuggled goods..

Dismantle the Air Drop Operations

PREREQUISITE: TALK TO PABLO DUARTE

INTERROGATE RADIO OPERATOR

Travel to the Holland Bros. Shipping & Freight yard **(4)** on the waterfront up in northeast Tickfaw Harbor. From the west entrance, move through the first warehouse; no hostiles are present here, just workers. Exit via the loading dock in back and cross the yard to the second building, a covered dry dock with a ship inside, the *Zavi's Sky*. Climb the stairs to enter the second level office area.

Use Intel View to spot your target marked with an "Interrogate" icon overhead. Sneak down the walkway and turn left to take down the guard at the window. Then proceed into the control room to knock down and interrogate the radio operator. He tells Lincoln about a fellow named

Butterbean who coordinates all airdropped drug shipments from a small marina south of Tickfaw.

Be sure to rob the control room, grabbing stacks of cash and raiding the two Weapon Lockers, before you retrace your route out of the dry dock. Or, if you want, you can clear out the entire building, which holds lots of cash and ten shipments of destructible smuggled goods. You can also find a Vargas painting hanging on the wall in the main office across the skywalk from the dry dock building.

UNLOCKS: KILL BUTTERBEAN

KILL BUTTERBEAN
PREREQUISITE:

INTERROGATE RADIO OPERATOR

Travel south to the island where the marinas are located. Go to the main marina and wiretap the Junction Box (circled in our shot) on the lower level of the pier. Then return to the road and head over to the smaller NBPD police boat dock **(5)** just to the west.

Here's a sneaky way in. Approach from the north and veer left to the small break in the trees. Go through the opening; you're right next to the dock, but you can't climb up. However, you can swim down the length of the dock to the first corner. Look for a guard next to a gas

pump further down the dock; he won't see you if you stay in the water. Swim around the corner, pull yourself onto the dock where it's lower, and dive into cover at the railing.

Observe the guards patrolling the dock then take down the fellow facing away from you near the building. (Use your Minimap to monitor enemy movement/facing to make sure you're not spotted.) Then climb the nearby ladder to the second level balcony.

You find a Manitou Model 67 sniper rifle here, if you want to take the shooting route. Otherwise, sneak around the balcony corner and take cover at the next corner. Lure over the two guards, one at a time, posted on the large patio.

Now take cover at the station door. Butterbean is just inside. Lure him over for a silent takedown, or rush him for a brutal takedown, or lean in the doorway and gun him down. Now you can either retrace your route quietly back to the road, or clear out the building and dock to collect loose cash and generate unholy mayhem.

Talk to Pablo Duarte (Second Time)

Return to Pablo's trailer **(1)** to learn that Pops Holland is trying to shape up his crew back at the Holland Bros. freight yard.

UNLOCKS:

CONFRONT WALTER "POPS" HOLLAND

Confront Walter "Pops" Holland

PREREQUISITE:

TALK TO PABLO DUARTE (SECOND TIME)

Return to the Holland Bros. Shipping & Freight yard **(4)** on the waterfront up in northeast Tickfaw Harbor. Here's a quick and violent way to reach Pops: accelerate hard into the west entrance and ram open the entry gates next to the Holland Bros. sign directly ahead! Shoot from your car to gun down the Sentry (circled in our shot) on the other side, then speed straight to the stairs leading up into the dry dock building. Hop out and sprint upstairs, gunning down the goon at the top.

RADIO BOBBY DUCKS

This is a great mission to call in your Hit Squad backup. They can engage Pops' men in the main lot between buildings while you push forward in search of Pops himself.

Inside, fight down the walkway through two doorways then turn left and proceed down the corridor into the control room. (Grab a Tac-Vest from the Weapons Locker there if you want.) Use the switch on the control panel to raise the *Zavi's Sky* out in the dry dock.

Hustle back down the same corridor and turn left through the doorway that leads out onto the dry dock walkway. Run down the walkway to the second ramp that leads to the boat's starboard side.

Use the ramp to board the raised *Zavi's Sky* and run across the boat's bow to the opposite ramp on the port side. Run across that ramp, turn right on the far walkway, then take the next doorway on the left onto the enclosed skywalk.

Here's a wide view of the dry dock (left) and the skywalk (circled) running to the office building (right).

Run across the skywalk to the office building. Pops is in the first office on the right. Take out the guard; then incapacitate Pops. Seize Pops and kill or recruit him to secure the Smuggling racket in Tickfaw Harbor. Assign it to one of your Underbosses.

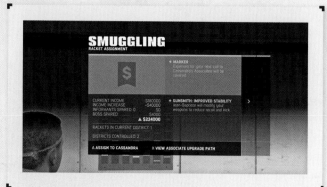

UNLOCKS STORY MISSION:
KILL FRANK PAGANI: THE TAKEDOWN

MISSION: "KILL FRANK PAGANI: THE TAKEDOWN"

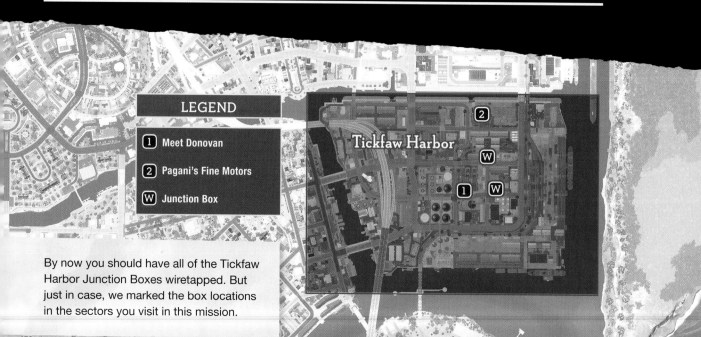

LEGEND
1. Meet Donovan
2. Pagani's Fine Motors
W. Junction Box

Tickfaw Harbor

By now you should have all of the Tickfaw Harbor Junction Boxes wiretapped. But just in case, we marked the box locations in the sectors you visit in this mission.

See Donovan for the Latest on Frank

PREREQUISITE:

COMPLETE BOTH TICKFAW HARBOR RACKETS ("AUTO THEFT" AND "SMUGGLING")

Activate this objective and follow the trip route to find John Donovan's blue van **(1)** parked next to the towering tanks and pipes of the chemical plant. Approach the driver's side door to talk to Donovan. The news: Frank Pagani is back in town, and Lincoln can use the tracking device to hunt him down. As Donovan

drives away, you can hear the tracker clicking.

Get to Pagani's Car

Open your Map to see a large yellow circle. This marks the area in which Pagani's car is located in Tickfaw Harbor. You can drive around the

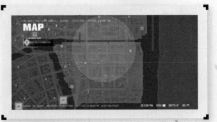

area while listening to the clicking of the tracker. When the clicking speeds up, you're getting closer to Pagani's car. Watch your map. When the clicking is fast and you see a cluster of red blips appear, head for them to find Pagani.

(Or you can just drive directly to the destination **(2)** marked on our district map.) You end up on the perimeter of Pagani's Fine Motors lot.

Make Your Way Inside

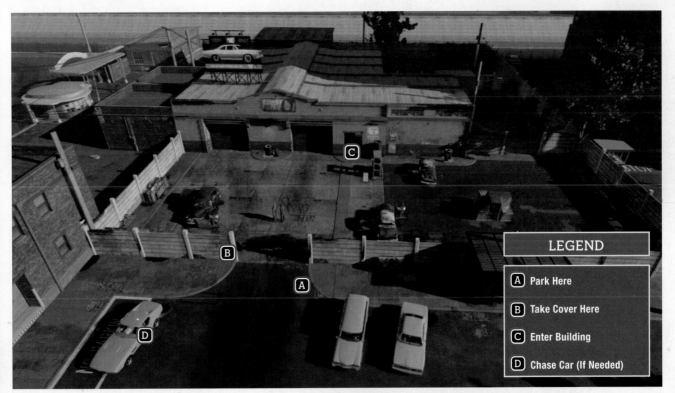

LEGEND

A	Park Here
B	Take Cover Here
C	Enter Building
D	Chase Car (If Needed)

Here's a quick, sneaky way to beat this mission. Park your car just outside the right post of the lot entrance **(A)** and plant a C4 charge on it. Sure, it sounds crazy, but you'll see why soon. Also note that spry green De'Leo Stiletto sports car sitting nearby **(D)**. You'll need that ride if your sneaky plan fails.

Take cover at the wall **(B)** to assess the situation with Intel View. Two guards stand nearby, so whistle them over in succession for silent takedowns. (If you wait too long and they separate, don't worry—get the first one by the entrance, then sneak through the nearby hut and take down the second guy from behind.)

Cross the lot to approach the front door **(C)**. Frank Pagani is inside the garage just to your left, next to his red De'Leo Traviata. When you do something to trigger an alert, Frank will hop in his car and flee. Several tactical options exist, but the easiest is to start by kicking open the door.

Get to Frank

Kicking the door hard alerts a guard, who comes running down the corridor just inside. Take cover behind the wall just outside the door and gun him down. Be ready to take out a possible second guard too. Then step into the corridor and look left through the security window to see Frank hop into his car. You can't shoot him through the window; it's glass is too thick.

Do Not Let Pagani Escape!

Immediately rush back outside and open fire on Frank's red sports car as it pulls out of the garage. You can inflict some damage here, but as Frank drives past you, don't forget your ace in the hole: your booby-trapped car just outside the gate. The moment Frank's car exits the gate and drives past your car, detonate the C4 charge. The explosion should destroy Frank's car.

Note that if you can't destroy Frank's car before he pulls onto the street, you'll have to chase him down. Sprint to the green Stiletto and hop in to give chase. Frank's car is fast and nimble, but so is your Stiletto. Shoot Frank's tires to disable the car, or ram him off the road and block his path. Then hop out and toss a grenade.

Kill Frank Pagani

If his car explodes, Frank will survive the blast and stagger out. Shoot him until he's incapacitated and goes down on one knee.

Confront Frank Pagani

Grab Frank to trigger the chapter-ending cinematics: Lincoln learns the truth about Sal Marcano's actual motive for robbing the Federal Reserve—Giorgi grabbed something more than just money from that vault. He also learns that Marcano has an expert Cuban counterfeiter named Alvarez working for him now.

Assign Tickfaw Harbor at the Sitdown

After the FBI's Maguire makes a stark pronouncement about Lincoln's true nature, you see another sitdown meeting. When the moment comes, assign the newly acquired district to one of your Underbosses. Keep in mind that loyalties will be strained if you aren't equitable in distributing favors.

Finally, Lincoln returns to Donovan's tac-ops center and fills in his ex-CIA associate on the new aspects of the situation. The pair agrees that finding Alvarez is a new priority. They also begin to focus on Tommy Marcano and his Southdowns rackets.

SOUTHDOWNS UNLOCKED

Completing your takeover of Tickfaw Harbor unlocks the two rackets in the Southdowns district: Gambling and Black Market. Now you can take down another capo and member of the virulent Marcano family, Tommy Marcano.

UNLOCKS: "GAMBLING" AND "BLACK MARKET" RACKETS (SOUTHDOWNS)

FRISCO FIELDS:
THE PRIVILEGED DIE SLOW
RACKET: "SOUTHERN UNION"

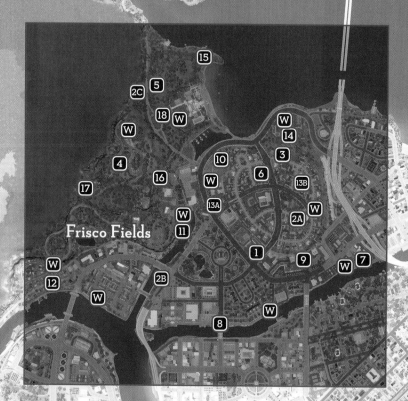

Frisco Fields

LEGEND

1	Briar Patch Restaurant (Jackie Grimaldi)	10	Enforcer (Uncle Andrew)
2	Informant	11	Enforcer (Uncle Thaddeus)
3	Supply Stash	12	Enforcer (Uncle Jude)
4	Supply Stash	13	Informant
5	Southern Union Camp	14	Bellaire's Grocery Store
6	Southern Union Residence	15	Fossats
7	Southern Union Heritage Center	16	Gaudets
8	Enforcer (Uncle James)	17	Coyote
9	Enforcer (Uncle Bartholomew)	18	Retrousse Yacht Club Entrance
		W	Junction Box

Talk to Jackie Grimaldi

PREREQUISITE:

SECURE BARCLAY MILLS DISTRICT

Travel to the Briar Patch restaurant **(1)** in Frisco Fields to meet Jackie Grimaldi, a Special Agent for the United States Department of the Treasury. She's investigating a man who works for Olivia Marcano named Chester Moreau, looking into his connection to the Southern Union.

Interrogate Southern Union Brothers

PREREQUISITE: TALK TO JACKIE GRIMALDI

Two Informants appear on the map **(2a, 2b)**. You only need to talk to one; once you interrogate one, the other one disappears from the map. If the Informant you choose escapes and you don't catch him, he ends up at the other Informant location.

BROTHER SIMON

Brother Simon and his crew hang out in the parking lot of the Southern Union's Church **(2a)**. Be sure to wiretap the Junction Box (circled in our screenshot) on the back of the church first. (Note that this wiretap also reveals the map locations of one "Southern Union Supplies" stash and one "Southern Union Gathering.") Then sneak carefully around the left side of the church.

Simon is in the bright green shirt and white pants and marked "Interrogate." Shoot to incapacitate Simon first so he can't escape, then take out this three companions. Interrogate Simon to learn that Chester Moreau's enforcers are working on a "big, secret job."

UNLOCKS:

KILL THE SOUTHERN UNION ENFORCERS

BROTHER PETER

Brother Peter and his Union boys hang out behind the gas station **(2b)** near the bridge in southern Frisco Fields. Peter stands right next to his shiny red ride, so target him immediately—if you spook him he'll hop in his car and speed away. (If Peter bolts, fire at the getaway car to disable it before it gets out of range.) Interrogate Peter to learn about Chester Moreau's enforcers.

UNLOCKS:

KILL THE SOUTHERN UNION ENFORCERS

BROTHER MATTHEW

Brother Matthew and his minions are based in a small trailer encampment (2c) down a rural road in the northwest corner of Frisco Fields. Sneak up to the blue trailer and take cover behind the woodpile on the side to survey the situation and listen to Matthew talk.

Quickly toss a grenade at Matthew's feet before he stops talking to incapacitate him and take out the associates nearest him. (If you wait too long, Matthew steps to the barbecue grill and his partners move away.) Gun down any surviving goons then interrogate Matthew to learn more about Chester Moreau's operation.

UNLOCKS:

KILL THE SOUTHERN UNION ENFORCERS

Destroy Southern Union Supplies

PREREQUISITE: TALK TO JACKIE GRIMALDI

The Southern Union has two stashes of racist propaganda materials that they peddle for good money. Neither one appears on your map until you wiretap its sector. Both are stashed in garages next to small ranch homes in a nice neighborhood.

BACKYARD BARBECUE

To put this location on your map, wiretap the sector's Junction Box on the back of the Southern Union's Church (2a). Approach the house (3) and use Intel View to spot the stash in the garage as well as the two gunmen behind the house. The gunmen are mixed with other guests at a backyard barbecue. You can avoid them by sneaking around the garage's far side.

Enter the back door and grab the cash on the table first. Then stand near the garage door and target the red gas can (circled in our shot) next to the three stacks of racist supplies to destroy all three with one shot. Sprint out of the garage and escape the neighborhood before being detected.

WILDERNESS SHACK

To reveal this spot **(4)** on your in-game map, you must wiretap the nearby Junction box inside enemy turf at a PCP lab! It's not as tough as it looks at first. Stalk around the outside of the rustic cabin to the box (circled in our shot). The guard over on the next porch won't spot you as you complete the wiretap. Then sneak back around the cabin and check your map to find the new objective icon just down the road to the south.

Head south to the shack and hustle to cover behind the blue panel truck. Use Intel View to see only four gunmen with just one destructible crate, talking with some local rednecks. The odds are good if you want to engage in a simple frontal assault. Fight your way into the shack and blast the crate for racket damage. Pick up stacks of cash in the cabin too.

Raid Southern Union Gatherings

PREREQUISITE: TALK TO JACKIE GRIMALDI

The Southern Union is a social network with regular gatherings of a casual nature as well as official agenda meetings. Disrupting such activities will reverberate up the hierarchy and flush out leaders. In each objective, you complete the "raid" when you destroy any one of the supply stacks in that location.

SOUTHERN UNION CAMP

To find this camp on your map you must wiretap the Junction Box (circled in our shot) on the front entry gate of the Retrousse Yacht Club **(17)**. Once that's done, activate this objective and follow the trip route the short distance from the club to the Southern Union Camp **(5)** in a clearing surrounded by trees.

Enter from the main road heading east and take cover. Use Intel View to spot the two supply crates in the shelter on the left. Two fools stand side by side target shooting, and two others converse near the shelter entrance. If you can land a Screaming Zemi right between the two pairs, they will converge to examine it, and you can follow with a grenade. Go destroy the supply crates to complete the objective.

SOUTHERN UNION RESIDENCE

To put this location on your map, wire-tap the sector's Junction Box on the back of the Southern Union's Church **(2a)**. Travel to the Everson home **(6)**, a nice suburban ranch style with a detached garage. The Eversons bribe cops for the Southern Union—note the police cruiser parked on the street, and the Confederate battle flag hanging on the garage door. Sneak up to the front of the house and use Intel View to spot the stuff highlighted in the garage with one gunman guarding it. Three more goons mix with folks at a backyard barbecue…as do a pair of cops outlined in blue!

You must destroy at least one stack of supplies in the garage to "raid the gathering." Sneak around the garage's far side and take cover at the back corner. Whistle to lure out the gunman for a silent takedown then duck into the

garage's back door. Grab the cash first. Then stand near the door and target one of the red gas cans on the floor next to the lawn mower. Shooting a can ignites the two stacks of supplies and completes the objective. Sprint away to avoid the cops.

SOUTHERN UNION HERITAGE CENTER

Wiretap the Junction Box (circled in our shot) on the side of this old warehouse **(7)** down on the riverfront in southeast Frisco Fields. Your map then reveals that it's the Southern Union Heritage Center—something that needs wrecking, to be sure. After you nail the first two guards, sneak inside and use Intel View to spot the four crates marked for destruction.

Use your favorite tactics to clear the warehouse: whistle and takedown; toss a Screaming Zemi then a grenade; call in a Hit Squad. To "raid" the center and complete the objective, destroy at least one of the marked crates. Target nearby red gas cans to detonate the destructible crates. Then loot any cash you can find.

Kill the Southern Union Enforcers

UNCLE JAMES

Uncle James and his hooded clan harass folks on the waterfront walkway under the bridge **(8)** to Downtown. Take cover at the bottom of the stairs and toss a Screaming Zemi into their midst to draw them even closer together. Then follow up with a Molotov cocktail to toast the racist bastards. Nail James for a racket damage bonus.

UNCLE BARTHOLOMEW

Travel to the Midtown Lanes bowling alley **(9)**. Head around the right side, take cover at the first stack of crates, and peek around to find Bartholomew watching his boys kick the crap out of some poor fellows just for the fun of it.

Lure the nearest guard away from the yellow pickup truck for a silent takedown. Then push forward and take cover behind the yellow truck. From there you can keep luring over marks, including Bartholomew himself.

UNCLE ANDREW

Uncle Andrew and crew are beating up a guy in a dirt lot **(10)** at a Cavar construction storage site. Approach from the street and eliminate the guard up the hill at the gate opening. Take cover at the gate and view the beating to see that Andrew and his thugs are crowded closely around the victim—salivating, no doubt.

You can be heartless and just toss a grenade or Molotov into their circle to kill them all and their victim too. Or you can be slightly less heartless and lure them over one by one for brutal face-knifing takedowns, letting their victim escape.

UNCLE THADDEUS

Uncle Thaddeus and his big crew enjoy a pool party at a cliff-side mansion **(11)** overlooking the waterway. Wiretap the Junction Box (circled in our shot) on the side of the garage. Then climb over the low brick wall and take cover behind the souped-up car. Lure over the thug guarding the driveway for a silent takedown. Proceed to the back corner where he stood and whistle to pull more gunmen away from the pool.

Move down to the next corner near the pool and continue your sneaky whistling. Thaddeus, in his bathing suit and carrying a beer, will be one of the first fools who check out the sound. Take him down for racket damage. If you want to take out the whole crew, your reward is another $3500 in cash waiting for pickup on the table near the barbecue. And for added fun, you can drive away in the Samson Opus sports car sitting in the driveway.

UNCLE JUDE

Jude and his band of hooded miscreants harass a lone man in the parking lot of the old church **(12)** down in southwest Frisco Fields. Wiretap the Junction Box on the Swift Deli next door then use Intel View to see that Jude has a good-sized crew. Take cover behind the junked car or the trailer between the church and deli, then start trying to lure over thugs for silent takedowns.

HEY, JUDE

Uncle Jude and his boys are clumped together tightly as they beat the man in the parking lot. You can toss a grenade or Molotov into their midst and nail Jude and three or four of his men. However, you'll also kill their poor victim.

Interrogate Southern Union Brothers (Second Time)

After you inflict the required racket damage, a new Informant appears on the map in one of two spots **(13a, 13b)**. If the Informant escapes and you don't catch him, he ends up at the other Informant location.

BROTHER PAUL

Brother Paul and crew hang out at the Everyday Laundromat **(13a)** in central Frisco Fields. (Wiretap the sector at the Junction Box on the back of the nearby Thrift Mart.) Go to the locked back door and pry it open, but don't enter! Two thugs are right inside, so take cover outside and whistle to lure each of them for takedowns.

Slip inside, turn right, and go to the next door. Take cover beside the door and open it. Paul and two of his guys are just on the other side, so if you rush in nail Paul first to incapacitate him, or else he'll flee quickly. A better move is to whistle all three goons through the doorway for silent takedowns. Interrogate Paul to learn about something going on afterhours at the Bellaire's supermarket.

UNLOCKS:

TALK TO JACKIE GRIMALDI (SECOND TIME)

BROTHER LUKE

Luke hangs out at a backyard party **(13b)** over in east Frisco Fields. Sneak through yards and approach from the east, taking cover behind the trailer behind the party. Toss a Screaming Zemi next to the barbecue and wait until Luke and his boys gather to

investigate it. Then toss a grenade or Molotov into their midst for a group takedown. Approach the incapacitated Luke and interrogate him to learn about something going on afterhours at the Bellaire's supermarket.

UNLOCKS:

TALK TO JACKIE GRIMALDI (SECOND TIME)

Talk to Jackie Grimaldi (Second Time)

PREREQUISITE: INTERROGATE SOUTHERN UNION BROTHERS (SECOND TIME)

Return to the Briar Patch restaurant **(1)** and talk to Jackie Grimaldi again. She reports that something's happening at the Bellaire supermarket at 10 PM that night. Jackie recommends a quiet infiltration to learn exactly what's going on.

UNLOCKS:

INVESTIGATE BELLAIRE'S GROCERY STORE

Investigate Bellaire's Grocery Store

PREREQUISITE:

TALK TO JACKIE GRIMALDI (SECOND TIME)

WAIT FOR NIGHTFALL

Travel to the Bellaire's supermarket **(14)** in the Value Plaza shopping center up in northeast Frisco Fields. Wiretap the Junction Box just across the lot, if you haven't done so already. Then follow the objective marker to the spot by the wall next to two folding chairs

on the side of Carlyle's Furniture store, just across from Bellaire's. Press the Action button to wait there, then watch the cutscene as night falls and Southern Union boys arrive in a truck. They go in Bellaire's side door.

GET INSIDE BELLAIRE'S

Sneak in the same door and take out the goon with his back to you. Pick up the Tac-Vest from the floor nearby. Find the staircase just around the corner and work your way upstairs to the meeting.

INTERROGATE MASON CARTER

In a small meeting room on the second floor, Lincoln comes upon a terrible sight: a man is being sold as a slave to bidders in the audience. The gentleman running the slave auction is Mason Carter, and he has only two Southern Union bodyguards, so you can lean around the doorway into the meeting room and gun them down quickly. Then incapacitate Carter.

Let the miserable bidders go, or make them pay by tossing a Molotov into the audience. Grab the $3500 cash sitting on the desk. Then interrogate Mason Carter. He admits that Chester Moreau has more slaves imprisoned around the district. When Lincoln ends the conversation with Carter, he inflicts a large amount of damage to Moreau's racket.

> **BELLAIRE PICKUPS**
>
> Before you leave the grocery store, explore to pick up loads of cash plus a copy of *Repent* magazine and a Vargas painting in the main office.

Rescue Human Trafficking Victims

PREREQUISITE:

INTERROGATE MASON CARTER

THE FOSSATS

Travel up to the compound **(15)** at the northwest tip of Frisco Fields. Your Intel View reveals a squad of five Southern Union guards posted between you and the cabin. Work your way through them, stealthily or violently, depending on your preference. In either case, take out the Sentry in the garage before he can call in reinforcements. Go through the garage and out its back door. Open the green door on the shack to release the Fossat family.

Work your way up the left side of the house and take down the pacing guard from behind. Then sneak up on the guard at the tunnel entrance and take him down too.

THE GAUDETS

The placement of the in-game map icon for this objective is somewhat misleading because the location is underground. To reach it, you must travel to the huge house **(16)** just east of Cleavon Duvall State Park. Your goal is to work your way to a tunnel opening (circled in our screenshot) behind the mansion.

Descend the stairs down the tunnel to an underground meeting hall. Several Southern Union gunmen are at the hall's far end. Use your favorite tactic to get past them. Continue into the back room to find a $1250 pile of money. Then open the green door to discover and liberate the Gaudet family.

Rob the Coyote

PREREQUISITE: Interrogate Mason Carter

Be ready for a surprise here. Activate the objective and follow the trip route to a hut **(17)** with a big red propane tank out front. Kick open the hut's door and find a big $10,000 pile of cash sitting unguarded on the back desk. Easy, right?

Of course not. As you grab the money, two angry pairs of good ol' boys from the Southern Union pull up in pickup trucks to claim their cash. Hustle to the doorway and shoot the red propane tank as soon as you can to inflict some hurt. Take cover at the doorway, use Intel View to assess the incoming threat, then start gunning them down. When the way is clear, get back to your vehicle and escape.

Talk to Jackie Grimaldi (Third Time)

Return to the Briar Patch restaurant **(1)** and talk to Jackie one more time. She tells Lincoln that Chester Moreau is holed up at the grocery store.

Kill Chester Moreau

Return to the Value Plaza shopping center where the Bellaire Supermarket **(14)** is located, but this time park on the road to the east and approach the store from the back. Climb the ladder over the brick perimeter wall and work your way past any guards across the loading yard to the service door (circled).

Move past the receiving desk and through all the stacked boxes, then take two right turns to find the staircase. Climb to the second floor and turn right.

Work your way back to the main office where Chester is holed up. Incapacitate Chester then seize him for a final confrontation with the disgusting human trafficker. Assign the Bellaire's-based racket to an Underboss—no more slave trade in Frisco Fields.

RACKET: PCP

Frisco Fields

LEGEND

1	Quik Lodge Motel (Bear Donnelly)	**4**	PCP Cook ("Beaks" Brunner)	**7**	Duvall Hall Science Center
2	Informant	**5**	PCP Cook (Lonnie Grima)	**W**	Junction Box
3	PCP Cook (Gabe Chauvin)	**6**	Priority Cabs Garage	●	PCP Chemicals

By now you should have all of the Frisco Fields Junction Boxes wiretapped—but we put their locations on this map, just in case.

Talk to Bear Donnelly

PREREQUISITE:

SECURE BARCLAY MILLS DISTRICT

Activate this objective and follow the trip route to the seedy Quik Lodge Motel **(1)** in southwest Frisco Fields. Follow the objective marker to the room upstairs and enter to meet Bear Donnelly, your old contact from Pointe Verdun. Bear tells Lincoln about Olivia Marcano's PCP racket in Frisco Fields, run by a top-notch chemist named Bobby Bastian. The operation is so well-integrated that licensed taxicabs are delivering the goods to bored housewives with expendable income.

Interrogate Bobby's Dealers

PREREQUISITE: TALK TO BEAR DONNELLY

Two Informants appear on the map **(2a, 2b)**. You only need to talk to one; once you interrogate one, the other one disappears from the map. If the Informant you choose escapes and you don't catch him, he ends up at the other Informant location.

RODNEY PREJEAN

Rodney Prejean hangs out at the Drive-In restaurant **(2a)**, looking to push his powder on kids. Park in back near the dumpsters and sneak leftward around the circular building. Hide behind the stack of boxes and spot your mark just ahead with a lone sidekick. Shoot to incapacitate Rodney so he can't escape, then take out his companion. Interrogate Rodney to learn that Bastian is keeping the cash drops from his drug taxi deliveries at the Priority Cabs dispatch garage.

UNLOCKS: ROB THE TAXI GARAGE

"TIPS" KERNAN

Tips Kernan and his gang loiter in the common area of a tenement row **(2b)** in southwest Frisco Fields. Use Intel View to see that two of his guys lean up against the building on the left. A good approach is to circle around that building to the corner by the basketball court. Start whistling to lure his men to the corner for silent takedowns. When you go for Tips, incapacitate him quickly or he'll run! Interrogate Tips to learn that Bastian is storing the cash drops from his drug taxi deliveries at the Priority Cabs dispatch garage.

UNLOCKS: ROB THE TAXI GARAGE

Find and Eliminate PCP Taxis

PREREQUISITE: TALK TO BEAR DONNELLY

Priority Cabs taxis driven by a drug courier will spawn periodically in front of you. The courier is marked with a "Kill" icon overhead, visible above the taxi. To complete this objective, you must kill the courier (the driver), so you don't need to destroy the vehicle. However, the taxi carries three hostile gunmen as well, so if you destroy the car, you can take out the entire team.

Look for the "Kill" icon overhead to spot a PCP taxi. The driver is a drug courier.

The PCP taxis are usually in the oncoming lane, driving toward you. Try to swing your vehicle across the taxi's path, then hop out and either shoot the driver through the windshield or toss a grenade under the taxi. If the taxi gets past you, chase it down, shooting at its tires to disable it. Then hop out and target the driver. Taking out each "Kill"-marked driver inflicts damage on Bastian's PCP racket.

Target the driver first! Once he's eliminated, the objective is complete.

PCP taxis continue to spawn until you talk to Bear Donnelly the second time.

Find and Destroy PCP Chemicals (5)

PREREQUISITE: TALK TO BEAR DONNELLY

Bastian's PCP business depends on a steady supply of the chemicals needed to produce the drug. These chemicals are warehoused in five different sites in Frisco Fields. Each site appears on your map only if you've wiretapped that sector. So if you haven't already, wiretap all of the Junction Boxes in the district. (For your convenience, the PCP chemical storage sites are also marked on our district map for this racket.)

Each PCP chemical site features stashes of explosive chemicals in barrels that you can destroy, plus a big green "Industrial-Strength Chemical" truck that you can blow up for even more damage.

Kill Bastian's PCP Cooks

PREREQUISITE: TALK TO BEAR DONNELLY

GABE CHAUVIN

Gabe Chauvin cooks in a boarded-up ranch house **(3)** on a quiet suburban cul-de-sac. Head around the right side and take cover at the back corner for an Intel View scan. Silently take down the goggled cook who steps outside, then sneak in and take down two more cooks in the back room. Proceed into the front room and terminate Gabe, the guy in glasses and a blue jumpsuit. This inflicts a hefty amount of racket damage. Don't leave before destroying the drums of chemicals for additional damage.

"BEAKS" BRUNNER

Travel out west to the enclave of "rustic" (i.e., decrepit) cabins **(4)** and trailers that Beaks Brunner has turned into a veritable cooking school. (If you haven't wiretapped the box on the cabin at the far end of the enclave, do so now.) Work your way across the encampment to the building where your Intel View shows Beaks and his boys are gathered. Toss a Screaming Zemi to draw them out, and toss a Molotov to warm things up. Target Beaks if he survives the attack—he's the guy in the blue jumpsuit.

LONNIE GRIMA

Lonnie and his cooks have a "kitchen" in an old warehouse **(5)** next door to the Locksmith and Fresh Dairy shops in an industrial block down in southeast Frisco Fields. You can see the cooking smoke pouring out of the garage doors! Work your way around to the open garage door, number 9, and take a quick Intel View of the premises.

All those cooks are armed, so your best bet is to take cover just outside the open door and start whistling over folks one by one. Sooner or later, Lonnie himself comes to investigate. Take him down for ten grand in damage! Clear out the others too, then loot the place for cash.

Rob the Taxi Garage

PREREQUISITE:
INTERROGATE BOBBY'S DEALERS

The Priority Cabs depot **(6)** is a big place with a number of buildings. Bastian's cash stash is in the middle garage (circled in our photo) in the row of three. Approach from the west, climb the low brick wall between buildings, and move down the alley through the chain-link gate. Use Intel View to scan the area.

Turn right and sneak along the long building to nail the gunmen pacing by the cabs. Then take cover outside the open garage door of the middle garage. Two goons are seated inside to the left, including a Sentry. Creep up behind each or lure them over with whistles for silent takedowns. (Another option is to shoot both with a silenced weapon, if you have one available.)

Now go to the locked chain-link gate and use your Pry Bar to open it. Sneak in and take down the lone guard inside. Then pry open the blue strongbox on the desk to pocket a cool $20,000 cash.

Talk to Bear Donnelly

Return to the Quik Lodge Motel **(1)** and head back up to Bear's shabby room to talk. Bear says that Bobby Bastian has taken personal control of the main laboratory, trying to get production back up to speed. Time to pay him a visit.

Confront Bobby Bastian

Travel to the Duvall Hall Science Center **(7)**, enter the front doors, and take cover immediately. Bastian is up on the second floor, in a back office. Work your way across the main lobby—stealthily if you can—then climb the stairs to the next level.

Follow the green signs that point the direction to the research area. Work your way through a series of equipment-filled labs. Keep in mind that you can shoot through windows into labs next door. Also note the red explosive canisters sitting everywhere; if you get into a gunfight on the way, target the canisters when foes are next to them.

Find Bobby Bastian in or just outside the main office in the back. Kill or recruit him to complete Lincoln's takeover of the PCP racket in Frisco Fields, then assign it to an Underboss.

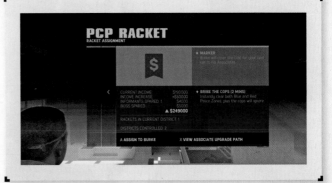

RESEARCH PERKS

Don't miss the $3500 stack of cash and the Vargas painting in the Duvall Center's main office.

UNLOCKS STORY MISSION:
KILL REMY DUVALL

FRISCO FIELDS:
THERE'S A WAR GOIN' ON

MISSION: "KILL REMY DUVALL"

LEGEND

1. Blue Gulf Motel (Donovan)
2. Start Search for Deacon
3. Cleavon Duvall State Park

Donovan's Got More on Remy Duvall

PREREQUISITE: Secure Both Frisco Fields Rackets ("Southern Union" and "PCP")

Travel down to the Blue Gulf Motel **(1)** in Delray Hollow to meet with Donovan in his tac-ops center. Donovan has a recording of a raw conversation between Remy Duvall and Oliva Marcano. It appears that Remy and his Southern Union brothers are gearing up to make a move. Now Lincoln needs a way to track down Duvall.

Find a Southern Union Deacon

Activate this objective and follow the trip route back to Frisco Fields **(2)**. When you arrive, check your map: a large yellow search circle has appeared. Drive around within this circle and keep an eye on your Minimap. When you spot a Southern Union icon appear on the Minimap, drive toward it until the yellow circle disappears and you get a new objective.

Interrogate Southern Union Deacon

The icon marks the location of a Southern Union Deacon. Find the deacon and shoot to incapacitate him. When he falls down on one knee, gun down any of his armed associates. Then interrogate the deacon. Lincoln learns that Remy has called a meeting of his Union boys up by the old lookout point that night. The deacon calls it "putting together a huntin' party."

Go to the Southern Union Rally

Call your Arms Dealer and pick up a scoped rifle. Then travel to Cleavon Duvall State Park **(3)**. Night falls automatically as you arrive, and you get a new objective.

Kill Remy Duvall

Instead of following the torch-lit parking arrow sign that points leftward up the road to the parking lot, veer to the right of the sign and follow the walking path. It leads uphill to a chain-link side gate.

From here, you can see Remy Duvall on the stage, whipping his Union brothers into a frenzy of hatred. Hop over the fence and take cover in the stone ruins. Wield the scoped rifle and nail Remy with a couple of headshots. He collapses to one knee.

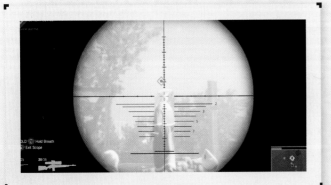

Kill the Remaining Southern Union Soldiers

Once you've incapacitated Remy, you can turn your attention to the other lowlife. Not all of the Southern Union members are armed; use Intel View and your Minimap to find the red-marked gunmen. Toss grenades, Molotovs, whatever you've got. Take them out—all of them. When the last one falls, the objective changes again.

Confront Remy Duvall

Approach Remy and hold the button indicated to trigger a pair of cutscenes: Remy remains an unrepentant racist to the bitter end. And then you see live TV reports of the grisly aftermath.

UNLOCKS STORY MISSION:
KILL OLIVIA MARCANO

FRISCO FIELDS:
CERTAINLY WAS EXCITING

MISSION: "KILL OLIVIA MARCANO"

LEGEND

1. Meet Donovan
2. Stephen Degarmo
3. Briar Patch Restaurant (Donovan)

Meet Donovan to Get Into Remy's Wake

Travel up to the entrance road to the Retrousse Yacht Club and find Donovan's blue van **(1)** parked down a short lane just off the road. The van has new signage: "Ms. Ya-Ya's Restaurant & Catering." Open the passenger side door; Donovan says Olivia Marcano is in the country club.

This triggers a series of cutscenes: first, Donovan tells the Senate hearing what he suspects about Olivia's motivations. Then you see a scene between Sal and his sister-in-law: as it turns out, Remy Duvall's will has bequeathed the casino land to an unknown nephew, Stephen Degarmo, tossing a magnum-size monkey wrench into Sal's plans. Finally, Donovan explains to the Senators how Lincoln, dressed as a waiter, snuck into the country club for Remy's wake.

Infiltrate Remy's Wake

Donovan delivers Lincoln to the service entrance. Just walk inside the door. Easiest objective so far—but don't let that dampen your feeling of accomplishment.

Go to the Manager

Veer rightward to meet the manager, who's talking to an employee. Follow the manager through the kitchen area.

Dose the Wine Bottle

When you reach the pantry, the manager moves ahead to direct wine pourers into the reception. Approach each of the three wine bottles sitting on

the counter and hold the button indicated to spike it with the syringe of LSD solution. Lincoln picks up the third bottle after you dose it.

Serve the Manager

When the manager returns, he's holding a wineglass. Approach him to pour some of the spiked wine into his glass.

Serve the Mourners

Move out onto the floor. Approach marked attendees holding empty glasses and serve them wine as Olivia Marcano speaks to the crowd.

Serve Olivia's Bodyguards

After Olivia's speech ends, follow the objective markers to three of her bodyguards (the fellows in the light-colored suits) and serve them wine too.

Take a Smoke Break

After you serve the third bodyguard, follow the objective marker back into the kitchen area to see how the dosed wine is affecting the manager. Continue back through the kitchen until you reach the threesome of workers near the exit door

who invite Lincoln to smoke with them. This break gives the dosages time to work out on the floor.

Follow Olivia

Head back through the kitchen and out into the reception area again. Things have changed a bit. Spot Olivia Marcano on the first landing of the staircase and follow her upstairs with the one bodyguard who didn't drink spiked wine. Follow them upstairs and into the back office.

Put Down the Wine Bottle

Olivia tells Lincoln to put the bottle on the bar. Approach the bar and hold down the button displayed to set down the bottle.

Kill Olivia's Bodyguards

Use Intel View for a quick survey of the room. Everybody here including Olivia is a target. Pick up the Masterson Phoenix pistol just to the right on the bar's lower shelf, and open fire. Use the bar for cover and gun down all of the guards.

Subdue Olivia

Olivia is tough and hard to hit. Shoot until you incapacitate her and she goes down on one knee.

Confront Olivia

Approach Olivia and hold the button prompted to trigger a cinematic: Lincoln is relentless at first as he seeks information from Olivia. But in the end, out of pity and disgust, he shows her mercy.

Find Stephen Degarmo

Exit the side door into a service corridor where you can raid a couple of Weapon Lockers. Then kick open the exit door in that corridor and take down the guard waiting on the other side.

Take cover just down the walkway and whistle for the guard at the far end to lure him for a silent takedown. Sneak up on a second guard with his back to you for another takedown.

Head down the staircase at the end of the walkway and open the door at the bottom to trigger a cutscene: poor Stephen Degarmo is facing some mob coercion tactics to sign over the land he received in the Remy Duvall's will.

Rescue Stephen Degarmo

Degarmo is across the courtyard, about 80 meters away. A quick Intel View scan reveals a number of hostile mobsters out in the courtyard garden. Check out our overhead shot to get a wider perspective on where you start and where you finish at the toolshed where Degarmo is being held.

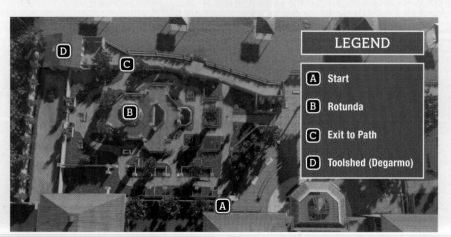

LEGEND
A Start
B Rotunda
C Exit to Path
D Toolshed (Degarmo)

You start at the doorway **(A)**. Move out and veer to the left toward the open rotunda **(B)** up on a raised patio. Again, the courtyard is crawling with gunmen. Your goal is to work along the far wall to reach a side path via the open exit gate **(C)** then turn left and get into the toolshed **(D)**.

There are many ways to move across this space. By now you should have developed a favorite approach. Use it! Sneak all the way using stealth and silent takedowns, if you want. Or gun down every miserable goodfella roaming the garden. Note that several gunmen are posted near the exit gate you're trying to reach.

When you finally reach the toolshed's garden entrance door, kick it open and immediately open fire on the torturing goon inside. Then approach poor Stephen Degarmo to untie him.

Escape with Degarmo

Open the exit door to the driveway and get into Degarmo's red De'Leo Stiletto, a nimble vehicle for escape purposes. Wait until Degarmo gets in the passenger seat and then drive past the funeral hearse, smashing directly through the Duvall portrait next to it. Police cars arrive as you pull out into the main driveway. Turn right at the barricade and barrel through the yacht club's entrance gate, swerving to avoid arriving police vehicles.

Lose the Cops

By now you should be proficient at evading police pursuit. Use your police dispatcher associate (if available) to call off the chase once you get off the yacht club grounds onto the city streets. Once you get out of the Police Zone, you get a new objective.

Get Degarmo to Donovan

Follow the new trip route to the destination marker in the parking lot of the Briar Patch restaurant **(3)** (next to the Lautner's store). Donovan waits for you there in his surveillance van.

Your arrival triggers a series of chapter-ending cinematics, including a look at Olivia Marcano's unfortunate hospital recuperation, and Sal Marcano's realization that he must make an uncomfortable phone call.

IN COMES SANTANGELO IF...

In Mafia III, you must take down all three of Sal Marcano's capos—his brothers Tommy and Lou, and his sister-in-law Olivia Marcano[md] after taking control of their respective districts: Southdowns, French Ward, and Frisco Fields. You can do this in any order.

Whatever order you choose, Killing the first Marcano capo triggers a cutscene where Sal calls for help from the Mafia's "Commission" led by Leo Galante. This phone call has no in-game consequences.

Killing the second Marcano capo, however, motivates Sal to bring in outside help. You see a cutscene where Sal makes a deal with Nino Santangelo, the heroin dealer and assassin. This cutscene triggers a new game chapter, "In Comes the Devil," and its lone mission, "My Name Is Lincoln Clay...".

In our walkthrough, we tackle Frisco Fields and Olivia Marcano first. In this order, bringing down Olivia prompts Sal's phone call to The Commission. We go after Southdowns and Tommy Marcano second, so we list the Santangelo cutscene and mission there. Again, if you were to take down Frisco Fields and Olivia second instead of first, the Santangelo content would appear here, right after Olivia's demise.

Assign Frisco Fields to an Underboss

Then the scene switches to another sitdown at the bayou mansion. Assign the newly acquired Frisco Fields district to one of Lincoln's Underbosses. Feathers will be ruffled, but that's the price of admission for the show that Lincoln is now running.

SOUTHDOWNS: THE FISTS AND THE FLAMES

RACKET: GAMBLING

LEGEND

1. Meet "Sweet" Danny Little
2. Informants
3. Enforcer (August "Bulldog" Perotta)
4. Enforcer (Rocky Torani)
5. Enforcer (Shane Fordham)
6. Eddie Kenner
7. Willcock's Sports Bar
W. Junction Box
 Slot Machines

Southdowns

Bayou Fantom

Talk to "Sweet" Danny Little

PREREQUISITE:

SECURE TICKFAW HARBOR DISTRICT

"Sweet" Danny is up on the roof of a building **(1)** across the street from The Acadia, a boxing venue. Enter the green door next to the fight posters and climb the stairs to the roof.

"Sweet" Danny is a top-level boxer, but he's having trouble with one of Tommy Marcano's men, a fellow named "Two-Dicks" Peralta who runs a sports gambling operation out of the Willcock's Saloon. Two-Dicks wants Danny to take a dive in his next fight; he also recently kidnapped Eddie Kenner, a promising up-and-comer who may be forced into an illegal fighting circuit.

Interrogate Two-Dicks' Runners

PREREQUISITE:

TALK TO "SWEET" DANNY LITTLE

Informant icons appear on the map in these four locations **(2a, 2b, 2c, 2d)**. You only need to interrogate one Informant; once you do, the other three icons disappear from the map. If the Informant you choose escapes and you don't catch him, he ends up at one of the other Informant locations.

UNLOCKS: RESCUE EDDIE KENNER

LOUIE "LAMPS" ZUCCO

Louie "Lamps" auditions fighters at a back alley venue **(2a)** in central Southdowns. A crowd watches the battle as Lamps and five of his men keep an eye on things. A good approach is up the alley from the south. Then use the green door between the dumpsters. Follow the corridor through the next door then proceed down the next alley. Take cover at the corner and observe the fight crowd.

Use Intel View to distinguish the goons from the gawkers. To go in loud, toss a grenade at Lamps to incapacitate him and eliminate a couple of his guys in the process. Then let the crowd scatter a bit before you gun down the other guards. Go interrogate Lamps to see what he knows.

"MONK" O'HALLORAN

Monk O'Halloran runs a high-stakes card game in the backyard of his childhood home **(2b)**, a house with blue shutters up on the north side of Southdowns. Monk and his only associate chat in an equipment shed while a foursome plays cards nearby on a patio table. Toss a grenade or Molotov right into the shed!

This incapacitates Monk and takes out his partner. Let the card players flee and snag the cash they leave behind on the table. Then interrogate Monk to learn what he knows. Afterwards, destroy the stash of gambling equipment in the corner of the shed to inflict damage to the Gambling racket.

Inside, work around the stacked crates, taking down anyone you encounter. When you can see the makeshift casino across the big room, you can lure over Joey (marked with the Informant "i" icon) and incapacitate him. Interrogate him to learn what he knows. Now you can either leave or, much better, wreak havoc on the casino where you can inflict thousands of dollars of damage on the Gambling racket.

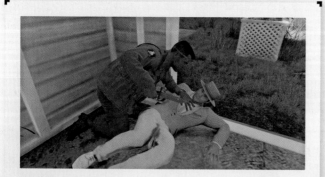

JOEY FINCH

Two-Dicks has a secret casino operating out of a Bayside Shipping warehouse **(2c)** on the northwest waterfront, with Joey Finch as the pit boss. Work your way around the outside from corner to corner to silently take down guards. Then pry open the locked door (circled in our overhead shot) on the backside and sneak in.

WELCOME TO THE WAREHOUSE

You can find a Vargas painting hanging behind the reception desk at the garage door entrance into Joey's casino.

NUNCIO LOMBARD

Nuncio Lombardi runs numbers for Two-Dicks. Based on an open patio near a seafood market **(2d)** up on the north shore of Southdowns, Nuncio is easy to incapacitate if you've got a high-powered rifle with a scope. Just nail him from a distance until he goes down on one knee.

Now take cover and pick off Lombardi's men. Target the Sentry first, if you can! Once the area is cleared, interrogate Lombardi to learn what he knows.

Kill Two-Dicks' Gambling Enforcers

PREREQUISITE:

TALK TO "SWEET" DANNY LITTLE

AUGUST "BULLDOG" PEROTTA

The Bulldog and his men oversee Two-Dicks' makeshift casino inside a pair of outbuildings **(3)** on the western edge of Southdowns. Approach the head of the alley where a "Rocco's Retreat" sign hangs on the fence next to the NB Liquor Store.

Start by wiretapping the Junction Box (circled in our shot) on the hut just down the alley; you have to eliminate the gunman guarding the alley approach first, but he turns his back to you, so it's an easy takedown.

Once the box is wiretapped, do an Intel View scan of the area ahead. You can see the casino's slot machines inside the hut, and spot Perotta and crew in the garage down at the alley's far end, where the poker tables are set up. Work from cover around the alley and try to get silent takedowns on as many guards as possible. Pry open the hut door and lure out the lone guard inside. Then go seek out the Bulldog.

If you trigger an alert, the gamblers scatter and flee in panic, and the Bulldog and his men come after you. Once the casino is cleared, destroy the five pairs of slot machines in the hut. Then loot all of the cash from the garage with the poker tables.

ROCKY TORANI

Rocky runs a high-stakes poker game, with a card table set up under an open shelter in the loading lot behind (among other businesses) Tuneville Records **(4)** in south-central Southdowns. Your best approach is to find the well-hidden Junction Box (circled in our shot) just a few yards away, tucked between a brick hut and a blue trailer. Now you can see the distribution of goons with your Intel View.

SHANE FORDHAM

Shane Fordham and his rude crew **(5)** run the sports book for Johnny Two-Dicks out of Neil A. Arthur Stadium. They've got a lot of customers lined up, so we suggest you first approach from the north end of the stadium and wiretap the Junction Box (circled in our shot) under the east stands. That way you can tell the bad guys from the bettors by using Intel View, even through walls.

Work your way around the area, taking out Rocky's boys one by one. Scoop the $2750 cash off the card table and the $1250 bag of money just around the corner, sitting on a crate in the fenced enclosure. Torani and a squad of gunmen (including a Sentry) are keeping watch on the loading dock in a covered alley across the street from the Food Circuit Grocery. Take him down for racket damage.

Work through the area clearing out the thugs silently if you can, using the Swift Drink trailer as cover. Then find Shane with an associate behind the betting table. If you haven't triggered an alert, he has his back to you. Take him down from behind for racket damage then finish off his partner and search the area for cash pickups.

Destroy Slot Machines (9)

PREREQUISITE:

TALK TO "SWEET" DANNY LITTLE

"Two-Dicks" Peralta makes good money from crooked one-arm bandits installed inside local Southdowns institutions such as Joey's All American Diner, Frank's Blue Land Jazz Club, Fareham Grocery, Shooters Bar, and even an Everyday Laundromat. You can find map icons marking the locations of these rigged nickel slots once you get their Southdowns sectors wiretapped.

Each site has just two goons posted to oversee operations, so you can approach aggressively and take them out. Then destroy the bank of three slot machines to inflict more damage to the Gambling racket. Watch out for witnesses rushing off to call the police.

Bust Up Street Games

PREREQUISITE: TALK TO "SWEET" DANNY LITTLE

Peralta also runs a big "dice alley" gambling site on the streets of Southdowns. Once you get the site's district sector wiretapped, an icon pops up showing the location of the back-alley craps game. The place is well-guarded, with half a dozen gunmen keeping an eye on things, plus two tough bosses with a "Kill" icon overhead.

Obviously, caution is advised when approaching this gathering. Use patience and stealth to work around the site, using silent takedowns to even up the odds a bit before engaging in gunplay. Afterwards, clean up the considerable amount of cash littered around the area.

Rescue Eddie Kenner

PREREQUISITE: INTERROGATE TWO-DICKS' RUNNERS

Activate this objective and follow the trip route out of Southdowns to its end in the Bayou Fantom. The location you seek **(6)** is on a small island, so find a boat on the docks and motor across the gap, following the objective marker.

When you reach the dock, hop out and take cover. Lure down the gunman standing guard at the locked front door of the cabin and take him down. Use your Pry Bar to unlock the door but take cover outside the door. Inside, a guard faces away from you, staring at a cage where Eddie Kenner is held captive. Sneak behind him and take him down.

Take a second to loot the cash in the room because it's a considerable amount. Then open the cage door and hold the button indicated to free the prisoner. He takes off running. Retrace your route back to your boat to leave the area.

Talk to "Sweet" Danny Little (Second Time)

PREREQUISITE: RACKET DAMAGE TOTAL TO $0

Return to "Sweet" Danny up on his rooftop **(1)** to learn that Two-Dicks is back at Willcock's, threatening his fighters.

Confront Johnny "Two-Dicks" Peralta

Travel to Willcock's Sports Bar **(7)**. Peralta is upstairs in his office, and a lot of armed tough guys are spread around the premises. You can avoid most of them by taking this route: First, go behind the building to find the back door (see our shot) into the bar's storage area, a long room with stocked shelves and a black/white tiled floor. Take cover just outside the doorway.

Whistle to lure any guards posted inside to the doorway for a silent takedown. Move through the room to the bar entrance on the right, checking with your Intel View to make sure the way is clear. Take cover at the doorway and peek into the bar to see stairs just ahead on the right. You want to get up that staircase, but preferably without being detected.

Whistle any nearby goons to the storage doorway for takedowns, then sneak into the bar and head up the stairs on your right. Watch for a guard patrolling the balcony; wait until he paces away then take him down from behind. Now you've got a clear path to the office at the far end of the balcony.

Inside, Johnny "Two-Dicks" chats with an associate. Whistle to lure out the associate and take him down. Then lure Johnny out for a takedown too. Seize the incapacitated boss and either kill or recruit him to take control of the Gambling racket in Southdowns.

Assign the racket to an Underboss.

RACKET: BLACK MARKET

LEGEND

1. Grant Purdue
2. Informants
3. Enforcer (Santo Clemente)
4. Enforcer (Alfredo "Fred" Pace)
5. Black Market Money Stash
6. Mama Righetti's Bakery
7. Purdue's Warehouse
W. Junction Box
○. Black Market Products

Southdowns

Talk to Grant Purdue (First Time)

PREREQUISITE: SECURE TICKFAW HARBOR DISTRICT

Select this objective and follow the route to the corner building **(1)** under the Swift sign. Enter the green door right on the corner and talk to Grant Purdue. Purdue tells you about an insurance scam being run with his excess inventory by a guy named Artie Higgins.

Interrogate Artie's Hustlers

PREREQUISITE: Talk to Grant Purdue

Informant icons appear on the map in these three locations **(2a, 2b, 2c)**. You only need to interrogate one Informant; once you do, the other two icons disappear from the map. If an Informant escapes and you don't catch him, he ends up at one of the other Informant locations.

UNLOCKS: Retrieve Grant Purdue's Truck

PASCAL "THE ROMAN" LINZA

Linza operates in the alley **(2a)** right behind the building where you met Grant Purdue. When you arrive, he's watching two of his boys kick the crap out of a delivery truck driver. Take cover in front of the truck and toss a Screaming Zemi at the thugs. Let them gather close, then toss a Molotov or grenade. Rush the incapacitated Linza and interrogate him.

LETO TIERI

Leto Tieri and his crew are unloading stolen goods from a truck parked in a loading alley **(2c)** behind a row of businesses in south-central Southdowns. From the street out front, unlock the green door (circled in our shot) in the brick wall; it leads into a liquor storage garage. Sneak forward to the barrels to see Leto through the open garage door just ahead of you.

Whistle to lure him over for a takedown and interrogation. Afterwards, stay behind the barrels, popping up to nail Leto's men as the fools try to funnel through the garage door bottleneck to get at you. Once the area is clear, scour the area for cash pickups.

HENRY "THE CHINK" ORIENTE

Henry Oriente and his gang hang out in the loading yard outside the Food Circuit Grocery **(2b)** in southern Southdowns. Slip into the yard via the gate in the chain-link fence (circled in our shot) out behind the building. Take cover behind a crate near the big water-tanker truck, and silently

take down the pair of pacing guards.

Henry is chatting with an associate near the front of the big truck. Whistle to lure him over for a takedown and interrogation, but watch out for another guard patrolling on the opposite side of the truck.

Destroy Black Market Products (7)

PREREQUISITE:
TALK TO GRANT PURDUE

Artie Higgins is trying to move stolen TVs. You can hurt his racket by destroying them. The TVs are stashed in Holland Bros. crates around Southdowns, but the in-game map icons marking their locations appear only when you wiretap the sectors they're in. (Our district map includes their locations.) Each site features two crates of TVs (each marked with a destructible icon), plus a fairly large crew of Artie's men.

As always, if you can find a clear angle to each stash from a distance, you can snipe them and run. Or you can work close enough to toss explosives and still escape. But each site also features plenty of cash pickups, so you may want to systematically clear the area of Artie's soldiers, then loot it.

Kill Artie's Hijackers

PREREQUISITE: TALK TO GRANT PURDUE

SANTO CLEMENTE

Santo and gang are hosting a yard sale of stolen goods **(3)** next to a garage in a residential neighborhood in north-central Southdowns. Sneak into the garage and quietly take down the goon inside from behind. Drop behind the crate and whistle to lure in the next guard for a silent takedown.

Here, watch your Minimap and Intel View for guards coming around the outside of the garage and entering the big door behind you. Go take cover inside the door if they make this move. Then move to the garage's

back door and continue your whistling ways to thin out Santo's crew. When you finally encounter Santo, take him down then scour the yard sale for piles of cash.

ALFREDO "FRED" PACE

Fred and his fools are selling hot electronics out of a backyard alley **(4)** in another residential neighborhood. Looks like all kinds of respectable folks are buying stolen goods. Climb over the white picket fence, take cover, and lure the Sentry and another guard for takedowns. Keep whistling until you get Fred's attention then end his sales career abruptly.

Steal the Black Market Money Stash

PREREQUISITE: TALK TO GRANT PURDUE

Travel to the big Louisiana Shipping Company warehouse (5) down in southern Southdowns. As you can see by the two icons side-by-side on your in-game map, there are actually two separate money stashes at this site.

Each stash is locked in a blue strongbox atop a table on the ground floor, one on either end of the warehouse. Pry them open—each holds $5000. The warehouse is full of loose cash and crates of black market goods, too. So you can really hammer Artie's racket by thoroughly scouring this site.

Retrieve Grant Purdue's Truck

PREREQUISITE:

INTERROGATE ARTIE'S HUSTLERS

You can damage the Black Market racket in two ways at Mama Righetti's Bakery (6), which happens to be Artie Higgins' main hideout complex. If you can eliminate Artie's best fence, Freddie, you cripple Artie's ability to sell what he steals. And if you can pilfer the truckload of Purdue's stolen goods, Artie's insurance scam collapses too.

KILL FREDDIE THE FENCE

Freddie the Fence is out in the lot, marked overhead with a crosshairs icon. Here's a violent but efficient way to take him out. Enter the area from the south and go through the storefront of Mama Righetti's Bakery. A guard is posted in the back hallway. But instead of a silent takedown, shoot him down. This triggers an alarm,  so take cover at the doorway leading from the bakery to that back hall. Now Artie's men start rushing to attack.

Keep your position at the doorway, and use Intel View and your Minimap to see them coming and be ready. Some descend from the stairs just around the corner to your left, and others come from outside through the doorway at the end of the back hall. All are easy targets! When the bodies stop piling up in the hall, head outside through that far door.

Locate Freddie just ahead in your Intel View, not far from the big semi loaded with crates. (Note: This is Grant's truck— see the next objective.) Watch for an approaching Sentry then attack Freddie and gun him down for a large amount of racket damage inflicted.

STEAL GRANT'S TRUCK

Now you're in position to steal the big truck too. However, the immediate area is full of killers, cash, and crates full of goods. If you're still far from the Damage limit, by all means go crazy on Artie's complex. Otherwise, hop in the truck and follow the trip route back to Grant Purdue's warehouse (7).

Carloads of hostile gunmen harass you along the route, but just focus on driving the big rig. Ram enemy cars, veer side to side to run pursuers off the road, and smash through the two-car roadblock they set up. When you see the green destination marker, turn into the alley and pull into the red circle to complete the objective.

Talk to Grant Purdue (Second Time)

PREREQUISITE:
Racket Damage Total to $0

Return to Purdue **(1)** to learn that Artie Higgins is at his headquarters in Mama Righetti's Bakery.

UNLOCKS:
Confront Artie Higgins

Confront Artie Higgins

PREREQUISITE: Talk to Grant Purdue (Second Time)

Return to Mama Righetti's **(6)** and enter through the bakery's front door, dive into cover at the counter, then quietly take down the guard behind the counter. Exit into the rear hall, turn left, and open the door. Raid the Weapon Locker if you want then sneak through the next doorway and climb the stairs to the second floor.

At the top, silently eliminate the lone gunman guarding the doorway. Move through the office to the next closed door, take cover beside it, and pull it open to see a roomful of stolen electronics and a guard staring out the window to the right. Shoot him if you have a silenced weapon; otherwise, sneak up for a silent takedown. Then take cover halfway across the room and whistle to lure guards on the other side.

Move to the doorway into the storage room and take out anybody who's left. Then sneak to the office door on the left to confront Artie Higgins and take control of the Black Market racket in Southdowns.

MAMA'S VARGAS

Don't miss the Vargas painting on the wall in Artie Higgins' office on the second floor of Mama Righetti's.

UNLOCKS STORY MISSION: "Jesuit in New Mexico"

SOUTHDOWNS:
JESUIT IN NEW MEXICO
MISSION: "RESCUE ALVAREZ"

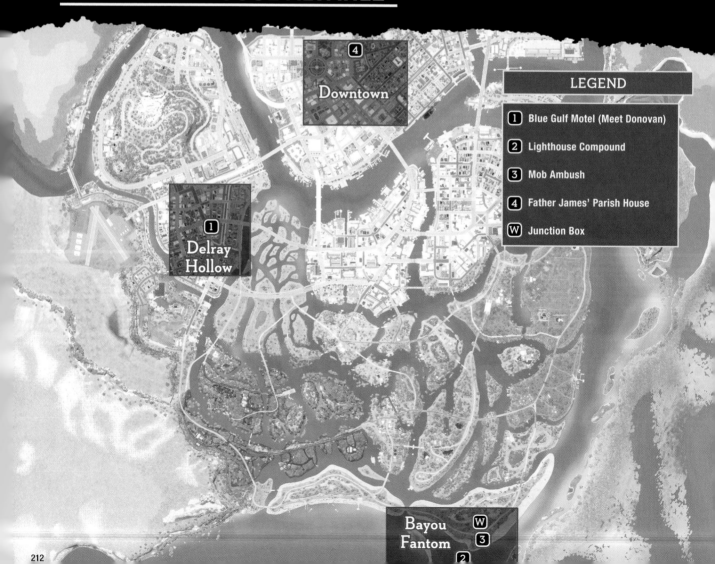

Downtown

Delray
Hollow

LEGEND

1	Blue Gulf Motel (Meet Donovan)
2	Lighthouse Compound
3	Mob Ambush
4	Father James' Parish House
W	Junction Box

Bayou
Fantom

Talk to Donovan About Alvarez

PREREQUISITE:

SECURE BOTH RACKETS IN SOUTHDOWNS

Travel to the tac-ops center in the Blue Gulf Motel **(1)** back in Delray Hollow to hear Donovan's latest intel on Sal's plan to use the Federal Reserve plates to print money. Marcano's Cuban counterfeiter, Alvarez, has gotten cold feet and wants to go back home. He's waiting down at the Bayou Fantom lighthouse for a boat. But Sal has gotten wind of this, and things won't turn out well for Alvarez unless Lincoln can intervene.

Go to the Lighthouse

Make sure you have a fast, nimble car for this mission. Follow the long trip route from Southdowns into the Bayou Fantom. Before you approach the lighthouse, wiretap the sector Junction Box (circled in our shot) on the wall of the Best Oil garage next door to the Trago Full Service gas station. (We marked the box location on our map too.) It helps to have enhanced Intel View because this is a night mission.

Continue down the road and across the bridge to the lighthouse compound **(2)**. As you approach, the game automatically cycles the time to nightfall.

Save Alvarez

Cross the bridge and move past the first buildings to the pickup truck in the lane. Take cover behind the truck and do an Intel View scan to see the first pair of guards highlighted red up ahead, both with their backs to you. Both are easy takedowns.

Push forward through the huts and use Intel View to spot two more guards up on the raised walkway leading to the lighthouse. When they split up, take down the guard who paces toward you, then hustle down the walkway to the barrel for cover. The other guard climbs stairs to the porch of the hut at the base of the lighthouse.

Two more of Marcano's men are on that porch trying to break down the door, calling for Alvarez to come out. These are the last enemies of this segment, so the odds are good if you want to just open fire and pick them off.

Approach the hut door and kick it open to trigger a cutscene: Lincoln convinces Alvarez he's come to help, and in return the Cuban spills the beans on Marcano's counterfeiting operation, located in "a boxing ring that Tommy Marcano owns." As they leave the hut, several truckloads of Marcano's men arrive down in the lane.

Escape with Alvarez

It's dark, so use Intel View to help find targets. The porch railing provides good cover and high ground for the early part of this gun battle, so let the first wave of goons come to you and pick them off. Then start pushing across the bridge walkway, diving forward from cover to cover.

Once you get across the bridge, you can work your way up the left side of the compound to a hut with a ladder on the porch. Climb the ladder to reach a balcony overlook with good cover, providing excellent firing angles at the thugs below. When the area is clear, you can hop in any vehicle to escape; Alvarez will join Lincoln in the passenger   seat. Unfortunately, the mob arrived in clunky pickup trucks, so if you drove a good car and parked it here, use it now. Drive across the bridge to exit the lighthouse compound.

Two things happen after you drive across the exit bridge:

First, when you reach the light pole on the far side, a timer appears onscreen next to your Minimap. It starts counting down from 8:00 minutes. You must reach Father James' parish house in the French Ward within that amount of time or else you fail the objective and jump back to the checkpoint at the bridge to try again.

Second, as you approach the intersection (3) at the Trago gas station, three more carloads of Marcano's men converge on you. Two pull up in front to cut off your escape, and another pulls up behind you.

Even though the timer is running, a good tactic here is to hop out of your vehicle and toss grenades, then open fire with a rifle at the cars. Or (if you're stuck driving one of the lumbering pickup trucks) you can sling grenades at two cars, let the shooters climb out of the third car, gun them down…and then borrow their car, since they don't need it anymore. Remember to wait until Alvarez joins Lincoln inside the car before accelerating away.

Get Alvarez to Father James

TIME LIMIT: 8:00 MINUTES

Now it's a controlled race against time. Again, the timer started the moment you crossed the bridge from the lighthouse compound. Follow the trip route, accelerating hard on the open stretches of road. If you make every turn as directed and avoid accidents, you should make it with time to spare.

Your arrival on Father James' doorstep (4) triggers a cinematic: Lincoln appreciates the Father's generosity, but the wedge driven between them has clearly grown wider.

UNLOCKS STORY MISSION:

KILL TOMMY MARCANO

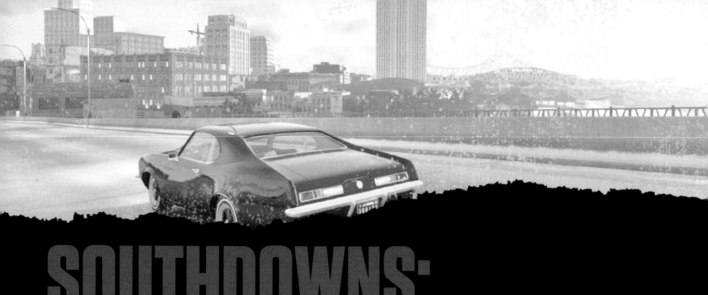

SOUTHDOWNS:
BURN LIKE NAPALM
MISSION: "KILL TOMMY MARCANO"

LEGEND

1 Drive-In Restaurant (Meet Donovan)

2 Briar Patch Restaurant

3 The Acadia

W Junction Box (The Acadia's Sector)

French Ward

Southdowns

See Donovan for More on Tommy Marcano

PREREQUISITE: COMPLETE "RESCUE ALVAREZ"

Find Donovan's blue van in the parking lot **(1)** of the Drive-In restaurant and approach the passenger side window.

This triggers a series of cutscenes: The Marcano brothers bemoan the loss of Alvarez, but still don't take Lincoln Clay as seriously as they should. In the Senate hearing, Donovan explains how Lincoln planned to use a former associate of Sammy Robinson to get into Tommy Marcano's boxing club, The Acadia.

Talk to Alcee Bennett

Follow the trip route to the Briar Patch restaurant **(2)** on the western edge of the French Ward district. Enter and approach Alcee Bennett, the man wearing the white hat in the booth on the right. He agrees to go for a ride with Lincoln.

WIRETAP THE ACADIA

If you haven't already done so, be sure to wiretap the Junction Box for the sector where The Acadia is located before you go inside the club.

Go to the Acadia

Walk outside the restaurant, get in your car, and wait for Alcee to join Lincoln. Then follow the trip route to The Acadia **(3)** in Southdowns. Listen to the dialogue en route—you get some backstory on Alcee and his days in Delray Hollow, and he explains how things work at The Acadia.

Enter the Acadia

Pull around to the side across the street from the stadium. Exit the car and go down the stairs into The Acadia's side entrance.

STORY MISSIONS

Submit to Pat-Down

Approach the guard on the right and press the button prompted to trigger a pat-down.

Go to the Locker Room

Follow Alcee through the double doors and turn right. Proceed to the doorway at the end of the corridor and veer rightward into the Locker Room.

Change Your Clothes

Go to the marked locker and press the button indicated to change clothes for the fight and trigger a short conversation with Alcee.

Enter the Ring

Follow Alcee through the stage door. When the two guards move aside, go through the next doors into the ring area. You can choose to "Work" or "Insult" the crowd, then walk into the ring.

Defeat Nick "Boom-Boom" Beaumont, Bobby Ledoux, and Gravedigger Vaughn

Now you engage in a series of three fights which are essentially the same, except the opponent gets tougher each time. Keep moving and use your melee controls to punch until Lincoln unleashes his punishing brutal head-butt. Avoid getting trapped in corners by the bigger opponents.

Return to the Locker Room

Follow Alcee out of the ring then go through the open doors and head straight into the locker room. This triggers a cutscene: Tommy Marcano and a few friends are waiting for Lincoln.

Fray the Rope

Use the controls displayed onscreen to move Lincoln's arms up and down. Do it quickly and relentlessly to fray the rope against the metal rack. Watch the screen carefully and quickly press the button shown when prompted to break free and grab `the gun from Tommy's boy.

Kill Tommy Marcano

Take cover beside the doorway and target the shooters in the next room, including Tommy. Shoot Tommy until he falls on one knee, incapacitated.

Confront Tommy Marcano

Pick up the dropped Riot 550 shotgun then approach the fallen Tommy Marcano. Hold the button indicated to trigger a  cutscene: Lincoln grabs the money plates then applies the same grand solution to both Tommy and the printing press.

Reach the Street

Fight down the hallway and around the corner to take cover at the doorway that leads into the grandstand. Use Intel View to spot the gunmen ahead as the fire and smoke start to spread through The Acadia. Pick off a few foes then climb left up the stairs to the top of the grandstand where it's more protected. Move along the railing and use the trash cans for cover as you work across to the corridor on the opposite side of the room.

Now fight down the hallway as more of Tommy's men swarm toward you. Be patient—the fire won't engulf you. Just keep pushing steadily ahead from cover to cover spot. Use Intel View to find Medicine Cabinets too; there's one on the wall at the end of the first row of seats in the stands. Take cover at the front railing and pick off shooters over in the next grandstand. You need to pass through that area next, so clear it out now.

Use the Medicine Cabinet in the lobby for health, and use the pillars for cover. One last squad of goons waits beyond the top of the exit staircase. Cover is scarce out there, so pick them off from the lobby then dive behind the wooden baluster at the bottom of the stairs. Watch out when you reach the glass trophy case—gunmen can shoot you through the glass! Push all the way to the final exit doors leading out to the street, where a final few hostiles are waiting for you.

Escape the Area

Just as you grab your first breath of fresh air outside, cop cars start arriving. A yellow circle appears on your in-game map; once you get outside of it, you're clear, as long as you've avoided any police pursuit. Sprint around the corner to the left to where you parked on the side of The Acadia. Grab a car and start evasive maneuvers to escape the Blue Police Zone.

FOLLOW THE MARKER

In the smoke and confusion of The Acadia blaze, look for the diamond-shaped objective marker to guide you from checkpoint to checkpoint through the holocaust.

Continue around the corner and proceed through the next grandstand to the exit. An explosion rocks Lincoln, but keep moving down the staircase. At the bottom, kick open the door to the floor level around the ring. After the left side of the arena suddenly collapses (burying a quartet of hostile gunmen), fight your way around the right side using the two bars for cover. Continue on to the lobby.

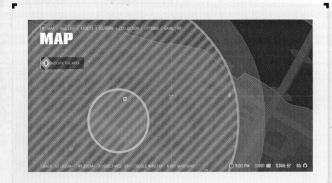

IN COMES SANTANGELO IF...

In Mafia III, you must take down all three of Sal Marcano's capos—his brothers Tommy and Lou, and his sister-in-law Olivia Marcano—after taking control of their respective districts: Southdowns, French Ward, and Frisco Fields. You can do this in any order.

Whatever order you choose, Killing the first Marcano capo triggers a cutscene where Sal calls for help from the Mafia's "Commission" led by Leo Galante. This phone call has no in-game consequences.

Killing the second Marcano capo, however, motivates Sal to bring in outside help. You see a cutscene where Sal makes a deal with Nino Santangelo, the heroin dealer and assassin. This cutscene triggers a new game chapter, "In Comes the Devil," and its lone mission, "My Name Is Lincoln Clay...".

In our walkthrough, we tackle Frisco Fields and Olivia Marcano first. In this order, bringing down Olivia prompts Sal's phone call to The Commission. We go after Southdowns and Tommy Marcano second, so we list the Santangelo cutscene and mission here. Again, if you were to take down Southdowns and Tommy first instead of second, Sal's phone call to The Commission would appear here, right after Tommy's death and Lincoln's escape from The Acadia.

Sal Calls in Santangelo

When you kill Tommy Marcano and escape the area, you trigger a cutscene: Donovan discusses the Treasury's money plates with the Senate Commission. If Tommy is the second capo you've killed (as in this walkthrough), then Lincoln's escape after Tommy's death also triggers another cutscene: Sal Marcano calls in Nino Santangelo, the heroin dealer, to help finance his attempts to make gambling legal for his casino project. He also wants Santangelo to eliminate Lincoln Clay.

Assign the Southdowns District to an Underboss

The scene shifts to the bayou mansion where Lincoln has another sitdown with his lieutenants. Award control of the Southdowns district to one of them.

NEW BORDEAUX:
IN COMES THE DEVIL
MISSION: "MY NAME'S LINCOLN CLAY..."

PREREQUISITE: KILL THE SECOND MARCANO CAPO

Draw Out Santangelo

Once this mission is triggered, the relentless assassin Nino Santangelo begins to hunt Lincoln across the city. It doesn't take much to "draw out Santangelo"—just go about your business, and he will soon arrive with carloads of vicious killers. His arrival is marked by the red "Retaliation" banner that appears across the top of the screen.

Kill Santangelo

This next objective doesn't exactly describe your task. Here you actually "incapacitate" Santangelo. When he and his crew arrive to attack Lincoln, the objective marker tracks Santangelo's location. If you get him in your gun sights, shoot until he drops to one knee. He can't move after that, so you can concentrate on the next objective.

Kill Santangelo's Men

This objective appears if any of Santangelo's men are still alive after you incapacitate their boss. Hunt them down and kill them, and then return to the fallen Santangelo.

Confront Santangelo

Here you simply approach the incapacitated Santangelo and hold the button prompted to trigger a cutscene: Lincoln utters the phrase that gives title to this mission.

FRENCH WARD:
EVIL THAT MEN DO

RACKET: DRUGS

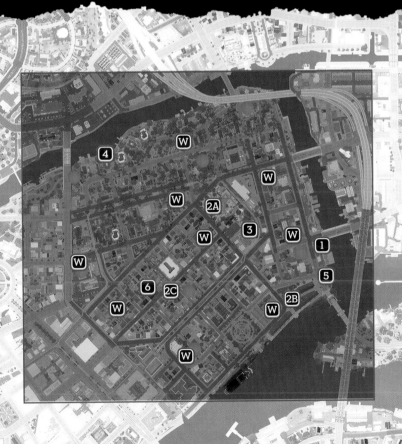

LEGEND

1. Big Jim McCormick
2. Informant
3. Enforcer (Lester Terriot)
4. Mansion Drug Delivery
5. Boathouse Drug Delivery
6. Cistern (Under Big Mouth Jazz Club)
W. Junction Box
● Street dealer

Talk to Big Jim McCormick (First Time)

PREREQUISITE: SECURE DOWNTOWN DISTRICT

Find Detective Jim McCormick in a small waterfront warehouse **(1)**, down the ramp from the street. Big Jim is tired of scum like Doc Gaston who push drugs across the French Ward; Gaston is the biggest pusher in New Bordeaux, but nobody knows where he or his operation is based. He's got a big supplier coming in town for a meeting, and Big Jim wants Lincoln to sniff it out.

> **WIRETAP THE ENTIRE DISTRICT**
>
> This should go without saying by now, but we'll say it again just in case. All Junction Boxes in the French Ward appear on your map after you talk to your first district contact. Go wiretap every box! Wiretapped sectors reveal a lot of useful information.

Interrogate Pushers

PREREQUISITE: TALK TO BIG JIM MCCORMICK

UNLOCKS:

TAIL BAGMEN TO FIND GASTON'S CASH

Three Informants appear on the map **(2a, 2b, 2c)**. You only need to talk to one; once you interrogate one, the other two disappear from the map. If the Informant you choose escapes and you don't catch him, he ends up at one of the other Informant locations.

EUGENIO CALABRESE

Travel to the cemetery's southwest entry **(2a)** and take cover at the gate. You can spot Calabrese's big crew just inside, using Intel View. You can push forward to the stone bench without getting spotted, then whistle to lure both Sentries and the others to silent takedowns. Calabrese himself is posted around the corner to the right, beyond a row of mausoleums. Move toward him along the mausoleum on the right but stay in cover, luring more of his guys to their doom. Interrogate Calabrese to learn about the stash site used by Gaston's bagmen.

> **CEMETERY PICK UP**
>
> Look for a copy of *Repent* magazine sitting on top of one of the low stone walls surrounding the big central crypt and statue.

FRANK NERO

Frank and three burly goons work the lot **(2b)** by the newspaper boxes in southeast French Ward. Your best bet is to set up on the busy street with a scoped rifle and target Frank, firing until he's incapacitated and can't run. Then pick off his companions and approach. Interrogate Frank to learn about Gaston's network of mobile bagmen delivering their take to a central stash site.

KURT DANO

Kurt Dano hangs out at the Les Trois Pattes Bar **(2c)** in south-central French Ward. He has only one companion, but if you nail that guy first, Dano will make a run for it. Don't let him escape! Interrogate him for knowledge of Gaston's bagmen and stash.

Kill Gaston's Enforcer

PREREQUISITE: TALK TO BIG JIM MCCORMICK

LESTER TERRIOT

Lester runs a makeshift drug den out of a pair of garages **(3)** between a collapsing brick building and the railroad tracks. He has a lot of product—six separate stashes—with most of it stored in a small brick hut (circled in our shot). He also has a big support crew that includes a Sentry.

Start on the street to the northeast and take an Intel View of the situation. Use your Pry Bar to unlock the garage's back door; the Sentry is just inside, so quickly take cover outside before he spots you. Now you can start luring victims through the doorway for silent takedowns.

Alternatively, you can head around the collapsing building and down the alley behind it toward the den, working your way through the lot using dumpsters, barrels, and parked cars for cover. Lester is by himself in the garage next to the den, so if you clear the lot of all his men, you isolate him for an easier takedown.

Dropping Lester inflicts lots of racket damage, but don't stop there! Each drug stash you destroy is worth even more. Open the brick hut's door and target the red explosive tanks to detonate all five of the drug shipments stored inside for tons more damage. You can find a *lot*

of cash laying around too. So this site really helps you send a message to Doc Gaston.

Kill Gaston's Street Dealers (7 Pairs)

PREREQUISITE: TALK TO BIG JIM MCCORMICK

Doc Gaston has a platoon of dope dealers out working the back alleys and dark corners of the French Ward district. Dealer icons don't appear on your map until you wiretap their sector, but we've marked all seven spots on our district map. Two dealers (each marked with the "Kill" icon overhead) work each site, with one or two other armed associates lurking nearby, so approach carefully.

Before you make a plan of attack, conduct an Intel View scan of each area to identify dealers and their crew. You clear the site from the map once you kill one dealer, but might as well get them both since their demise is worth racket damage. Afterwards, scoop up their $500 bag of cash as well.

WIRETAP TO FIND DEALERS

Each dealer location is marked on the map, but only if the location's sector Junction Box has been wiretapped.

Destroy the Drug Resupply Boats

PREREQUISITE:
TALK TO BIG JIM MCCORMICK

RAID MANSION DRUG DELIVERY

Travel to the green waterfront mansion **(4)** up in northwest French Ward. Your target is the drug resupply boat (circled in our overhead shot) that's upside-down on the dock behind the mansion. Out front, start by taking cover behind the middle section of brick wall. Then whistle over the two guards, one from the front porch and another from the driveway or side porch.

Sneak around to the back patio and take cover behind a planter box. Use Intel View to see many guards down in the dock area, including a Sentry. You can try engaging a firefight, or toss a Screaming Zemi toward the dock to gather curious guards around it and then follow up with a Molotov cocktail. But we suggest maintaining your stealth and working for silent takedowns. When the odds are more manageable,

you can open fire on the remaining gunmen. Then go toss a grenade at the boat on the dock.

RAID BOATHOUSE DRUG DELIVERY

Travel to the boathouse with the red-checked roof **(5)** down in the southeast corner of the district. Use the Pry Bar to unlock the front door then duck inside and take cover behind the stack of barrels and crates. Whistle to lure over any guards who will come for silent takedowns.

Now move closer to the threesome of goons who sit together at the cash-covered table across the room. Lure them over one at a time too, or just toss a Molotov on top of them. Grab the cash (lots of it!) then nail the last guards down on the dock. Finally, toss a grenade into the drug resupply boat at the dock. (Or you can shoot the gas can next to the boat to ignite the vessel, as well.)

Tail Bagmen to Find Gaston's Cash

PREREQUISITE: Interrogate Pushers

As you learned from the Informant, Doc Gaston has a crew of bagmen who deliver the dealers' cash to Doc's stash site. Each bagman drives a red De'Leo Stiletto marked with an overhead "Follow" icon. When you see one, follow it to the meeting site and fight your way in to find a fat stack of Gaston's cash.

FINDING BAGMEN

Patrol the streets around French Ward in your car until you spot the red De'Leo Stiletto marked "Follow." Don't follow too close or drive erratically! If you call attention to yourself, the bagman flees.

Talk to Big Jim McCormick (Second Time)

PREREQUISITE: RACKET DAMAGE TOTAL TO $0

Return to Big Jim **(1)** and chat with him to learn that Doc Gaston is holed up in the Cistern (an underground club) beneath the Big Mouth Jazz Club.

Confront Doc Gaston

PREREQUISITE: TALK TO BIG JIM MCCORMICK (SECOND TIME)

Travel to the front of the Big Mouth Jazz Club **(6)** and take an Intel View to see targets below you, underground. To get down into the Cistern, go in through the jazz club's front door and head directly back to the kitchen. Get ready to do a lot of whistling for silent takedowns. Cross the kitchen, take cover at the cutting table by the other door, and lure the two thugs guarding the top of the stairs.

Important: guards are everywhere, so keep checking your Intel View as you progress. Go downstairs to take cover outside the next doorway and lure the next guard over. At the top of the next staircase, take cover against the right railing and sneak down to the bottom. There, lure over yet another guard for a takedown. Raid the Weapon Locker then move through the hole in the wall past the grinning kid.

Head down the sloped passage to take cover outside the next chamber full of party folk. A Sentry and another gunman are posted here, so lure them over too. (This may spark a panic amongst the clientele, but ignore it for now.) Proceed through the chamber and take cover again, at the top of the next stairs. More guards, more whistling, more takedowns.

Continue downward, following the carpets until you reach the main cistern chamber, a large circular, high-ceilinged area full of chairs and couches with a bar at the far end. Intel View shows you two gunmen (one a Sentry) sitting and drinking at the bar with their backs to you, plus two more standing, one off to each side of the chamber. Your goal is to get through the open iron gate (circled in our screenshot) just to the left of the bar. Choose your method: stealth, shooting, explosives, or any combination that suits you.

This view from the balcony shows the two guards drinking at the bar, the other guards, and the iron gate (circled) where you're headed.

Once you get through the gate left of the bar, veer leftward through the next opening and climb the short staircase. Then veer left again through another iron gate and turn left up the next stairs.

At the top, turn left and climb one last staircase. Take a quick Intel View here: you can see Doc Gaston (marked by the star icon) in an office to your right, but he has a bodyguard nearby. You should be able to target Doc through the curtain-draped doorway to incapacitate him. Then wait for his guard to return fire through the draped doorway and nail him too.

DOC'S VARGAS

Before you deal with the fallen Gaston, grab the Vargas painting hanging on the wall in his office. A $3500 stack of cash sits on the table in a side room off the office, too.

Finally, go seize Doc Gaston and kill or recruit him to take control of his Drugs racket. Assign the racket to an Underboss.

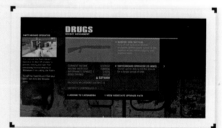

RACKET: SEX

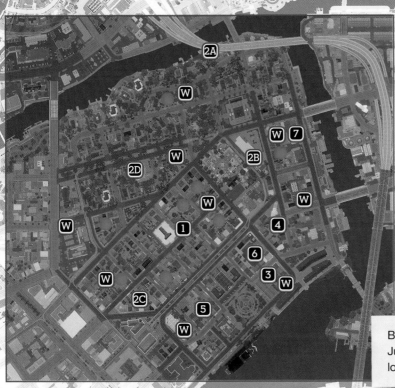

LEGEND

1. Harold Cauley
2. Informants
3. Enforcer (Irving Pichot)
4. Enforcer (Ernie Lupo)
5. Enforcer (Oscar Sabato)
6. Plow House (Kinky VIPs)
7. Un Bel Jardin (Rob Orgy)
W. Junction Box
○ Stag Flicks

By now you should have all of the French Ward Junction Boxes wiretapped—but we put their locations on this map, just in case.

Talk to Harold Cauley (First Time)

PREREQUISITE: SECURE DOWNTOWN DISTRICT

Activate this objective and follow the trip route to Les Dames Rouges club **(1)** where you find Harold Cauley, the muckraking reporter for *The Tattler*, at the bar. He points Lincoln toward "Handsome" Harry Robicheaux, the man who runs the sex rackets in the French Ward for Lou Marcano. His infamous sex hotel, Un Bel Jardin (better known as the Plow House), is rumored to be a hotbed of scandal for the city's powerbrokers.

Interrogate Pimps

PREREQUISITE: TALK TO HAROLD CAULEY

INTERROGATIONS UNLOCK: "KILL THE KINKY VIPs" AND "ROB THE ORGY"

After you talk to Cauley, Informant icons appear on the map in three of these four locations **(2a, 2b, 2c, 2d)**. You'll need to talk to two of them in order to unlock two new objectives. Your interrogations will reveal two useful bits of information: Handsome Harry has some kinky VIP customers coming to Un Bel Jardin for rough sessions of fetishistic fantasy. And second, a big sex orgy is raging in a secret site, so money is probably stacked all over the place.

ONLY TWO INFORMANTS NEEDED

Once you interrogate two of the three available Informants, the third Informant icon disappears from the map. If one of the Informants you visit escapes and you don't catch him, he ends up at one of the other Informant locations.

BILLY ZACCARO

Billy oversees the set for a pornographic movie shoot in a small warehouse **(2a)** underneath the freeway bridge to Pointe Verdun in northeast French Ward. Take out the guards and interrogate Billy to learn what he knows.

Find three destructible crates in the garage (circled) next door to the film shoot.

MARCO VINCI

Marco Vinci and two of his boys lurk in an alley **(2b)** next to the Yvonne St. Augstin Boutique. If you approach the alley by moving across the front of the boutique, Marco stands with his back to you. Sneak up to the goon at the corner for a fast takedown then quickly incapacitate Marco and dispose of his other buddy. Now you can interrogate Marco and learn what he knows.

Afterwards, destroy Billy's five crates of filmmaking equipment. Two crates are in the film studio garage, but three more sit in the garage next door (behind a garage door marked "Caution"). Don't miss them!

PIETRO IOVINE

Pietro Iovine runs his business from the middle of a hotel courtyard (2c) down in southwest French Ward. Approach from the south, moving up the alley past the working girls. Take cover outside the open doorway into the courtyard and use Intel View to pinpoint the locations of Pietro and his thugs.

Toss a grenade or Molotov at Pietro to incapacitate him, gun down the two goons to the right, then set up at the bottom of the staircase to nail the last gunman who rushes downstairs from the upper balcony. Then interrogate Pietro to find out what he knows.

FREDDIE "THE BULL" TORO

Freddie the Bull pimps his girls by an alley dumpster (2d) next to a Bellaire's Supermarket in northern French Ward's garden district. Shoot Freddie from the street to incapacitate him then take out his two armed companions. Interrogate Freddie for his information.

Kill "Handsome" Harry's Enforcers

PREREQUISITE: TALK TO HAROLD CAULEY

IRVING PICHOT

Find the entry doorway to the L-shaped courtyard (3) of the sleazy hotel where Irving Pichot bases his escort service for Handsome Harry. Irving is upstairs in a room with one of his girls.

Sneak into the courtyard all the way to the trash can enclosure against the left wall; you can see two guards up ahead (circled in our shot). Lure over the first guard for a takedown. Then creep up the stairs just ahead and take down the gunman facing away from you.

Work your way across the courtyard until you can climb the stairs to the second floor; Irving is in the very first room. After you drop him, grab that money bag on the floor.

ERNIE LUPO

Ernie Lupo and his sick crew use the Best Oil warehouse (4) as a base of operations. A quick Intel View reveals four heavies (including one Sentry) plus five boxes of destructible porno materials inside—three downstairs and two upstairs. Find the stairs in back that lead down to a lower-level door and use your Pry Bar to open it. Inside, you find the three stacks of porno materials.

One option: take cover behind the three barrels, facing the interior doorway. Destroy all three porno stacks for racket damage. You get detected and Ernie's men, with guns drawn, rush downstairs to investigate. But the doorway is a bottleneck for them, so from cover behind the barrels, pick off goons as they try to come through, including Ernie himself.

The drawback is that if you don't tag the Sentry, he will make a run for the upstairs phone to call in Reinforcements. So another option is to stay stealthy and hold off on shooting the destructible boxes; instead, take cover at the doorway and start whistling to lure down goons one at a time, including the Sentry and Ernie. When you finally clear the building, head upstairs and destroy the other two boxes of materials.

OSCAR SABATO

Oscar Sabato and his lowlife buddies run a brothel out of a fountain courtyard (5) between apartment buildings over in southeast French Ward. Approach up the alley past a blue pickup truck and take cover at the narrow doorway leading into the courtyard. Whistle over the nearest thug for a takedown then survey with Intel View. Oscar is seated upstairs, with four more gunmen spread across the yard.

Push forward to the white crosshatch planter; from here, you can lure over two more of the gang. Sneak leftward to the fountain to get the last two. (Be sure to nail the Sentry before he's alerted—he's posted by a phone box, so he can make a quick call for Reinforcements.) Now you can climb the white staircase and end Oscar's miserable existence.

Kill Limo Patrons

PREREQUISITE: TALK TO HAROLD CAULEY

As you learned from Harold Cauley, Handsome Harry ferries his upscale customers to Un Bel Jardin in limousines. These limos randomly pass you on the street; the VIP passenger in the back seat is marked with an overhead "Kill" icon that appears over the limo. When you see one, get on its tail and open fire, targeting tires to disable the vehicle. When it stops, hop out and toss a grenade under the grille. Gun down the VIP passenger if he emerges alive.

Find and Destroy Stag Flicks (8)

PREREQUISITE: TALK TO HAROLD CAULEY

Handsome Harry has quite a film business, with filmmakers working nonstop to produce stag flicks featuring "Bare Nudity!" (as the posters proclaim). Boxes full of finished film reels and posters are stored in eight places around the French Ward. We marked the locations on our district map, but note that their icons won't appear on your in-game map until you've wiretapped their sector.

Some locations seem to be unlikely porn stashes—garages of mansions, etc. Before you raid each site, conduct an Intel View scan of the area to identify enemy numbers and locations. You clear the site from the in-game map once you destroy the box of stag flicks. Afterwards, be sure to grab any stacks of cash laying around as well.

WIRETAP TO FIND DEALERS

Each dealer location is marked on the map, but only if the location's sector Junction Box has been wiretapped.

Kill the Kinky VIPs

PREREQUISITE: INTERROGATE PIMPS (FIRST TIME)

Travel to Un Bel Jardin (AKA the Plow House) **(6)**, a hotel transformed into a sex playground for VIPs with unusual tastes. Enter via the doorway (circled in our shot) next to the black iron gate that leads to the garage area.

Inside, follow the left turn and use the service entrance. Mob gunmen are everywhere, so use Intel View and check your Minimap regularly as you proceed. Climb the stairs to the second level, go through the hole in the wall, and follow the hall to the hotel bar on the second floor.

HOTEL ART BONANZA

You can find a Vargas painting sitting between the liquor shelves behind the hotel's second-floor bar. Another Vargas hangs in the game room where the pool and poker tables are located.

As you search the hotel for VIPs, don't miss a number of money pickups and collectible items, including the $3500 cash sitting on the credenza (circled in our shot) next to the pool table in the game room. You can also find a pair of Vargas paintings (see our Tip).

Your goal: hunt down and kill three "kinky VIPs," high-rollers who pay top dollar to indulge their sexual fetishes. Nailing these rich perverts puts a big hit on Handsome Harry's racket take. Two of the three "Kinky VIPs"—Brother Superior and Neighbor Phil—are in rooms on the second floor, both not far from the hotel bar. Go room to room to find them and gun them down. (Note that if you've triggered an alert, the VIPs may get proactive and come hunting for you, so be wary.)

The third VIP—Captain Pennies, the sickest puppy of them all—is downstairs prepping for work in a room off the wine cellar. Terminate his fantasy quickly.

Brother Superior

Neighbor Phil

Captain Pennies

234

Rob the Orgy

PREREQUISITE: Interrogate Pimps (Second Time)

Head to the unmarked warehouse (7) over on the eastern edge of French Ward that's been converted into a sex club. Something big is clearly going on—black limos, traffic cones, armed guards. Approach from the back and climb the exterior stairs to the second floor entrance. This leads into an office area with a pair of guards.

Snuff them both silently then move out onto the balcony overlooking the wild festivities below. Use Intel View to spot the two gunmen down on the floor, one on either side. Turn right, sneak down the stairs, and then quietly terminate the Sentry. Now you can grab the big $20,000 stack of cash (circled) sitting on the cabinet next to the refrigerator cases. Retrace your way out—or crash the party, if you want.

Talk to Harold Cauley (Second Time)

PREREQUISITE: Racket Damage Total to $0

Return to Harold in Les Dames Rouges (1) to learn that Handsome Harry has arrived at Un Bel Jardin to assess the situation.

Confront "Handsome" Harry Robicheaux

PREREQUISITE: Talk to Harold Cauley (Second Time)

Travel back to Un Bel Jardin (6) and take the same route in that you used for "Kill the Kinky VIPs." Harry is holed up in the game room upstairs, the room with the pool and poker tables. Hunt him down and kill or recruit him to take control of the Sex racket in the French Ward. Assign the racket to an Underboss.

UNLOCKS STORY MISSION: "Kill the Judge"

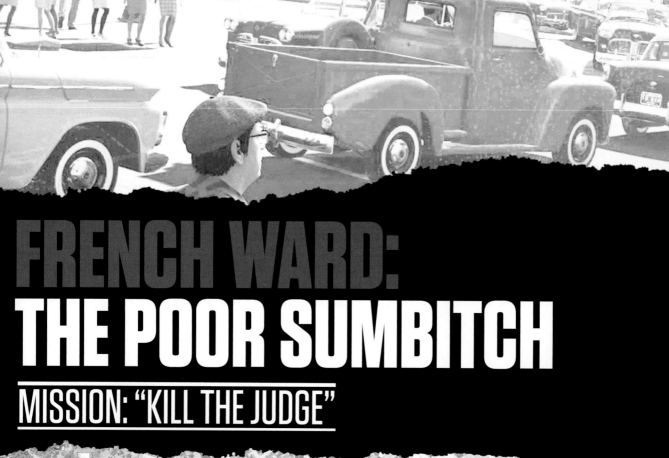

FRENCH WARD:
THE POOR SUMBITCH

MISSION: "KILL THE JUDGE"

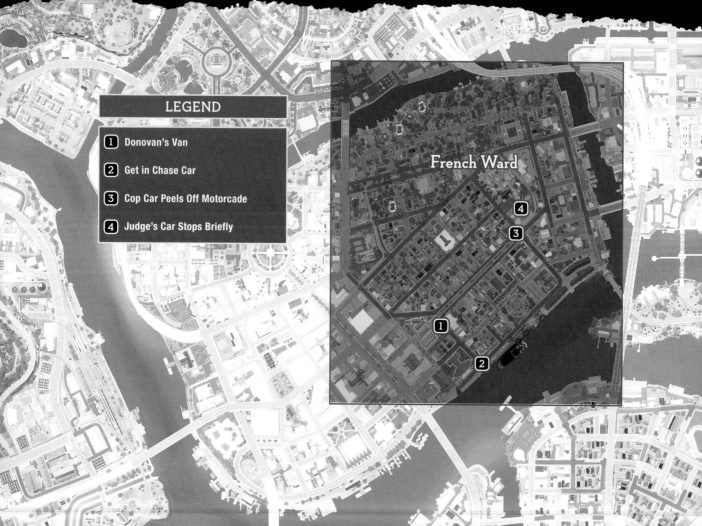

LEGEND

1. Donovan's Van
2. Get in Chase Car
3. Cop Car Peels Off Motorcade
4. Judge's Car Stops Briefly

French Ward

See Donovan for the Latest on the Judge

PREREQUISITE: SECURE BOTH FRENCH WARD RACKETS ("DRUGS" AND "SEX")

Before you start this mission, make sure you've got a full supply of grenades in your weapon inventory. Then find Donovan's blue Marquis' Fine Liquors van **(1)** parked in front of the movie theater and get in the passenger side door. Donovan has news: a wiretapped conversation revealed the identity of the Circuit Court judge who's playing ball with Uncle Lou Marcano. Turns out Judge Cornelius Holden is presiding over a controversial federal case and leaving the courthouse with a police escort. Taking him out won't be easy. Donovan points out the armored vehicle.

Kill Judge Holden

Donovan drops off Lincoln in front of the Everyday Laundromat **(2)** near the courthouse. Hop in the red De'Leo Traviata parked in the lot. Watch as the judge's car leaves the courthouse with police cruisers in front and back.

Follow the motorcade. You can attack anytime you want, but the judge's car is well-armored and the cops are well-armed. If you want to strike early, accelerate in front of the judge's car then veer across its path to cut it off. Hop out and quickly toss as many grenades as you can at the target. If you can detonate the car while the judge is still inside, you kill him and complete the objective.

But another option is to patiently follow the motorcade and wait for a better opportunity. Stay right on its tail; at an intersection a few blocks away **(3)**, the trailing cop car peels off the motorcade. Swerve around the cop and speed to get behind the judge's car as it takes a right-hand turn through a covered passage into an alley.

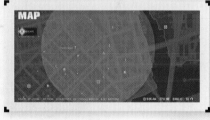

Stay close until the judge's car makes a wide right turn

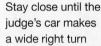

in the alley and halts briefly **(4)**. Hurry! It stops for only a few seconds, so hop out of your car and immediately sling multiple grenades at the target. If you toss in time and detonate the car, Judge Holden meets his just end.

Escape

A big yellow circle appears on your map, marking the zone you must escape. Hop back into your hot red Traviata, back up into the street, and drive like a madman until you're outside the yellow map circle.

UNLOCKS STORY MISSION:
KILL "UNCLE" LOU MARCANO

FRENCH WARD:
REAL NICE TIME

MISSION: "KILL "UNCLE" LOU MARCANO"

LEGEND

1. Meet Donovan
2. Coal Dumper
3. Fall Off *Delphine* Here
W. Junction Box

Talk to Donovan About Uncle Lou

PREREQUISITE: COMPLETE "KILL THE JUDGE"

Activate this objective and follow the trip route to Donovan's van **(1)** parked just off the road down in the Bayou Fantom. Enter via the driver's side door.

This triggers a series of cutscenes: The Senate hearing mulls over the aftermath of the Judge Holden murder, and the Marcano brothers discuss their next move. Looks like your next destination is a riverboat.

Reach the Coal Dumper

Now you take control of Donovan's van. Listen to the conversation as you follow the new trip route. Donovan explains that Uncle Lou always sails the same course with his riverboat, the *Delphine*. Lou's boat will pass an old coal dumper where Donovan has planted explosives; Lincoln needs to connect a detonator to each C-4 block. When you arrive at the coal

dumper site **(2)**, exit the van and climb the ladder up the railcar to get past the gate.

Connect the Primer Cords

Before you wire the explosives, wiretap the Junction Box (circled in our long shot) on the platform for enhanced intel. Then use Intel View to help find each of the four C-4 blocks where you must connect the primer cords.

Wiretap the Junction Box on the coal dumper before you detonate the explosives.

You can also see three hostile bayou rednecks posted at the far end of the dumper platform—two guys fishing, and another working the barbecue grill. If you want to work uninterrupted, you can take them out.

Two C-4 blocks are planted down low on the platform floor—one on a support strut, the other on a big gear housing.

The other two C-4 blocks are located up the ramp on the upper platform.

Detonate the C-4

When all four blocks are wired, follow the objective marker (or follow the wiring) to the control hut. Pry open the locked door, go through the hut to the back porch, and flip the detonator switch.

Sit back and enjoy the show as the *Delphine* takes a broadside hit from the coal dumper's falling superstructure. Uncle Lou tries to direct State Senator Jacobs upstairs to safety. Then he deploys his men throughout the boat, suspecting more than an accident.

Get to Uncle Lou

Uncle Lou and Jacobs are on the *Delphine*'s top level, so you need to work your way up. Run to the end of the dock, dive into the bayou, and swim to the ladder (circled in our shot) in the middle of the boat.

FOLLOW THE MARKER

Progress through the *Delphine* includes a number of waypoints set along the route through the riverboat. So when in doubt, follow your onscreen objective marker!

Get to the Second Deck

Climb aboard the *Delphine* and step through the doorway on your right. The engine room is directly ahead, but it's a dead end. Instead, turn hard left and go straight through two open doors across to the opposite side of the boat. Turn left through the next door and follow the long passage along the gunwale until you see passengers fleeing out an open door ahead and jumping into the bayou. That leads into the riverboat's big casino room.

Before you enter the casino, take a quick Intel View to see that a large squad of Lou's men are posted inside. Fight your way through the gaming tables to the wide staircase on the far side and climb up to the next deck. Immediately dive for cover behind the bar at the top, because more gunmen deploy up ahead.

Get to the Third Deck

Fight through the lounge area out onto the stern (rear)—you can see the boat's big paddlewheels spinning. Now head around the corner to your left and fight your way up the long walkway. At the far end, climb the stairs to the third deck. When you get there, an explosion rips through the windows to your right!

Keep moving forward to the big bar out on the bow (forward) area where another large squad of Uncle Lou's goons wait for you. Clear them out, then enter the doorway that leads back inside into a library. Keep pushing through rooms (including one with a scale model of the riverboat) until you reach another staircase leading up. At the top, turn left and proceed through three more doorways until you find a staircase going back *down* a level.

Get through the Dining Room

Head down the stairs and follow the passage until you spot Uncle Lou and Senator Jacobs. Run to the doors and kick them open! Your targets flee

through the dining room ahead. As you open the next door and follow them, another large squad of mafia killers arrives. Clear out the gunmen, climb the ladder at the back of the dining room, and approach the door hatch.

Open the hatch to trigger a scene: Lincoln finally has Uncle Lou and the Senator at gunpoint. Lou tries to take Jacobs hostage, but Lincoln doesn't care about the politician. Suddenly, an engine room explosion engulfs everyone!

Follow Lou. Lincoln is injured so you can't move fast, but Lou is worse off and his shots are wild and inaccurate. Just keep following Uncle Lou relentlessly until you catch him. This triggers a series of chapter-ending cutscenes: Lincoln uses Uncle Lou to "send a message" to Sal Marcano.

IN COMES SANTANGELO IF...

In Mafia III, you must take down all three of Sal Marcano's capos—his brothers Tommy and Lou, and his sister-in-law Olivia Marcano—after taking control of their respective districts: Southdowns, French Ward, and Frisco Fields. You can do this in any order.

Whatever order you choose, killing the first Marcano capo triggers a cutscene where Sal calls for help from the Mafia's "Commission" led by Leo Galante. This phone call has no in-game consequences.

Killing the second Marcano capo, however, motivates Sal to bring in outside help. You see a cutscene where Sal makes a deal with Nino Santangelo, the heroin dealer and assassin. This cutscene triggers a new game chapter, "In Comes the Devil," and its lone mission, "My Name Is Lincoln Clay...".

In our walkthrough, we tackled Frisco Fields and Olivia Marcano first, thus, Olivia's fall prompted Sal's phone call to The Commission. Then we went after Southdowns and Tommy Marcano second, so we listed the Santangelo meeting and mission after Tommy's fall. Securing French Ward last and then killing Uncle Lou Marcano triggers a new chapter, "Yet Here We Are"—the final confrontation with Sal Marcano.

Confront Uncle Lou

Lincoln ends up groggy on the ground **(3)**, next to the burning riverboat, with only his Combat Knife as a weapon. Up ahead, Uncle Lou, still packing his pistol, staggers away through the forest.

Assign the French Ward to an Underboss

Once Lou Marcano is dead, the game cuts to another sitdown meeting at the abandoned bayou mansion. Assign the French Ward district to Burke, Vito, or Cassandra. If you've steadfastly ignored one or

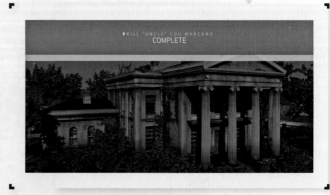

more of your Lieutenants, they may rebel at this point. Check out the section on "The Betrayal Missions" in our Optional & Other Missions chapter.

HOTEL PARADISO:
YET HERE WE ARE
MISSION: "KILL SAL MARCANO"

LEGEND

1. Blue Gulf Motel (Meet Donovan)
2. Northlake Bridge Toll Plaza
3. Hotel Paradiso Casino

Delray Hollow

Pointe Verdun

Discuss Marcano's Whereabouts with Donovan

Travel to Donovan's tac-op center **(1)** to find the former CIA agent preparing the place for a cleansing immolation. He has one last wiretapped recording for Lincoln to hear: Sal and Giorgi are circling the wagons at their Hotel Paradiso casino. Time to go exterminate the king rat and his son.

Go to the Casino & Get Inside

Follow the trip route through the Northlake Bridge toll plaza **(2)** and continue across the bridge to Sal's casino, the Hotel Paradiso **(3)**. When you arrive, head to the right side of the front entrance to find scaffolding and climb its stairs. At the top, make a quick Intel View scan to see lots of Marcano's men inside.

Find Giorgi

Enter the casino and take cover at the first crate by the balcony railing. Two guards chat a short distance down the balcony. When you whistle, *both* come over to investigate! Do a regular takedown of the first guard who arrives, then perform a Brutal Takedown on the second one to quickly silence him and avoid gunfire.

Proceed along the balcony and nail another guard looking over the railing with his back to you. Move cover to cover around the balcony level and silently take down two more guards on patrol. Now the upper level is cleared.

Sneak down the stairs leading to the main floor lobby. But before you reach the bottom, hop over the left railing and drop into the foliage next to the staircase. From here you can surprise another guard pacing past the ferns. Then start sneaking your way around the main floor, pouncing on patrols from behind or whistling to lure them to your secluded hiding spots. You can clear the entire main lobby this way. If you do get spotted and trigger a gunfight, you can find plentiful cover in the lobby.

Kill Giorgi

GET TO THE CASINO FLOOR

Work your way into the back hallway behind the reception desk and continue into an office area, where your objective changes. You must be getting close! Continue past the office desks and turn left through the exit door.

CASINO VARGAS

Don't miss the Vargas painting propped up on a couch in the waiting room of the casino's office area.

Climb the stairs to discover a "Win This Car" display. Hop into the De'Leo Stiletto on the podium and accelerate hard down the hall to hit the wooden ramp and fly through the "Paradiso" glass display onto the casino's main floor. (This move isn't mandatory, but it sure is fun.)

FIND THE BACK STAIRS

Hop out of the car and take cover behind the row of slot machines, then hustle over to the low wooden wall that encircles the main floor. A squad of gunmen are posted behind the circular desk in the middle of the room, underneath the big chandelier. You can maneuver around them while staying behind the low wall, but watch out for reinforcements coming down the stairs on both sides of the room.

As you clear out the main floor, watch for goons who burst through a door on the raised "Paradiso" stage behind the main bar (where a piano sits). Gun them down and go through the door they left open. Backstage, climb the stairs.

GUN DOWN GIORGI

Watch out for a crew of gunmen just outside the doorway at the top! Giorgi is holed up nearby in the casino's main operations booth. Eliminate his three guards, then shoot down Giorgi in the doorway of the booth. When he falls, your fighting is finished.

Confront Marcano

Climb the curving staircase to see Sal Marcano standing at his office window, overlooking the casino entrance twelve stories below. Approach Sal to trigger a final scene. We won't spoil the conversation, but when it ends, you have a choice to make.

Approach the fallen Giorgi and hold the button displayed to trigger a scene: Lincoln ties up loose ends with his old heist partner. Afterwards, he takes Giorgi's elevator key and rides up to the executive office level.

Marcano's Fate

Your choice: Go after Sal yourself…or just watch Sal handle his own fate.

Leave the Casino

Now head back downstairs. Stepping into the elevator triggers another cutscene: Lincoln meets Leo Galante, chairman of "The Commission," the American Mafia's governing body. Leo delivers a message to Lincoln, and makes an offer. Is it an offer that Lincoln can refuse?

UNLOCKS STORY MISSION:

"BEFORE THEY BURY YOU"

FRENCH WARD:
BLIND EYES OF GOD

MISSION: "BEFORE THEY BURY YOU"

LEGEND

1. St. Jerome's Catholic Church
2. Northlake Bridge Toll Plaza
3. Bayou Mansion

2 Pointe Verdun

French Ward 1

3 Bayou Fantom

Discuss Your Next Move with Donovan and Father James

PREREQUISITE:
COMPLETE "KILL SAL MARCANO"

Travel to St. Jerome's Catholic Church **(1)** and enter to trigger a long scene with Donovan and Father James. Lincoln listens to their respective points of view on the current power vacuum in New Bordeaux's underworld. Now you have another momentous choice (or two) to make.

Take the Throne or Leave Town

EITHER LEAVE NEW BORDEAUX...

If you choose to leave this town and its mayhem behind, drive up to the Northlake Bridge **(2)**...and keep going. Listen as Jonathan Maguire, former Assistant Director, Criminal Enterprise Branch, delivers the game's epilogue.

...OR DRIVE TO THE PLANTATION HOUSE

But if you choose to "take the throne," drive down to the abandoned bayou mansion **(3)** for another sitdown with your Underbosses. Here's where you make your final choice.

If you choose RULE TOGETHER, Assistant Director Maguire once again wraps up the story, along with a final emotional word from Father James.

But if you choose RULE ALONE, you must walk away from the mansion's front door and get in your car to end the tale. In this case, Father James speaks first, with Maguire delivering the final address.

KEEP WATCHING

Don't miss the game's true epilogue after the credits. Surely you want to see how John Donovan's testimony at the 1971 hearing before the Senate Select Committee on Intelligence turns out?

OPTIONAL
& OTHER
MISSIONS

THE BETRAYAL MISSIONS

When distributing districts during a sitdown meeting, you can either make an Underboss (Vito, Burke, and Cassandra) extremely grateful or you can make them very mad. If you continually ignore one of your Underbosses, eventually that Underboss will storm out and quit the team. This can even happen if the Underboss already controls one district. What makes an Underboss even more perturbed is when you take away a Racket that you've already assigned them by assigning the district it's located in to another Underboss during a sitdown meeting.

When you tick off an Underboss and they leave your group, you are tasked with killing that Underboss. Sad but true. You will infiltrate their hideout (where you collect Kickbacks), fight through their cronies, and eliminate your ex-friend. Instead of losing the Optional Missions they offer, their Lieutenant will carry on their operation. So don't worry about missing out on those. For example, if you kill Vito at his restaurant, Alma will carry on the hits that you would have done for Vito. This is a sad outcome, so we suggest trying to keep everyone happy—if it works into your strategy.

DELRAY HOLLOW:
CASSANDRA

MISSION: ".45 IN MY HAND"

Barclay Mills

[2]

Delray Hollow

[1]

LEGEND

[1] Cassandra's

[2] Truck Warehouse

Steal Weapons Shipment

PREREQUISITE: COMPLETE MISSION "AN EMOTIONAL ATTACHMENT" IN CHAPTER "BAYOU FANTOM: SITDOWN"

TALK TO CASSANDRA

Head to Cassandra's voodoo shop **(1)** in Delray Hollow. Enter through the front door and a cinematic introduces the mission. She's afraid the Hollow cannot protect itself and wants you to steal stashes of guns from around the city.

STEAL WEAPONS SHIPMENT

Access the map and highlight the first task in Cassandra's ".45 In My Hand" objectives panel. This will mark a route to the truck you need to hijack in the northwest **(2)** in Barclay Mills. The location is marked with a purple submachine gun icon on the map. Approach the building from the high ledge on the warehouse's southeast corner. Use Intel View to spot the truck inside and your first two targets patrolling the narrow alley. A silenced weapon is a great way to eliminate the enemies quickly.

Jump off the ledge and approach the large, open front door. Cover behind the crates or the entryway. Use Intel View to spot the remaining five enemies in and around the backside of the warehouse. Pick them off one by one, then get into the truck. This will keep the truck from taking bullet damage as you drive off.

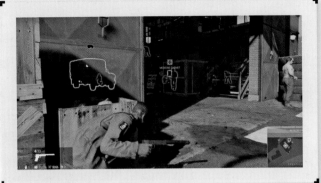

DELIVER THE TRUCK TO CASSANDRA

A route on the map leads the way back to Cassandra's when you get behind the wheel of the Potomac 5500 truck. Follow the route to your destination; and don't worry, you'll encounter no opposition along the way unless you get in trouble with the cops. Park the truck in the red marker beside Cassandra's shop and exit the vehicle to complete the delivery.

Return to Cassandra who is now on the top floor office, sitting on the couch. Collect any accumulated Kickbacks by picking up the envelope on the coffee table. Talk to Cassandra to complete the mission. Talk to her again to start the next optional mission.

MISSION: ".45 IN MY HAND"

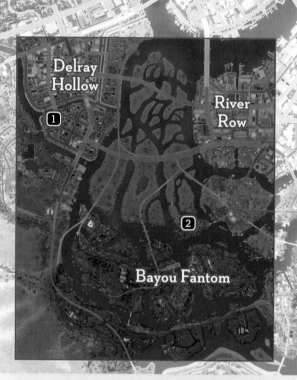

LEGEND

1. Cassandra's
2. Dixie Gun Stash Truck

Steal Dixie Gun Stash Truck

PREREQUISITE: COMPLETE ".45 IN MY HAND: STEAL WEAPONS SHIPMENT"

TALK TO CASSANDRA

Talk to Cassandra in her second floor office in the voodoo shop **(1)** in Delray Hollow. She'll request that you steal a Dixie gun stash in the Bayou. Open the map and select this option from the Objectives Panel to set your route to the location of the stash marked with a purple submachine gun icon.

STEAL DIXIE GUN STASH TRUCK

Stop outside the compound **(2)** in the Bayou and go in on foot as not to alert any hicks. The compound is completely surrounded by a wall with barbed wire. Sneak up to the opening on the northwest side and crouch down beside a short wooden fence beside a trailer. Whistle for and silently take down the two rednecks on the other side.

This leaves three enemies remaining. Shoot the rifleman on the rooftop to your left, and then finish off the other two goons that come running from around the truck parked at the back of the lot.

DELIVER THE TRUCK TO CASSANDRA

Enter the truck and follow the route back to Cassandra's voodoo shop **(1)**. Park in the marker and exit the vehicle. Return to the second floor to speak with her to finish the mission.

MISSION: ".45 IN MY HAND"

Delray Hollow
①

River Row

Southdowns
②

LEGEND
① Cassandra's
② Police Station

Steal Police Van

PREREQUISITE: COMPLETE ".45 IN MY HAND: STEAL DIXIE GUN STASH TRUCK"

TALK TO CASSANDRA

Talk to Cassandra in her second floor office in her Delray Hollow voodoo shop (1). She'll request that you steal weapons from the police. Open the map and select this option from the Objectives Panel to set your route to the location of the police van marked with a purple submachine gun icon in Southdowns.

STEAL POLICE VAN

Park in front of the Southdowns police station (2) and sneak around the west side of the building and silently take down any patrolling cops in the driveway on your way to the guard booth at the gate.

Whistle or use a Screaming Zemi to draw cops out of the booth window while you hide beside it in the little brick wall nook. When the cops start arriving, enter the booth and creep up to the exit. Use the Police Dispatcher option if things go badly.

Stealthily work your way through the back lot and into the open garage. Draw the nearby cops around the corner near the exit gate into a kill zone. Silently take down the cops as they round the garage corner. The one cop that is hard to draw out is the one behind the police van you must steal.

Approach him using the police van as cover between the two of you. We suggest getting in the armored vehicle and just driving off through the gate. Or you could rush the police officer and catch him off guard with a brutal takedown.

DELIVER THE TRUCK TO CASSANDRA

Get into the Samson Rhino (police van) and crash the gates following the route to Cassandra's (1). You will surely have the police on your tail, so either lose them with skilled driving or use the Police Dispatcher option to delete the heat. Follow the route back to the voodoo store, park in the marker, exit the vehicle, and talk to Cassandra.

RETURN TO CASSANDRA

Head into the voodoo shop and run up the stairs. When you reach the top of the stairs, a cinematic begins. After Lincoln's and Cassandra's heated conversation, the ".45 In My Hand" Optional Missions come to a conclusion.

CONTINUING CASSANDRA OPTIONAL MISSIONS

When you assign Cassandra a second district, another Optional Mission in ".45 In My Hand" is unlocked: Raid Weapons Warehouse. You must steal a drug truck from a warehouse and deliver it to her voodoo shop. When you complete this mission, ".45 In My Hand" is completed and Cassandra shares a little more personal history with Lincoln, thus creating a little more trust between them.

DELRAY HOLLOW:
EMMANUEL LAZARE

MISSION: "ARE WE COOL"

Barclay Mills

Delray Hollow

LEGEND

| 1 First Baptist Church Boathouse | 2 Smuggling Dock | 3 Drug Drop Location | 4 Friendly Racket (De & Boot Delivery) | 5 Friendly Racket (Inland Truck Delivery) |

Our Losses

PREREQUISITE: COMPLETE MISSION "AN EMOTIONAL ATTACHMENT" IN CHAPTER "BAYOU FANTOM: SITDOWN"

TALK TO EMMANUEL

Head to Emmanuel at the boathouse **(1)** behind the First Baptist Church in Delray Hollow. Emmanuel, Cassandra's Lieutenant keeps a steady supply of weed coming into the city, and he's very cautious when it comes to new acquaintances. This Haitian priest/drug runner and Lincoln don't exactly hit it off, but they agree to work together.

Emmanuel's jobs consist of driving to a drug boat location and defeating enemies around the boat (if present), and then taking the boat into the bayou and picking up airdropped drug crates. Once you've picked up three crates, drive to the nearest friendly boat dock and exit the boat. Then drive the automatically transferred shipment to a friendly Racket marked on the map.

GET TO THE SMUGGLING DOCK

Access the map and highlight the first task in Emmanuel's "Are We Cool" objectives panel. This creates a route to the small shack and Smuggling Dock **(2)** on the easternmost riverbank in the bayou. Stop your car away from the house and approach on foot. With Intel View you'll spot three rednecks in and around the house.

GET IN THE BOAT

You can hop through the open front window and rush and brutally take down the redneck in the house before he knows what's going on. Next, instead of opening the backdoor and alerting the redneck on the other side of it, simply jump out the back window and take him down quickly. Sneak up to the last redneck who's standing at the end of the dock facing the smuggling boat. Take him out and enter the boat.

DRIVE TO THE DROP LOCATION & WAIT FOR THE DROP

Drive the Samson Raider toward the purple Fleur-de-lis icon out in the river **(3)** heading northeast. Look to the skies and you'll see a prop-plane fly over and drop crates in the water. Follow the marker on the minimap to the nearest floating crate of weed.

TAKE THE WEED DELIVERY

Slow the boat down (you can't pick up the crates if you are going fast) and stop over the crate. Press down on the D-Pad to pick up the crate. Pick up all three crates this way.

DELIVER THE WEED TO A FRIENDLY RACKET

Once you've picked up all three of the drug crates, open the map menu and look for the friendly Racket dock location(s). They appear on the map as purple down arrows. As you look at your map, you'll notice you may have multiple friendly Racket dock options. Study the possible routes that you'd need to take to reach the nearest docks, and then decide which would be the easiest route for you. In our case, it's the dock to the north **(4)** in Southdowns.

Drive along the river or channels taking the most direct route to the nearest friendly Racket dock, and then park the boat in the red marker. When you stop, you and the drugs are automatically transferred to the drug smuggling truck. Now open the map and purple down arrows will point out all the inland friendly Rackets where you can deliver the drugs.

You can choose to go to the nearest friendly Racket, which for us is just north over the bridge in Tickfaw Harbor **(5)**. Or you could choose to go to a Friendly Racket near Emmanuel **(1)** in Delray Hollow. This way, after you make the delivery, Emmanuel will be nearby in case you want to pick up the next job. However, if you fear you may wreck the vehicle, we suggest delivering the drugs to the nearest racket to where you parked the boat.

Stop the truck in the red marker at the friendly Racket and get out of the truck to complete the delivery. You can continue the Trafficking  operation to increase the Earn for your Underbosses' Rackets. Helping your Underbosses expand their Rackets with Trafficking runs increases their Loyalty to you, while also allowing them to improve their net worth of Associates, and increase your potential Kickback.

RETURN TO EMMANUEL

Use your Valet to bring you a fast car, and then drive it to Delray Hollow to speak to Emmanuel **(1)** who is now in the back office inside the fellowship building  behind First Baptist Church. After the cinematic, Emmanuel remains in the office. You can talk to him to pick up the next trafficking job. He has two more jobs very similar to this one. The only difference is the boat location and the amount of enemies guarding it.

POINTE VERDUN:
THOMAS BURKE

MISSION: "I.R.A. DON'T ASK"

LEGEND

1 Burke's Iron & Metal

2 A Samson Richmond-Lux location

Pointe Verdun

Tickfaw Harbor

Steal 3 Orange Samson Richmond-Luxes

PREREQUISITE: COMPLETE MISSION "AN EMOTIONAL ATTACHMENT" IN CHAPTER "BAYOU FANTOM: SITDOWN"

TALK TO BURKE

Head to Burke's Iron & Metal **(1)** in Pointe Verdun. Enter the garage to find Burke working under a lifted car. Burke needs more cars to keep his IRA connections happy. Steal them and bring them back to the salvage yard.

FIND 3 ORANGE SAMSON RICHMOND-LUXES

This first mission of Burke's has you hunting New Bordeaux for three orange Samson Richmond-Luxes, luckily if you open your map you can find a plethora of spawn locations dotted all over the map with green screwdriver and wrench icons. There are three locations in each district except for the bayou. We suggest starting with the nearest marked (possible) location **(2)** to Burke's salvage yard. That way you won't have far to drive.

BLIP IT USING OBJECTIVES PANEL
There's a much greater chance of finding a vehicle at a tool icon marked position if you access the map and bring up the Objectives Panel for the mission and select the "Find 3 Orange Samson Richmond-Luxes" option. This draws a route to a location that very likely holds what you're looking for.

When you reach the location of the marker, access Intel View and you'll see the car you are looking for highlighted in yellow with a green vehicle icon hovering overhead. This picture shows the Orange Samson Richmond-Lux you are looking for.

DELIVER THE CAR TO BURKE

Simply jack the car and drive it back to Burke's place marked with a green down arrow. The route is automatically marked when you enter the vehicle. Drive the car under the crane structure and into the red marker. Exit the vehicle and look for the next two vehicles.

RETURN TO BURKE

When you've delivered the third one, enter the shop and talk to Burke. This completes the mission. If you talk to him again, you can pick up the next job.

MISSION: "I.R.A. DON'T ASK"

LEGEND
1   Burke's Iron Works
2   Southdowns Police Station
3   Frisco Fields Police Station
4   French Ward Police Station

Steal 3 Red De'Leo Capulets

PREREQUISITE: COMPLETE "I.R.A. DON'T ASK: STEAL 3 ORANGE SAMSON RICHMOND-LUXES"

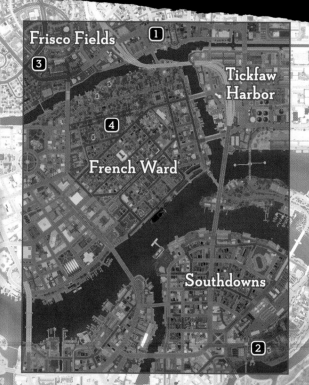

TALK TO BURKE

Head to Burke's Iron & Metal in Pointe Verdun **(1)**. Enter and find Burke behind the counter drinking a beer. Talk to him to pick up the second car theft job. This time Burke is looking for three Red De'Leo Capulets.

STEEL 3 RED DE'LEO CAPULETS

This job is naturally a little more difficult than the previous car theft job. This time you are looking for sports cars that have been impounded and are located in police station back lots… Police Territory. Open the map and you'll notice only one green tool icon blipped on the map. It's located over the Southdowns police station **(2)**.

Stop near the police station and use Intel View to spot the cops in and around the police station. You spot the green car icon over the target vehicle behind the open garage. There's a very easy way to steal this vehicle. Simply walk through the garage like you own the place and call the Police Dispatcher the moment an alert is created. Then jump in the car and drive off. Or you could sneak around and silently take down all the cops, using the Screaming Zemi to aid your strategy.

DELIVER THE CAR TO BURKE

Enter the red sports car and smash through the gates to escape the police station. Follow the route back to Burke's **(1)**, stop the car under the crane, exit the vehicle, and then look for the second Red De'Leo Capulet using the Objectives Panel.

FIND THE SECOND RED DE'LEO CAPULET

The second Red De'Leo Capulet is impounded at the Frisco Fields police station **(3)**. The target vehicle is heavily guarded. If you want to go the easy route, simply use the Police Dispatcher service and take the vehicle as if it were your own. If you don't want to waste a Mark or want to save money (or just like a challenge), go in stealthily through the window of the guard booth, taking out the cop inside from behind. Exit the booth, creep behind the police car and take out one of the cops as they walk away past the back entrance to the garage.

Sneak along the garage exits and hide in the nook past the garage. Throw a Screaming Zemi into the back corner of the lot so the remaining cops will gather and look away from the red sports car. Dash to the passenger side of the car, enter and drive it off the lot.

DELIVER THE CAR TO BURKE

Smash through the gates to escape the police station. Follow the route back to Burke's **(1)**, stop the car under the crane, exit the vehicle, and then look for the third Red De'Leo Capulet using the Objectives Panel.

FIND THE THIRD RED DE'LEO CAPULET

The third Red De'Leo Capulet is impounded at the French Ward police station **(4)**.

As with the previous challenges, you can either use the Police Dispatcher to take the easy way out, or use stealth and a Screaming Zemi to challenge yourself a bit. Again, enter through the gate guard booth and take out the nearby cop from behind. Enter the lot and immediately toss the Screaming Zemi in a back corner beyond the red sports car, which is parked to the left, midway in the lot.

The Zemi diverts the remaining cops' attention while you enter the sports car and tear off the lot through the gate at the guard booth.

DELIVER THE CAR TO BURKE

Follow the route back to Burke's **(1)**, stop the car under the crane, and exit the vehicle.

TALK TO BURKE

Enter Burke's shop and talk to him to finish this job. Talk to him again to pick up the next car theft job.

MISSION: "I.R.A. DON'T ASK"

LEGEND

1. Burke's Iron Works
2. Pointe Verdun Green Bullworth Aspen Location

Pointe Verdun

Steal 3 Green Bullworth Aspens

PREREQUISITE: PREREQUISITE: COMPLETE "I.R.A. DON'T ASK: STEAL 3 RED DE'LEO CAPULETS"

TALK TO BURKE

Head to Burke's Iron & Metal in Pointe Verdun **(1)**. Enter and find Burke behind the counter drinking a beer. Talk to him to pick up the third car theft job. This time Burke is looking for three Green Bullworth Aspens.

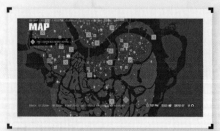

Open the map and check out all the green tool icons marked all over New Bordeaux. They pepper the map like they did in the first car theft job, plus there are even a few in the bayou. We suggest trying to find the target pickup trucks using the nearest icons **(2)** to Burke's. If you come up empty-handed, you can use the Objectives Panel objective selection to pretty much guarantee a find.

FIND 3 GREEN BULWORTH ASPENS

This is the truck you're looking for (see picture). They are not difficult to find using multiple possible locations marked on the map.

DELIVER THE CAR TO BURKE

Enter the truck and follow the route back to Burke's **(1)**, stop the car under the crane, and exit the vehicle. Repeat this process two more

times. You shouldn't meet any resistance around the vehicle.

TALK TO BURKE

Enter Burke's shop and talk to him to finish the mission. Burke discloses some personal issues he's dealing with, tightening the bond between the two characters and building trust.

UNLOCK ONE MORE BURKE JOB

If you give Burke a second district, the last of the car theft jobs will unlock in "I.R.A. Don't Ask." Go see Burke any time after assigning him a second district.

MISSION: "I.R.A. DON'T ASK"

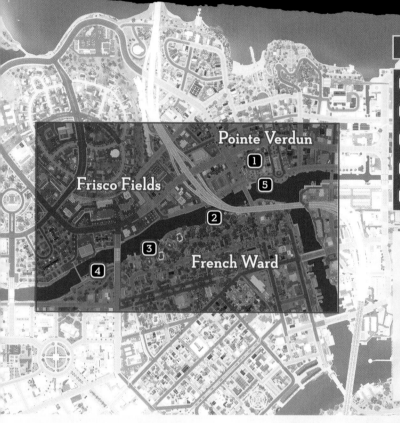

LEGEND

1. Burke's Iron Works
2. Possible Cutler 50 location
3. Possible Cutler 50 location
4. Possible Cutler 50 location
5. Burke's Boathouse

Pointe Verdun

Frisco Fields

French Ward

Steal 3 Cutler 50s

PREREQUISITE: COMPLETE "I.R.A. DON'T ASK: STEAL 3 BULLWORTH ASPENS" & ASSIGN BURKE A SECOND DISTRICT

TALK TO BURKE

Head to Burke's Iron & Metal (1) and talk to Burke. This time the I.R.A is looking for boat parts. Exit the shop and go to the Objectives Panel. Select "Find 3 Cutler 50s" and notice about three green tool icons representing possible Cutler locations in each district.

FIND 3 CUTLER 50S

We had a lot of luck finding all three Cutlers (2), (3) & (4) using the nearest icons to Burke's. Pictured here is a Cutler 50 so you know what you're looking for. It's very convenient to search and find the Cutlers along the channel that runs south of Burke's shop, since you must return it to his boathouse (5) once you've stolen them.

DELIVER THE BOAT TO BURKE'S DOCK

Route markers don't work on water, so open the map and look for the green down arrow on the shoreline just south of Burke's shop. This is his boathouse and dock (5). Drive the boat into the red marker and then exit the boat to complete the delivery. Do this three times, and then go talk to Burke (1).

TALK TO BURKE

Once you've delivered all three Cutler 50s to Burke's dock, head up his pier and through the salvage yard to talk to Burke. He rewards you with three Makers for completing this job! Talk to him again to unlock another job.

MISSION: "I.R.A. DON'T ASK"

LEGEND

1 Burke's Iron Works

2 Possible Samson Duke Location

French Ward

Steal 3 Blue Samson Dukes

PREREQUISITE: COMPLETE "I.R.A. DON'T ASK: STEAL 3 CUTLER 50S"

TALK TO BURKE

Head to Burke's Iron & Metal (1) and talk to Burke. This time the I.R.A is looking for Samson Dukes. Exit the shop and go to the Objectives Panel. Select "Find 3 Samson Dukes" and notice only about two green tool icons representing possible Samson Duke locations in a select few districts. Select one to get a route pretty much guaranteed to have the vehicle you're looking for.

FIND 3 BLUE SAMSON DUKES

This is the first time you will meet enemies (besides the police) at a vehicle steal location. When you get close to the target location, exercise caution. Use Intel View to spot red highlighted gangsters in the vicinity of the Samson Duke (see picture of Blue Samson Duke for reference).

Before you get close to the car, find a good location for cover. Then start picking off enemies with a weapon, or go stealthy. Either way, it's a good idea to eliminate the enemies before entering the vehicle, so they don't destroy it once you gain entry.

DELIVER THE CAR TO BURKE

Enter the blue sports car and follow the route back to Burke's (1), stop the car under the crane structure, and exit the vehicle. Repeat this process two more times. Expect to meet resistance around each vehicle you need to steal.

TALK TO BURKE

Once you've delivered all three Blue Samson Dukes to Burke's scrapyard, talk to Burke who's standing at the end of his shop counter. He tells you about Nicki wanting out of the family business and he's trying to raise enough money to help her do just that. He also reveals that he's dying of liver cancer. Lincoln and Burke build more trust, the I.R.A missions end, and you wind up with a little more cash in your wallet.

POINTE VERDUN:
NICKI BURKE

MISSION: "THE RIGHTEOUSLY F***ED"

Frisco Fields

Pointe Verdun

1

Steel The Moonshine Truck

PREREQUISITE: COMPLETE MISSION "AN EMOTIONAL ATTACHMENT" IN CHAPTER "BAYOU FANTOM: SITDOWN"

LEGEND

1 Nicki Burke

2 Dixie Mafia Distillery

Bayou Fantom

2

TALK TO NICKI

Talk to Nicki who is now starting a moonshine operation inside the "Butcher's" meat packing facility **(1)**. You can find her on the top floor in the large office doing some filing. She wants you to steal the moonshine from the rednecks in the bayou.

STEAL THE TRUCK

The Dixie Mafia is guarding a moonshine shipment **(2)** in Bayou Fantom. This area is marked with a jug of moonshine icon on the map. Take a fast car down to the bayou. You'll be traveling pretty much the longest route possible across the entire map to reach this remote location. Once you arrive, you will find yourself at a Trago gas station and garage compound. We suggest avoiding the gas station; there are many possible witnesses inside. Instead, hop the metal fence between the old carwash and the filling station (circled on this picture). Once you do, you will be trespassing in the distillery.

Turn right and defeat the rednecks on your way through the alleyway between the filling station and the large garage. The Eckhart Pioneer truck can be found around back to the left under a small shelter. Defeat any enemies around the truck to avoid bullet damage as you drive off. To escape the area, you could drive through the compound and crash through a gate or use the ramp shortcut directly in front of the truck (as you pull out of the shelter) at the privacy fence's corner.

DELIVER THE TRUCK TO A FRIENDLY RACKET

Once you're free and clear of the Dixie Mafia Distillery area, pull up the map and scan for the nearest Friendly Racket marked with a green down arrow. This location will vary depending on what rackets you have control over. Click on the arrow to create a route to the location. Once there, pull into the

red marker, park the truck, and get out to complete the delivery.

DENNY MCGILL UNLOCKED

"Denny McGill" is unlocked when you deliver the moonshine truck to a Friendly Racket. This is not a mission, but merely a conversation about a mutual high-school friend.

RETURN TO NICKI

Use your Valet service to order a vehicle that you can drive back to Nicki's hangout **(1)**. Talk to Nicki in her office. The two of you will chat about Denny McGill. This completes the mission. Continue stealing moonshine trucks from the Dixie Mafia and delivering them to a Friendly Racket for Nicki. The missions are very similar to each other, where the major difference is the unique location of Dixie Mafia's distillery. After a few more deliveries, "The Righteously F***ed" will be completed and rewards collected.

RIVER ROW:
VITO SCALETTA

MISSION: "I NEED A FAVOR"

Vito's Hit List

PREREQUISITE: COMPLETE MISSION "AN EMOTIONAL ATTACHMENT" IN CHAPTER "BAYOU FANTOM: SITDOWN"

Frisco Fields

French Ward

Downtown

Southdowns

River Row

LEGEND	
1	Vito's Restaurant
2	Stan "The Face" Caramanci
3	Chet "Lucky"

TALK TO VITO

Head to Vito's Italian Restaurant **(1)** and find him preparing a meal in the kitchen. Vito needs your help with some unfinished business. He needs some history buried so he can get his head straight. When the conversation ends, you find yourself in his second floor office of the house behind the restaurant. This is where you will collect Kickbacks and continue more missions. If you haven't done so already, collect the Vargas painting inside his office on the bookshelf.

INTERROGATE LUCKY'S OLD CRONIES

Grab a vehicle and follow the marker to a blue crosshairs icon on the map to find Lucky's first crony, Stan "The Face" Caramanci **(2)** located in the French Ward. You only need to interrogate this one crony to find out where your main target is located. Stan is alone in an alley between some buildings. Walk up to the guy with the interrogate icon over his head and press and hold **B** or **◉** until he succumbs to the knife death grip. You ask where you can find the councilman. He tells you he's supposed to be playing cards nearby. You can choose to kill or spare him.

KILL CHET "LUCKY" CARBONALE

Get into a vehicle and follow the marker to the northwest destination in Frisco Fields to find Lucky **(3)**, who won't be feeling very lucky for too much longer. You can find him inside a best oil service station on the corner.

You can enter through the front door and risk creating witnesses. If you go this route, take out the clerk and the mobster in the office with the shotgun. Or you can just break open the side door that leads directly inside the garage where Lucky is hanging out. He's the guy with the "Kill Lucky" message over his head.

There's a gambling game going on and all the mobsters are sitting down. They're not ready for you if you just rush in and grab Lucky from behind by pressing **B** or **◉** to break his neck. If you go this route, be prepared to battle the few cronies in the garage with him; they won't scare off after you kill Lucky. Raid the First Aid Kit in the garage, then get out of there before the cops are called.

RETURN TO VITO

Race back to River Row and go see Vito **(1)** in the stilt house behind the restaurant. Vito's jobs play out exactly like this one, but with different cronies and main targets.

KILL NESTOR ROURKE

His next target is Nestor Rourke. Pick one of his cronies (Patch, Smokey, or Leonard Ferrante) to interrogate to find out where Nestor is located. Turns out he's located in a garage in Southdowns. Follow the markers on the map and go and kill Nestor.

KILL PAULIE BIANCARDI

After Nestor, Paulie Biancardi is the next target. You don't have to interrogate anyone to find him. Simply mark the location indicated on the map in the Southdowns cemetery and drive there. With Intel View, you can stealthily snake your way through the cemetery without harming hardly any of his cronies (if you wish). You can just come up behind him on the mausoleum stoop and take him out stealthily from behind. Sprint out of the cemetery, and then report back to Vito.

KILL LUCA GUIDI & DARIO MURTAS

When you return to Vito, he thanks you and then sends you to kill Luca Guidi. This guy only has one rat you need to interrogate—similar to the earlier missions. Dario Murtas is last on the hit list. This guy is marked on the map (you do not need to interrogate anyone to find him). He's in a compound on the bayou. After this guy is killed, return to Vito to finally end the "I Need a Favor" missions.

Vito can't believe his past demons are dealt with and he reflects back on the passing of his friend Joe from *Mafia II*. Your relationship with Vito becomes more solid now.

RIVER ROW: ALMA DIAZ

MISSION: "ARE WE COOL"

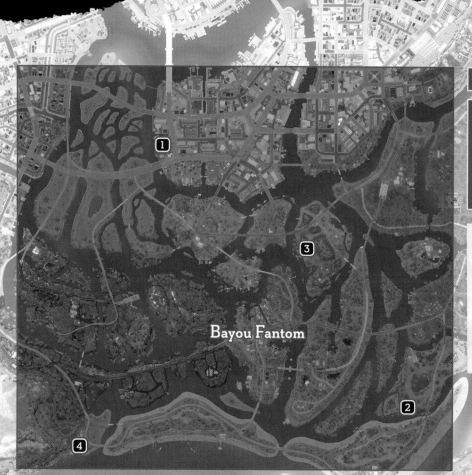

Bayou Fantom

LEGEND

1. Alma
2. Electronics Semi
3. Electronics Semi
4. Electronics Semi

PREREQUISITE:

COMPLETE MISSION "AN EMOTIONAL ATTACHMENT" IN CHAPTER "BAYOU FANTOM: SITDOWN"

TALK TO ALMA

Head to the second floor office of Alma's warehouse hangout **(1)** in River Row. You find Alma cleaning out her revolver when you enter her office. She says Vito wants her guys to double their runs. She needs you to keep the money coming into the warehouses and asks you to steal trucks that will be used to carry the contraband.

STEAL THE SEMI TRUCK

Open the map and check out the marked stereo icon **(2)** at the end of the long route to the bayou. This is the Dixie Mafia's semi full of stolen electronics that you are going to steal from the Dixie Mafia. When you get near the camp, exit your vehicle and go in on foot. You'll find a bunch of rednecks with guns guarding a semi-truck, semi-hidden under shelter.

Either go in guns blazing or work your way around the perimeter silently taking out bad guys with takedowns. Work your way around until you have a clear shot at the cab of the Bulworth Buckliner 500 in the shelter. Jump in and drive off.

DELIVER THE TRUCK TO A FRIENDLY RACKET

Much like other car theft missions from other allies, you must find a Friendly Racket in which to drop the load. You must drive carefully; if you lose or unintentionally drop the trailer, the delivery will not count. You need the trailer on the truck to complete the mission.

Open your map and search for blue down arrows. These represent the locations of Friendly (Vito) Rackets where you can deliver the truck. Mark one of the blue arrows and follow the route on the map to the racket. Pull the truck into the red marker. Get out of the truck to complete the delivery.

STEAL THE SEMI TRUCK

With Alma's missions, you do not need to return to her each time you steal a semi, similar to delivering cars to Burke. Just bring up the map after you make a delivery and use the Objective Panel to mark the next semi location **(3)**. The third semi **(4)** is in the southwest bayou.

RETURN TO ALMA

After delivering all the trucks to Friendly Rackets, square up with Alma **(1)** at her warehouse hideout.

COLLECTIBLES

There are multiple types of items scattered all over New Bordeaux just waiting to be discovered and collected. You will be searching for *Playboy* magazines, Vargas paintings, Albums, *Hot Rod* magazines, Communist Propaganda posters, and *Repent* Magazines.

All items are available from the start of the game. And when wiretapping junction boxes becomes available, all can be revealed on the map (as long as you have wiretapped the nearest junction box). We suggest going out of your way to find enough TL-49 Fuses to wiretap every single junction box so that all the collectibles on the map are revealed. However, if you want to save time, simply use our collectibles maps to find all the collectibles.

TL-49 COUNTER

The graphic in the bottom-left corner of the screen tracks how much money you have in your safe, how much money you are holding on your person, and the amount of fuses you are holding (the last number). Keep an eye on this before attempting a wiretap. You need three fuses to tap a junction box.

HOW TO WIRETAP

You first need to complete the "Story Mission: Smack" before attempting to wiretap a junction box. Next, you need three TL-49 Fuses; it takes three fuses to wiretap one junction box. There's usually at least one fuse in the vicinity of each junction box. (Fuses are also revealed in district sectors that have already been wiretapped.) Next, look for the nearest untapped junction box icon on the map. If you are headed to that district early and it's icon is not revealed on the map, then use our map to find the junction boxes. Look for a large green utility box attached to a wall in the environment. Walk up to it and press ✖ or ■ to begin the jimmying mini-game to pry the doors open.

JUNCTION BOX LOCK

The junction box lock will appear with a red "no sign" icon over it if you do not have at least three fuses in your possession. Find three fuses before attempting a wiretap.

STEP 1: FINDING THE SWEET SPOT

Rotate the Left Control Stick until a green highlight bar appears along the white circle covering the junction box. Move the control stick until you achieve the smallest green bar possible and then press ✖ or ■ to confirm the sweet spot. The smaller you can make the green sweet spot icon the easier the next step will be.

STEP 2: PRYING THE DOORS OPEN

Now that a very small green bar (representing the sweet spot) is locked onto the circular white prying indicator, a much larger green bar appears in its place. The smaller the green sweet spot bar you lock, the larger the pry area in this second step will be and the slower the prying needle moves, making it easier to execute the break-in.

Now the very thin white prying needle bounces across the white circle from the right to the left and back again. The smaller the sweet spot you created, the slower this needle moves. Stop the needle in the green bar. The easiest and quickest way to nail this step is to quickly press the ✖ or ■ as soon as it touches the green area instead of waiting for the needle to reach the middle of the green bar.

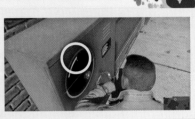

STEP 3: WIRETAP

The third step is an automatic action. Clay takes the fuse and wires it into the junction box creating a wiretap. After you close the doors, a green light on the fuse appears inside the junction box (seen through a small window), indicating that box has been wiretapped. If you access the Map Menu you'll see enemies (if any are near), and collectibles are now revealed on the map in the district's sector where that junction box is located. There are many junction boxes and fuses scattered throughout New Bordeaux. Find and tap them all to reveal the collectibles on the entire map.

JUNCTION BOX & COLLECTIBLE BREAKDOWN

Once a junction box has been wiretapped, the collectibles in that sector are revealed as blue blips. You can hover the reticle over these blips to reveal the type of collectible. The following is a breakdown of the junction box and collectible totals. And in case you are wondering, there are many more fuses scattered around the environment than you would ever need to hack all the junction boxes.

89 Total Junction Boxes

161 Total Collectibles

50 Playboys

33 Vargas Paintings

30 Album Covers

12 Hot Rod Magazines

31 Communist Propaganda Posters (there are only 8 unique poster styles)

5 Repent Magazines

AUTOMATIC JUNCTION BOX REVEAL

When you are sent to a new district through a story mission, all of that district's junction boxes are revealed on your map automatically.

DELRAY HOLLOW

LEGEND

- **5 Junction Boxes**
- **4 Playboy Magazines**
- **4 Vargas Paintings**
- **4 Album Covers**
- **1 Hot Rod Magazine**
- **2 Communist Propaganda Posters**

JUNCTION BOXES

1A JUNCTION BOX

Find this junction box on the west exterior wall of the Trago filling station in west Delray Hollow.

1B JUNCTION BOX

Tap this junction box to spy on Doug "Hatchet" Marcheti during the Smack Racket missions.

1C JUNCTION BOX

This junction box is on the exterior alley wall of the Everyday Laundromat. There's also a *Playboy* magazine inside the same Laundromat.

1D JUNCTION BOX

Wiretap the First Baptist Church using the junction box Donovan points out to you. This is the introduction to wiretapping.

1E JUNCTION BOX

Find this junction box on the side of the Perfect Waffle restaurant.

COLLECTIBLES

1 ALBUM COVER
(THE CHAMBERS BROTHERS)

Inside this northwestern Delray Hollow garage.

2 VARGAS PAINTING

On the first floor lobby on the left wall behind a counter as you enter Doucet's club through the front entrance. Grab this during "The Way Of Flesh."

3 VARGAS PAINTING

On the wall behind the desk in Merle "Trigger" Jackson's office of the Doucet's club. Grab this while freeing the strung-out girls during the prostitution missions.

4 ALBUM (EDDIE FLOYD)

On a shelf in the back of this garage. You are in this area when out to kill Deacon Caruso during Kincaid's Smack Racket.

5 COMMUNIST PROPAGANDA
(CUT DOWN CAPITALISM)

On the inside wall of this Delray Hollow train stop & ticket booth.

6 ALBUM COVER (CREAM)

On a filing cabinet in the back office of the Deep Dive Bar & Lounge. Rob the register and the cash box while you're there.

7 COMMUNIST PROPAGANDA
(EQUALITY FOR ALL)

Posted on the exterior front wall of this large government building.

8 PLAYBOY MAGAZINE (AUGUST 1966)

On the desk in the back office of the Everyday Laundromat. This is the same Laundromat with a junction box in the alley.

9 PLAYBOY (AUGUST 1964)

On a table in the basement of Sammy's Bar. Grab this after getting out of bed.

10 VARGAS PAINTING

Hung on the back of a support column in the basement bedroom of Sammy's Bar. Grab this after getting out of bed.

11 ALBUM COVER (CLARENCE CARTER)

On a desk in the back office of Delray Hollow's Warm Hearts neighborhood kitchen. Grab this before serving soup here during the Smack Racket.

12 VARGAS PAINTING

In the fellowship hall office of the First Baptist Church or better known as Kincaid's Smack Racket hideout. Find it hung on the wall behind the back corner office.

13 *HOT ROD* MAGAZINE (JUNE 1968)

On a desk in an office inside the Auto Service store on the corner. There are multiple entrances.

14 *PLAYBOY* (NOVEMBER 1967)

This magazine is on a desk in the living room inside this green ramshackle house.

15 *PLAYBOY* (MAY 1964)

Inside the Double Barrel Bar on the end of the bar counter.

RIVER ROW

LEGEND

🔌	**9 Junction Boxes**
◇	**7 Playboy Magazines**
◇	**4 Vargas Paintings**
◇	**2 Album Covers**
◇	**1 Hot Rod Magazine**
◇	**4 Communist Propaganda Posters**

JUNCTION BOXES

2A JUNCTION BOX

On the north side of the redbrick Rigolet's warehouse.

2B JUNCTION BOX

Just outside the front door of Vito's hideout, Benny's Ristorante Italiano.

2C JUNCTION BOX

On the north side of this office building. You'll want to hack this while destroying Union Trailers.

2D JUNCTION BOX

Find this junction box on the backside of the two-car garage opposite the United Dock Workers building.

2E JUNCTION BOX

On the south side of the multistory Dominik's Sugar building.

2F JUNCTION BOX

On the east side of the large multistory brick building where a Medical Supply Truck is located that needs to be stolen or destroyed.

2G JUNCTION BOX

On the south side of the large brick multistory Lunette Billiard building. It's good to tap this box when killing "Stitch" Gallo during the Union Extortion racket.

2H JUNCTION BOX

Located on the backside of the two-car garage beside the Tugboat Bar. Used to uncover targets during the Union Extortion racket.

2I JUNCTION BOX

On the south side of this warehouse in south River Row. Use it to spy on Nestor Pellegrini during the Contraband racket.

COLLECTIBLES

16 PLAYBOY (JULY 1964)

On a desk in a cage office inside this Bayside Shipping warehouse.

17 COMMUNIST PROPAGANDA (COMMUNISM REACHES THE STARS)

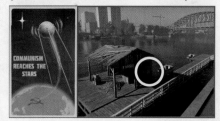

This poster is pinned up on the exterior wall of this pier shelter on the north tip of River Row.

18 VARGAS PAINTING

Hung on the wall of a second floor office in this Rigolet's Canning Company building.

19 ALBUM COVER (THE SUPREMES)

On a stack of boxes in a nook inside the Fresh Crab shack.

20 COMMUNIST PROPAGANDA (EQUALITY FOR ALL)

Posted on the side of this two-car, metal garage on the waterfront.

21 VARGAS PAINTING

This painting is on the floor leaning on the entry wall behind the entry greeting station inside Benny's Ristorante Italiano in River Row. Get it during "We Partners Now?"

22 VARGAS PAINTING

Leaning on a bookshelf inside Vito Scaletta's second story office behind Benny's Ristorante Italiano in River Row. Get it during "We Partners Now?"

23 PLAYBOY (JUNE 1966)

Behind the wall on a table in the kitchen area of the Fresh Crab shack.

24 PLAYBOY (MAY 1963)

On a corner filing cabinet inside the back office of the Baby Bear BBQ restaurant.

25 PLAYBOY (FEBRUARY 1966)

On a wooden table on the second floor catwalk of this large warehouse. This magazine contains an interview with Truman Capote.

26 PLAYBOY (MAY 1966)

On the floor inside the top of the stairwell of this small, two-story building. This rooftop offers a good vantage point when killing "Stitch" Gallo during the Union Extortion racket. Make sure to grab the fuse from the rooftop ledge while you're there.

27 COMMUNIST PROPAGANDA (COMMUNISM IS FREEDOM)

On the side of multistory Dominik's Sugars building.

28 VARGAS PAINTING

On the wall in the top floor office of this shipping warehouse on the riverfront. This is accessed during the "Roy's Contraband Racket" missions.

29 ALBUM COVER (BIG BROTHER & THE HOLDING COMPANY)

In the back office of Shooter's Bar.

30 HOT ROD MAGAZINE (MAY 1968)

Inside a train car near the wall that divides the train yard from the street.

31 COMMUNIST PROPAGANDA (FREEDOM IN COMMUNISM)

On the second story doorway of this small train depot.

32 PLAYBOY (OCTOBER 1967)

On a table in this shack in the River Row slums.

33 PLAYBOY (DECEMBER 1967)

Beside a wooden chair on the front porch of this riverfront home.

POINTE VERDUN

LEGEND

- 🎧 7 Junction Boxes
- ◆ 7 Playboy Magazines
- ◆ 4 Vargas Paintings
- ◆ 4 Album Covers
- ◆ 1 Hot Rod Magazine
- ⌄ 4 Communist Propaganda Posters

JUNCTION BOXES

3A JUNCTION BOX

On the southeastern side of the Pearl Edge motel.

3B JUNCTION BOX

This box is on the side of the restroom in the park near the lighthouse.

3C JUNCTION BOX

In a back alley behind Frederic's Delicatessen.

3D 3D JUNCTION BOX

On the side of this building in the road curve.

3E 3E JUNCTION BOX

On the side of this garage under the freeway.

3F 3F JUNCTION BOX

On the north side of the single-story Bail Bonds business.

3G 3G JUNCTION BOX

On the east side of this large warehouse structure used by Caesar De Angelis and his moonshine operations.

COLLECTIBLES

34 COMMUNIST PROPAGANDA (EQUALITY FOR ALL)

On this post at the northernmost pier in Pointe Verdun.

35 COMMUNIST PROPAGANDA (FREEDOM IN COMMUNISM)

On the side of the lighthouse in north Pointe Verdun.

36 PLAYBOY (JULY 1965)

On the bench facing the lighthouse.

37 PLAYBOY (AUGUST 1967)

Inside this green house. The magazine is on a table in the living room.

38 PLAYBOY (NOVEMBER 1965)

On a table outside a small home under the freeway.

39 VARGAS PAINTING

On a wall on the top floor office of the Bevers Moonshine headquarters.

40 PLAYBOY (SEPTEMBER 1968)

On a desk near a window on the second level of this large warehouse.

41 ALBUM COVER ("SMILEY SMILE" THE BEACH BOYS)

On a shelf outside a garage behind this large house.

42 COMMUNIST PROPAGANDA (COMMUNISM REACHES THE STARS)

On the front double doors of this school.

43 ALBUM COVER (THE ROLLING STONES)

Inside this green house on a desk in the living room.

44 VARGAS PAINTING

On the wall in the top floor office of Sonny Blue's Roberdeau Meat Packing Co building which is accessed during "The Blade Stained Red" protection mission.

45 COMMUNIST PROPAGANDA (COMMUNISM IS FREEDOM)

On the telephone pole beside this factory.

46 PLAYBOY (AUGUST 1965)

On a black couch inside the garage near a Bevers Moonshine location.

47 ALBUM COVER (JEFFERSON AIRPLANE)

On some boxes in the back room of this green row house. Enter through the door in the back alley.

48 HOT ROD MAGAZINE (JANUARY 1968)

On a workbench inside this Best Oil service garage.

49 PLAYBOY (OCTOBER 1965))

Inside the trailer office on the police station back lot. Use Zemis to distract and call the Police Dispatcher if you get spotted.

50 PLAYBOY (MAY 1967)

On top of a tool bench in the far corner of Burke's Iron & Metal garage.

51 VARGAS PAINTING

Hung on a wall in Burke's office behind the front counter in the main entrance to Burke's Iron & Metal.

52 ALBUM COVER (ROY ORBISON: CRYING)

On a vendor stand in the courtyard.

BARCLAY MILLS

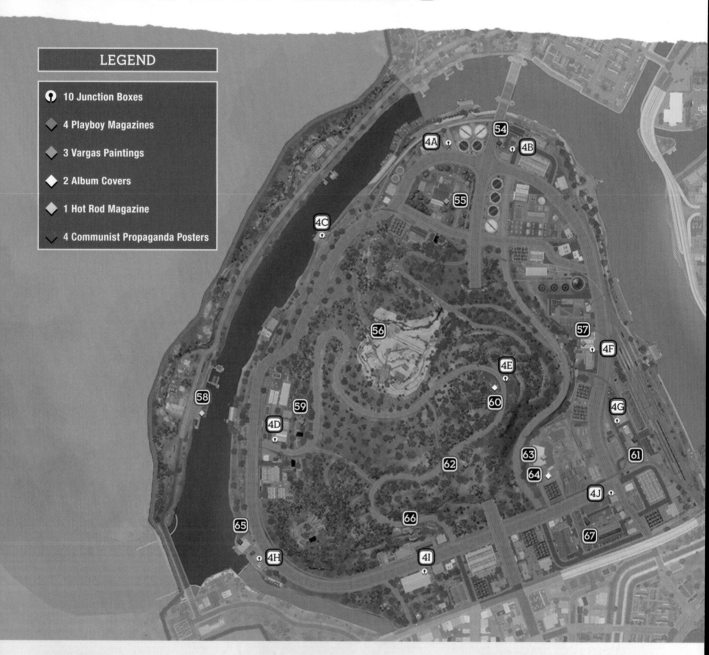

LEGEND

🔑 10 Junction Boxes

◇ 4 Playboy Magazines

◆ 3 Vargas Paintings

◆ 2 Album Covers

◆ 1 Hot Rod Magazine

⌄ 4 Communist Propaganda Posters

JUNCTION BOXES

4A JUNCTION BOX

On the east side of this three-story building on the corner.

4B JUNCTION BOX

On the east side of this short building near the bridge to Frisco Fields.

4C JUNCTION BOX

On the side of the riverside warehouse on the northwestern shore of Barclay Mills.

4D JUNCTION BOX

On the west side of this Best Oil service garage.

4E JUNCTION BOX

On the side of the radio tower building across the street from the bar.

4F JUNCTION BOX

On the corner of this four-story brick building with the Red Draft billboard on the rooftop. This is next to the large, open hangar/garage.

4G JUNCTION BOX

On the west side of this rail side building on the eastern rail yards of Barclay Mills.

4H JUNCTION BOX

On the north (road-facing) side of this water treatment facility.

4I JUNCTION BOX

On the northeast corner of this large warehouse.

4J JUNCTION BOX

On the north side of this two-story, corner building with the rooftop Black Suit billboard.

COLLECTIBLES

53 VARGAS PAINTING

Inside Nicki Burk's waterfront boat garage.

54 COMMUNIST PROPAGANDA (COMMUNISM REACHES THE STARS)

On the second floor patio balcony of this building near the bridge.

55 VARGAS PAINTING

This Halloween themed artwork is hanging on the wall in the main office on the second floor of the garbage dump headquarters, typically reached during "Puppy's Garbage Racket."

56 VARGAS PAINTING

Find this painting in the blue trailer office in the middle of the quarry. You typically access this area during "Meet Enzo Conti."

57 PLAYBOY (JANUARY 1964)

On a table behind the trucks parked in this large open garage in Barclay Mills.

58 HOT ROD MAGAZINE (JANUARY 1966)

Inside this rust bucket on the scrap barge across the river.

59 *PLAYBOY* (SEPTEMBER 1963)

This magazine is on a table in the middle of this wooden shack on the hill.

60 ALBUM COVER (STEPPENWOLF)

On a small table beside the front door of the Double Barrel Bar in Barclay Mills.

61 COMMUNIST PROPAGANDA (COMMUNISM REACHES THE STARS)

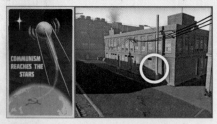

On the backside of this building near the tracks.

62 *PLAYBOY* (FEBRUARY 1964)

On a blue metal table on the porch of this cabin in the hills.

63 VARGAS PAINTING

Inside the train depot hideout, on the window wall behind the desk in the boss room.

64 ALBUM COVER (CREEDENCE CLEARWATER REVIVAL)

On a filing cabinet inside this blue trailer near the Barclay Mills railway turntable. Grab it during the Guns racket "The Dead Stay Gone."

65 COMMUNIST PROPAGANDA (EQUALITY FOR ALL)

On the backside of this building near the stairs that lead to the second story.

66 *PLAYBOY* (NOVEMBER 1963)

On the back porch of this ranch house on the hill.

67 COMMUNIST PROPAGANDA (COMMUNISM IS FREEDOM)

In the alley loading bay, on the wall of the multistory Locksmith Hardware & Service building between garages B2 and C3.

DOWNTOWN

LEGEND

- **10 Junction Boxes**
- 5 Playboy Magazines
- 3 Vargas Paintings
- 4 Album Covers
- 1 Hot Rod Magazine
- 4 Communist Propaganda Posters
- 1 Repent Magazine

JUNCTION BOXES

5A JUNCTION BOX

On a wall in the cut-through driveway of this cinema.

5B JUNCTION BOX

On the back corner of this Best Oil Auto Service station.

5C JUNCTION BOX

On the northwestern side of The Royal Hotel.

5D JUNCTION BOX

This junction box is on an alley wall on the building adjacent to the church.

5E JUNCTION BOX

This box is on a wall in the driveway cut-through in this building.

5F JUNCTION BOX

On the backside of the police station on police territory. Use Zemis and stealth to avoid detection.

5G JUNCTION BOX

This box is on the front side of this gas station on the corner.

5H JUNCTION BOX

This junction box is in the alley behind the ornate four-story building on the corner.

5I JUNCTION BOX

On the alley wall of this four-story apartment building.

5J JUNCTION BOX

This junction box is the underground parking garage in the south Downtown area.

COLLECTIBLES

68 *PLAYBOY* (JANUARY 1967)

On a desk in the Auto Service office.

69 VARGAS PAINTING

On the bookshelf in the back of this plush office on the top floor of the Imperial Health Club—typically accessed during Frankie's Blackmail racket. Enter through the main entry and work your way up using the stairs in the back of the lobby.

70 COMMUNIST PROPAGANDA (REVOLUCIÓN CUBA)

Hung on the side of the bridge. Access to the underground tunnels is found under the bridge.

71 *PLAYBOY* (NOVEMBER 1966)

In the sewers sitting on the bottom shelf on a small workbench. Easily accessed through the river tunnel just to the north of this location (near communist propaganda).

72 ALBUM COVER (DUSTY SPRINGFIELD)

On an oil drum inside this garage. The garage door must be opened to find it.

73 *PLAYBOY* (JUNE 1967)

This magazine is hidden in the flowers surrounding the park monument. The mag is sitting beneath the northeast palm tree.

74 ALBUM COVER (COUNT FIVE)

Inside this building at the bottom of the stairwell amongst a bunch of trash. This area is usually accessed during Frankie's Blackmail racket.

75 VARGAS PAINTING

Behind the check-in desk on the first floor of the Royal Hotel. You must get behind the desk to find it; it's propped up against the backside of the counter.

76 *REPENT* MAGAZINE (JUNE 11, 1968)

When you choose to sit on the sidewalk bench Downtown to speak with Donovan during the "Compromised Corruption" story mission, Donovan hands this magazine to you during the cutscene. However, do not forget to pick it up after the cinematic ends. You can also find it on this bench without activating this mission.

77 ALBUM COVER (ETTA JONES)

Inside a vendor booth in this parking lot.

78 *HOT ROD* MAGAZINE (JUNE 1966)

In the sewers on a workbench. Easy access can be had by entering the car garage below this building and entering the sewer passage doorway found in a caged office.

79 VARGAS PAINTING

On the northern end of the third story of the building under construction. Take the stairs all the way up and find the painting on the floor in the corner beside the stairwell. This area is accessed when you blow up the nearby crane in Cavar's Construction Racket mission.

80 *PLAYBOY* (APRIL 1965)

In the construction yard (behind Shaker's Jazz Club or Buck's clothing store) accessed during Cavar's Construction mission. Find the magazine on the desk inside the trailer office.

81 COMMUNIST PROPAGANDA (FREEDOM IN COMMUNISM)

Stuck on the north side of this very large government building.

82 *PLAYBOY* (DECEMBER 1964)

Inside this garage on the shoreline, find the magazine on a desk inside the office. This issue has an awesome interview with The Beatles.

83 ALBUM COVER (OTIS REDDING)

This one may not pop up on your radar until you approach it (even with wiretapping). Find this on the bow of the moored boat.

84 COMMUNIST PROPAGANDA (EQUALITY FOR ALL)

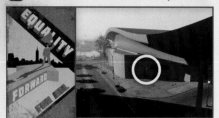

Stuck on the wall near the front entrance to this concert hall.

85 COMMUNIST PROPAGANDA (CUT DOWN CAPITALISM)

Hung on the side of this southern shipping warehouse facing the water.

TICKFAW HARBOR

LEGEND

- ○ 9 Junction Boxes
- ◆ 5 Playboy Magazines
- ◆ 3 Vargas Paintings
- ◆ 2 Album Covers
- ◆ 1 Hot Rod Magazines
- ◣ 4 Communist Propaganda Posters

JUNCTION BOXES

6A JUNCTION BOX

Located on the north side of this rail yard building.

6B JUNCTION BOX

On the backside of this two-story, white brick building.

6C JUNCTION BOX

On the north side of this tall brick warehouse near the large storage tanks.

6D JUNCTION BOX

On the side of this warehouse, which is filled with stolen vehicles during the Auto Theft racket.

6E JUNCTION BOX

On the east side of this blue warehouse. Find stashed vehicles inside during "Hot Rubber & Cold Blood."

6F JUNCTION BOX

On the south side of this shipyard warehouse.

6G JUNCTION BOX

On the south end of this very large waterfront warehouse.

6H JUNCTION BOX

On the ground floor of this parking garage on the wall just through the entryway. Drive to the top to find the communist propaganda poster.

6I JUNCTION BOX

On the north side of this long shipyard warehouse.

COLLECTIBLES

86 *PLAYBOY* (OCTOBER 1968)

Find this magazine behind the bar inside Shooter's Bar.

87 *PLAYBOY* (JULY 1967)

Find this magazine on the desk inside this small train depot.

88 ALBUM COVER (THE BOX TOPS)

This album is on the counter inside Joey's All-American Diner.

89 COMMUNIST PROPAGANDA (FREEDOM IN COMMUNISM)

On the south side of this long brick warehouse.

90 VARGAS PAINTING

Hung on wall inside the second floor office of this port warehouse, usually accessed during the Smuggling racket.

91 COMMUNIST PROPAGANDA (SCIENCE AND INDUSTRY SERVE COMMUNISM)

Hung on the side of this small utility building.

92 VARGAS PAINTING

Find this painting on the wall in the second floor office of the Best Oil corporate headquarters where counterfeiting apparently is going on.

93 *PLAYBOY* (JULY 1962)

On the rooftop ledge of this shipyard building. Use the stairwell to reach the rooftop.

94 ALBUM COVER (THE TEMPTATIONS)

This album is inside the rail depot. Kick in the door to access the interior.

95 COMMUNIST PROPAGANDA (REVOLUCIÓN CUBA)

On the stairwell enclosure of the multistory parking garage's rooftop level.

96 *PLAYBOY* (AUGUST 1962)

Find this magazine on the desk inside this trailer office at the shipyard.

97 *PLAYBOY* (MAY 1965)

On a desk inside this small trailer office on the waterfront.

98 VARGAS PAINTING

On the second level of this large Best Oil service station. It's on the wall in the office which you can reach from the service garage.

99 COMMUNIST PROPAGANDA (GLORY TO SOVIET SCIENCE & TECHNOLOGY)

On the door at the top of the lookout tower.

100 *HOT ROD* MAGAZINE (FEBRUARY 1965)

Find this magazine outside on the rooftop of this building. Use the metal exterior stairs to reach it.

FRISCO FIELDS

LEGEND

- 🔌 11 Junction Boxes
- ◆ 5 Playboy Magazines
- ◆ 3 Vargas Paintings
- ◆ 2 Album Covers
- ◆ 1 Hot Rod Magazine
- ▽ 2 Communist Propaganda Posters
- ◆ 1 Repent Magazine

JUNCTION BOXES

7A JUNCTION BOX

This box is on the side of the shack in the back of this camp.

7B JUNCTION BOX

On the Retrousse Yacht Club entry gate wall. Located to the right of the gate security booth.

7C JUNCTION BOX

On the side of this Griffin service station.

7D 7D JUNCTION BOX

On the side of a warehouse in an alley behind the Thrift Mart.

7E JUNCTION BOX

On the outer side of the brick gate around this plush home.

7F JUNCTION BOX

On the northeastern side of this round church.

7G JUNCTION BOX

On the side of the shack facing the nearby church where Southern Union racists conjugate during "The Privileged Die Slow".

7H JUNCTION BOX

On the south side of this tall, brick apartment building.

7I JUNCTION BOX

On the side of the Griffin filling station.

7J JUNCTION BOX

On the side of the bridge.

7K JUNCTION BOX

On the west narrow end of this long warehouse. Hack this box to spy on the racists using this building as a Southern Union Heritage Center.

COLLECTIBLES

101 *PLAYBOY* (APRIL 1967)

On the floor of this house on the lake.

102 VARGAS PAINTING

On a stack of folding tables in the left corner as you enter the Yacht Club's garden house.

103 VARGAS PAINTING

On a second floor office wall inside Bellaire's Grocery Store (entry is done at night by entering the marker next to the adjacent store named Carlyle's), usually accessed during a Southern Union mission.

104 *REPENT* MAGAZINE (JANUARY 10, 1968)

On a second floor office desk inside Bellaire's Grocery Store (entry is done at night by entering the marker next to the adjacent store named Carlyle's). It's in the room where the rally is broken up during Moreau's Southern Union Racket missions.

105 ALBUM COVER (JOHNNY CASH)

Inside this garage on a workbench. Open the garage door or kick in the backdoor (quicker) to gain entry.

106 ALBUM COVER (CREAM)

On a workbench in this garage with the trailer in the driveway. Break in the back door to enter quickly.

107 PLAYBOY (OCTOBER 1968)

On top of the tower sitting on the gazebo's short wall near the stairs. This is at Duvall Lookout, a historic Civil War site.

108 PLAYBOY (MARCH 1967)

On the table in the backyard in this nice subdivision.

109 PLAYBOY (MARCH 1965)

Under a pergola at the end of this large backyard in Frisco Fields. It's on the ground between lounge chairs.

110 PLAYBOY (SEPTEMBER 1965)

Inside this small shack.

111 HOT ROD MAGAZINE (DECEMBER 1968)

Find this magazine outside on a bench on the south side of this used car lot.

112 COMMUNIST PROPAGANDA (REVOLUCIÓN CUBA)

On an exterior column of this nice office building in Frisco Fields.

113 VARGAS PAINTING

When confronting Bobby Bastian during the PCP operation ("The Privileged Die Slow" story mission), you will infiltrate the PCP lab in the Duvall Hall Science Center. You can find this painting on the wall in Bobby's office on the second floor.

114 COMMUNIST PROPAGANDA (SCIENCE AND INDUSTRY SERVE COMMUNISM)

This propaganda poster is stuck to the front of this prestigious school.

FRENCH WARD

LEGEND

- ⚲ 9 Junction Boxes
- ◆ 4 Playboy Magazines
- ◆ 4 Vargas Paintings
- ◆ 4 Album Covers
- ◆ 1 Hot Rod Magazine
- ◣ 2 Communist Propaganda Posters
- ◆ 2 Repent Magazines

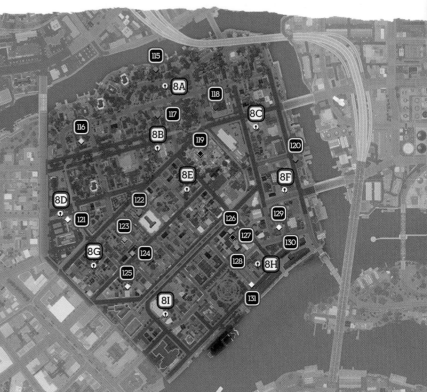

JUNCTION BOXES

8A JUNCTION BOX

On the side of this small brick shed in the backyard of a nice pink house.

8B JUNCTION BOX

On the back wall of the police station. This is on police territory so use stealth, Zemis to distract, and call the dispatcher if you get spotted.

8C JUNCTION BOX

On the side of the Super Rocket Diner.

8D JUNCTION BOX

On the front side of the Griffin filling station.

8E JUNCTION BOX

On the side of this building in the narrow alley.

8F JUNCTION BOX

This box is located in this narrow nook between buildings in the recessed walkway area.

8G JUNCTION BOX

On the side of this small building in this residential alley.

8H JUNCTION BOX

On the side of this brick wall in the residential alley with the sloped road.

8I JUNCTION BOX

On the back exterior wall of the Pawn & Loan store.

COLLECTIBLES

115 PLAYBOY (FEBRUARY 1962)

Next to the two lounge chairs near a brick shed beside this beautiful house.

116 HOT ROD MAGAZINE (MAY 1964)

On a workbench inside this residential garage.

117 PLAYBOY (FEBRUARY 1967)

Find this magazine on the workbench inside this residential garage.

118 COMMUNIST PROPAGANDA (GLORY TO SOVIET SCIENCE & TECHNOLOGY)

On the front door of this large building.

119 REPENT MAGAZINE (MARCH 10, 1968)

On the edge of a short wall around the central mausoleum in the cemetery.

120 120 PLAYBOY (APRIL 1961)

On the workbench inside this warehouse.

121 ALBUM COVER (DIANA ROSS AND THE SUPREMES)

Under this bench near the record store and the Griffin filling station.

122 PLAYBOY (NOVEMBER 1968)

On an outdoor grill under a pergola in the backyard of a large house.

123 VARGAS PAINTING

On the right wall as you enter the front door of the Big Mouth Jazz and Blues nightclub. You typically access this area when you are tasked to kill Leo "The Squid" Scutti during Gaston's Drug Racket.

124 VARGAS PAINTING

On the wall of the boss's office deep in the speakeasy tunnels under the Big Mouth Jazz and Blues nightclub. Take the stairs in the nightclub down into the tunnels. You usually access this area when you are tasked to kill Leo "The Squid" Scutti during Gaston's Drug Racket.

125 ALBUM COVER (ARETHA FRANKLIN)

On a table near an open window of this second story apartment.

126 VARGAS PAINTING

On a wall in the game room on the second story of this large motel. You typically enter this building when killing the Kinky VIPs during the "Handsome" Harry's Sex Racket in the "Evil That Men Do" missions.

127 *REPENT* MAGAZINE (JULY 12, 1967)

On a dresser in a room on the second floor of this motel. This room is just down the hall from the game room.

128 VARGAS PAINTING

On the shelf behind the bar on the second floor. There's also a stripper pole in this room. You typically enter this building when killing the Kinky VIPs during the "Handsome" Harry's Sex Racket in the "Evil That Men Do" missions.

129 ALBUM COVER (BARRY MCGUIRE)

On the shelf behind the bar inside Shooter's Bar.

130 COMMUNIST PROPAGANDA (SCIENCE & INDUSTRY SERVE COMMUNISM)

Plastered on the side of this one-story, yellow building near the water.

131 ALBUM COVER (QUESTION MARK AND THE MYSTERIANS)

On the second story balcony of this beautiful French Ward architecture. Reach it by using the sidewalk where it merges with this balcony.

SOUTHDOWNS

LEGEND

- 9 Junction Boxes
- 4 Playboy Magazines
- 3 Vargas Paintings
- 4 Album Covers
- 1 Hot Rod Magazine
- 2 Communist Propaganda Posters
- 1 Repent Magazine

JUNCTION BOXES

9A JUNCTION BOX

On the stair wall near the boat docks.

9B JUNCTION BOX

On the side of this Bayside Shipping warehouse.

9C JUNCTION BOX

Under the northeast covered walkway at Neil A. Arthur Stadium.

9D JUNCTION BOX

On the north end of Zachary Taylor High under the covered walkway. This is the basketball court side of the school.

9E JUNCTION BOX

On the side of this alley utility shack next to NB Liquors.

9F JUNCTION BOX

This box is on the train station wall facing the tracks.

9G JUNCTION BOX

On the south side of this small utility building in the alley.

9H JUNCTION BOX

On the backside of the police station. This is on police property so make sure to use a Screaming Zemi and stealth to get to the box. Call the dispatcher if you get in trouble.

9I JUNCTION BOX

On the back of this brick building near Chatham Ship n Store.

COLLECTIBLES

132 COMMUNIST PROPAGANDA (CUT DOWN CAPITALISM)

On a post on the end of the pier.

133 VARGAS PAINTING

Hung on the wall next to the safe in the shipping warehouse accessed during Peralta's Gambling Racket. The painting is near the northwest entrance facing the water.

134 ALBUM COVER (SAM COOKE)

On a stack of boxes at the top of the stairwell in this building. Use the green door on the south side of the building to gain access.

135 PLAYBOY (SEPTEMBER 1967)

In the stands at Neil A. Arthur Stadium.

136 VARGAS PAINTING

On the second floor office with the large safe in this old warehouse building.

137 PLAYBOY (MARCH 1968)

On a bathroom cabinet inside this green, shotgun home.

138 PLAYBOY (MARCH 1966)

On a table near the window in this second floor room in the Pearl Diver motel.

139 PLAYBOY (DECEMBER 1967)

This magazine is on a rooftop ledge. You can gain roof access using the stairwell, which is reached through either green door on the north or south side of the building.

140 COMMUNIST PROPAGANDA (REVOLUCIÓN CUBA)

Stuck on the side of this wall on a factory near the tracks.

141 ALBUM COVER (THE DUPREES)

On a low bookshelf in the dark basement of this Auto Service station.

142 ALBUM COVER (THE BEACH BOYS)

On the workbench inside this southern mansion's garage.

143 *HOT ROD* MAGAZINE (MARCH 1968)

On a workbench inside this industrial area garage.

144 ALBUM COVER (SAM & DAVE)

On a desk on the second floor of Hangar 13.

145 *REPENT* MAGAZINE (NOVEMBER 9, 1967)

This magazine is on the first floor of Willcocks Sports and Cocktails. It's on the counter in the middle of the bar area.

146 VARGAS PAINTING

In the main office on the second floor of Willcocks Sports and Cocktails.

BAYOU FANTOM

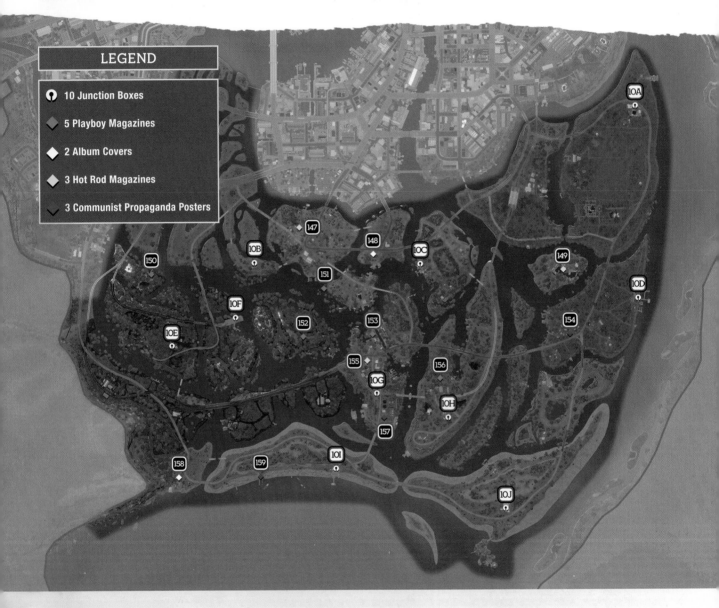

LEGEND

- 10 Junction Boxes
- 5 Playboy Magazines
- 2 Album Covers
- 3 Hot Rod Magazines
- 3 Communist Propaganda Posters

JUNCTION BOXES

10A JUNCTION BOX

On the side of the garage attached to the Tago filling station.

10B JUNCTION BOX

On the backside of this slat house with a water tank on the rooftop.

10C JUNCTION BOX

On the north side of this large boathouse.

10D JUNCTION BOX

At the entrance to this house on the water.

10E JUNCTION BOX

On the side of the small utility house near the water tower.

10F JUNCTION BOX

On the side of the bridge used to sabotage the paddleboat.

10G JUNCTION BOX

On the east side of this small depot.

10H JUNCTION BOX

On the south side of this cabin.

10I JUNCTION BOX

On the north side of this waterfront warehouse.

10J JUNCTION BOX

On the side of the Best Oil automotive workshop.

COLLECTIBLES

147 *HOT ROD* MAGAZINE (SEPTEMBER 1966)

On the picnic table under the shelter at this campsite.

148 ALBUM COVER (VANILLA FUDGE)

Behind the bar in the Double Barrel Bar.

149 *HOT ROD* MAGAZINE (NOVEMBER 1968)

On a cabinet in the back office of this shop.

150 *PLAYBOY* (JUNE 1962)

On a table inside this old shack on the bayou.

151 *PLAYBOY* (JUNE 1968)

On a workbench inside of this stilted shack over the water.

152 *PLAYBOY* (AUGUST 1968)

Sitting on a dresser inside the bedroom of this dilapidated shack.

153 *PLAYBOY* (JULY 1968)

On a picnic table under a covered porch of this riverfront home in the bayou.

154 COMMUNIST PROPAGANDA (SCIENCE & INDUSTRY SERVE COMMUNISM)

On the side of this small camper in this remote campsite.

155 *HOT ROD* MAGAZINE (AUGUST 1968)

On a workbench in the corner of the garage inside this Targo fueling station.

156 *PLAYBOY* (MARCH 1962)

Inside this shack in the middle of nowhere.

157 COMMUNIST PROPAGANDA (CUT DOWN CAPITALISM)

Hung on the south side of this remote dairy factory.

158 ALBUM COVER (CREEDENCE CLEARWATER REVIVAL)

On a corner shelf inside Shooters Bar's kitchen.

159 COMMUNIST PROPAGANDA (GLORY TO SOVIET SCIENCE & TECHNOLOGY)

Oddly enough, this poster is inside a structure; not on the outside like all others. Find it inside this riverfront shack just inside the front door on the left wall.

NORTH LAKE

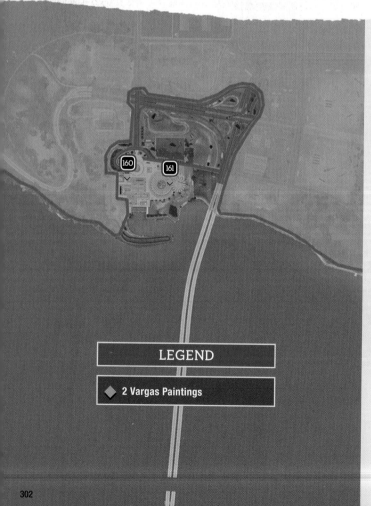

LEGEND

◆ 2 Vargas Paintings

COLLECTIBLES

160 VARGAS PAINTING

Inside Giorgi's casino. It's in a nook in the security office on the first floor. The painting is sitting on a couch; not yet hung on a wall. This is just before you reach the Stiletto giveaway (on the "Win This Car" platform).

161 VARGAS PAINTING

Inside Giorgi's casino. In the second level security room with the bird's-eye view of the gambling room below. This painting has also been set on a couch—not yet hung on a wall.

ACHIEVEMENTS & TROPHIES

NAME	DESCRIPTION	HIDDEN?	GAMERSCORE
Before They Bury You	Complete "Before They Bury You"	Yes	90
Pray on the Way Up	Complete "Pray on the Way Up"	Yes	15
It's a Brave New World	Complete "It's a Brave New World"	Yes	15
Fish Gotta Eat	Complete "Fish Gotta Eat"	Yes	15
Everyone Will Notice	Complete "Everyone Will Notice"	Yes	15
My Name is Lincoln Clay	Complete "My Name is Lincoln Clay"	Yes	15
Little Late for That	Complete "Little Late for That"	Yes	15
The Poor Sumb****	Complete "The Poor Sumb****"	Yes	15
Burn Like Napalm	Complete "Burn Like Napalm"	Yes	30
Certainly Was Exciting	Complete "Certainly Was Exciting"	Yes	30
Yet Here We Are	Complete "Yet Here We Are"	Yes	40
Somethin' I've Gotta Do	Complete "Somethin' I've Gotta Do"	Yes	15
For Old Time's Sake	Complete "For Old Time's Sake"	Yes	15
Cut & Run	Complete "Cut & Run"	Yes	15
We Partners Now	Complete "We Partners Now"	Yes	15
Sure Thing, Boss	Unlock all Associates	No	15
IRA Don't Ask	Complete "IRA Don't Ask"	No	25
I Need a Favor	Complete "I Need a Favor"	No	25
.45 in My Hand	Complete ".45 in My Hand"	No	25
Cash in Hand	Save $150,000 between your wallet and the bank	No	10
Baby, You're a Rich Man	Earn $500,000	No	10
Racketeer	Get the maximum earn from one of your rackets	No	15
We're in This Together	Keep all Underbosses alive until "Yet Here We Are"	No	15
Just You and Me	Keep only one Underboss alive until "Yet Here We Are"	No	15
Trust	Reach the Loyal state with one Underboss	No	15
Family	Reach the Loyal state with all three Underbosses	No	15
Hole in Your Pocket	Spend at least $500,000	No	10

NAME	DESCRIPTION	HIDDEN?	GAMERSCORE
Big Earner	Receive $10,000 in earn from one Underboss	No	15
The New Boss	Flip 16 Racket Bosses	No	15
Live Another Day	Spare all racket Informants	No	15
No Loose Ends	Kill all of the Racket Bosses	No	15
Can't Trust a Rat	Kill all racket Informants	No	15
Custom 358	Drive at 120 mph or faster for 20 seconds	No	15
Testing the Shocks	While driving, perform a 50-meter jump and land on your wheels	No	15
New Bordeaux Drifter	While driving, drift for at least 5 seconds	No	15
One Good Turn	Make a 180 degree turn at high speed without hitting anything	No	15
Wrecker	Execute 10 Vehicle Takedowns	No	15
Combat Specialist	Kill 300 enemies using Takedowns	No	15
Shh, shh	Perform 100 Stealth Takedowns on enemies	No	15
Closed Casket	Perform 50 Brutal Takedowns	No	15
Softened 'Em Up	Completely weaken a racket by killing all of its Enforcers	No	15
I'm Goin' In!	Attack a Racket without killing any Enforcers	No	15
Standard Communication Grid	Wiretap a Racket	No	15
Recruited to 5th SFG	Perform 5 headshots in 5 seconds	No	15
Bon Appétit!	Feed a body to an alligator	No	15
Next Time Swim Faster	Get eaten by an alligator	No	15
Sending A Message	Chain together 3 or more Brutal Takedowns	No	15
Code 112	Steal a Police car	No	15
Insurance Risk	Escape a Police Zone after being chased for 2 minutes	No	15
Never Saw it Coming	Kill an enemy within 2 seconds of kicking open a door	No	15
Flambé	Make 10 enemies light themselves on fire with their own Molotovs (shoot the enemy just before they throw)	No	15
Real Nice Time	Complete "Real Nice Time"	Yes	30
The Connection to Cuba	Complete "The Connection to Cuba"	Yes	15
There's a War Goin' On	Complete "There's a War Goin' On"	Yes	15
Jesuit in New Mexico	Complete "Jesuit in New Mexico"	Yes	15

TOP SECRET

NAME

NO.

NAME

NO.

BUILDING BACK ON SCHEDULE, SLOWDOWN OVE[R]

...my   sincerest   time   and
...hat things came   Cavar   re[...]
...head   with the   Gentleme[...]
...uring the con-   nothing
...n phase of our   wasting
...contribution to   your [...]
...own New Bor-   get ba[...]
...That is not how   he ad[...]
...refer to operate,   any
...you've got a   men[...]
...rout-

Birds Eye View, First Louisiana Bank & Trust, New Bordeaux.

First Louisiana Bank & Trust, New Bordeaux, LA.

dear l/xvii goddamned years
PQMDX JHUU SADDMYZQP KQMDE
after all this time youd think
MRFQD MXX FTUE FUYQ KAGP FTUZN
uncle sal would get tired of
GZOXQ EMX IAGXP SQF FUDQP AR
jamming his head up my ass like
VMYVUUZS TUE TQM GB YK MEE XUWQ
that's ever gonna change ill
FTMFE QHQD SAZZM OTMZSQ UXX
deal with it what i cant deal with
PQMX IUFT UF ITMF U OMZF PQMX IUFT
is how this place is a god damne[d]
UE TAI FTUE BXMOQ UE M SAD PMYZQP
sweat box you need me back in eb
EIQMF NAT KAG ZQQP YQ NMOW UZ QN
just say the word ill report back
VGEF EMK FTQ IADP UXX DQBADF NMOW
on our favorite uncle after i
AZ AGD RMHADUFQ GZOXQ MRFQD U
speak with him next week here
EBQMW IUFT TUY ZQJF IQQW TQDQ

New Bordeaux - A Modern City with Traditional Southern Values

POST CARD

getting together on april l/i
SQFF UZ'S FASQFTQD AZ MBDUX JUJ
at vili 8 pm
MF HUUU MY QF HUFA

FOWLER & WEBB FINE TAILORS
LITTLE ITALY 25
EMPIRE BAY 03491

JOHN F. KENNEDY

13¢ UNITED STATES

NEW BORDEAUX, LA
MAR 7 1967
09631

Cavar construction back on schedule

LOCAL UNION REP STILL MISSING, PRESUMED DEAD

NEW BORDEAUX — The search for Gus Borelli will be coming to a close, LT Clement Lindquist of the New Bordeaux PD announced today. It has been over a month since the local union rep was seen leaving a regularly-scheduled residence in the French Ward or at the union offices.

His sudden disappearance last month has triggered inquiries about alleged organized crime ties, but those claims remain unfounded according to sources within the New

forced to put this case on the backburner. More and more, officers are getting pulled in from around the city as an unrelenting mob war has escalated downtown.

Borelli's w Camille, who had adamant that he

tinued on A8

get,"
adies,
hate
than
me and
So let's
uilding."
out taking
nal com-
the press.
stands, the
lding will
a new admin-
hub for the
n the project is
d to be com-
in 1970. Some
functions of the
ng are expected
clude…

5 December, 1968

LOCAL UNION REP STILL MISSING, PRESUMED DEAD

NEW BORDEAUX – The search for Gus Borelli will be coming to a close, LT Clement Lindquist of the New Bordeaux PD announced today. It has been over a month since the local union rep was seen leaving a regularly-scheduled meeting with Local 1138 heads at the Perfect Waffle restaurant in Frisco Fields. Since then, there's been no sign of him either at his residence in the French Ward or at the union offices.

His sudden disappearance last month has triggered inquiries about alleged organized crime ties, but those claims remain unfounded according to sources within the New Bordeaux Police Department. With no leads at present time and many unanswered questions, it looks like the NBPD might be forced to put this case on the backburner. More and more, officers are getting pulled in from around the city as an unrelenting mob war has escalated downtown.

Borelli's wife, Camille, who had been adamant that he was a victim of foul play, has been uncharacteristically silent in the past few weeks as the search has dragged on.

Body Found During Downtown Demolition

om the
iated.

NEW BORDEAUX –

A body was found buried in the sub-basement of the Pappideaux building earlier today. The identity of the corpse remains a mystery since all potentially-distinguishable parts are still embedded in the concrete foundation. The building's controlled demolition earlier this week that revealed the body, loosened some of the concrete. Con-struction crews are now working closely with crime scene investigators to carefully clear debris.

City records show that Cavar Construction built the tower in 1968. The Company was suspected of having ties to the criminal underworld long before the construction company shut its doors in 2002. This discovery, though, has police officials baffled ...

e Best Beer in the ...

BON TEMPS BREWERY
BEST BEER IN THE SOUTH

ery bottle of Bon Temps
roud southern tradition
what makes our beer so
e on by the brewery where
s for spell and taste it for
times with Bon Temps beer.

AKIN AROUND TOWN"
By Bill Eakin

Marcano: Local Business
or Local Criminal?

You don't know Sal Marcano, but maybe you've heard the tale. A respected business man. A man who started off life in a shack along River Row, went to jail and turned his life around after getting out. A man who, over time, rose to become a land mogul, a Casino owner in Cuba in the 1950s, a local philanthropist and one of New Bordeaux's unknown heroes. Ask anyone from his old neighborhood and they

turkeys on the str... corner he used... hustle as a chil...

A truly self... proper gentle... the New ...

But much of... gilded f... sainte... many... you ...

POPULAR PIN-UP GIRLS HANG AROUND FRENCH WARD

always-jumping jazz joint "Big
th", was especially busy last
with lines out the door. Word
und that a season's worth of
girls (Miss **April**, **May** and
be specific) were making

their way through t
made it into the
thario and play
spending the
lovel

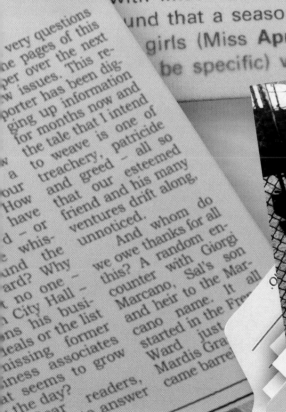

very questions
e pages of this
per over the next
w issues. This re-
porter has been dig-
ging up information
for months now and
the tale that I intend
to weave is one of
our treachery, patricide
How and greed – all so
have that our esteemed
– or friend and his many
e whis- ventures drift along,
und the unnoticed.
ard? Why And whom do
t no one – we owe thanks for all
n City Hall – this? A random en-
als or the list counter with Giorgi
missing former Marcano, Sal's son
iness associates and heir to the Mar-
at seems to grow cano name. It all
y the day? started in the Fre
Dear readers, Ward just
e intend to answer Mardis Gr
came barre

FRENCH OPERA HOUSE · STREET VIEW
NEW BORDEAUX · LOUISIANA

T-4 - POST CARD SPECIALTIES, NEW BORDEAUX, LA

TOOK ▮▮▮ ▮▮ IT ▮▮▮▮▮▮▮▮▮ LONG ▮▮▮ ENOUGH ▮▮▮▮▮▮▮ I
▮▮▮▮ ,BUT FINALLY ▮▮▮▮ ,GOT
A THAT BARTENDER ▮▮▮ MAKES
BLINDER, HALF-DECENT ▮▮▮▮▮ , THEN ▮▮▮▮▮▮
SOME ▮▮▮ LOCAL ▮▮▮▮▮ REPORTER
THROUGH ▮▮▮▮▮▮ COMES WANTING
UP ▮▮ .TO A WRITE
OF ▮▮▮ THE REVIEW RESTAURANT
SURE ,NOT WHAT ▮▮▮▮ THE
GUY'S ▮▮▮▮▮▮ ANGLE
HE ▮▮ SURE ▮▮▮ BUT SEEMED
TO LOVE ▮▮▮ THE
OF SEAFOOD. SPEAKING
THE OF ▮▮▮ WHICH
LAST COUPLE

NEW BORDEAUX, LA
MAY 3
1967
09681

JOHN F. KENNEDY
13c UNITED STATES

POST CARD

FISH ▮▮▮▮ YOU ▮▮▮▮ DOWN
SENT ▮▮▮▮▮ HERE.
FROM ▮▮▮▮ ,EMPIRE
BAY. ▮▮▮▮▮ DEALT
GOT ▮▮▮▮▮
AS WITH ▮▮▮▮ REQUESTED.

—V

FOWLER & WEBB FINE TAILORS
LITTLE MAW 25
EMPIRE BAY 03491

LL SAINT'S MASSACRE YEARS LATER

Quiet Sunday at the cemetery as we look back 33 years.

BORDEAUX – The men carried out an inauspicious the brutal attack in niversary for cold blood, timed to urbon City." A when fireworks were ter war broke out going off outside. mongst the crimi- The bodies weren't Bordeaux and it cul- even done dropping minated in the All before the killers left Saint's Day Massa- as quickly as they cre of 1934. It was came in, disappear- another lifetime for ing into a crowd of some, but those weekend revelers. with longer memo- The "Who" and ries of life in the "why's" behind the French Ward still re- crime scene still member the grue- remain a mystery some mass murder three decades after of 18 people in a hail the fact. One version gunfire – includ- of the story is re- ing former crime venge – four broth- boss Guiseppe Car- ers seeking retribu- illo. tion for the death of As the story their father. Another goes, a half-dozen story tells of gam- men, armed to the bling debts gone ▮▮▮▮ up just south. The only wit- ness of the attack, Carillo's ▮▮ one ▮▮▮▮

legend of the All Saint's Day Massa- cre. Organized crime still exists in our fair city, of course, but not since then have ▮▮▮ been such a

The Changing Face of New Bordeaux's Landlords: The Mob

By Louise Bossier

Sal Marcano's real estate photographed

Recently, New Bordeaux was robbed a great voice. A believer in what made the heart of our little "Bourbon City" tick. Bill Eakins was a deemed an accident, but we see it as a call to action. A call to dig deeper and uncover the truth.

That leads us to one big question our esteemed have failed to Why was Bill car found in River Row? never lived no family or friends in that area. Earlier that fateful day – before Eakins died – he was meeting with sources about some of the business facades in the French Ward. His investigation into mob-run drug dens hidden in plain sight… and hours later he's found in a car wreck.

Is it coin that his body up mere from whe subject of b story, Sal M spent his fo years? Sur We've laun investigatio Marcano's holdings properties throughou

FRENCH OPERA HOUSE, NEW BORDEAUX

WHEN IN NEW BORDEAUX, VISIT DOWNTOWN!

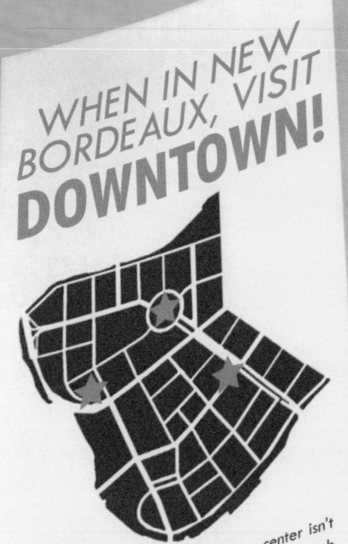

The bustling hub of Downtown's city center isn't to be missed when you're touring through "Bourbon City." New Bordeaux is growing everyday — you can see it on every street corner as brand new state of the art buildings are cropping up. When completed, our new City Hall will be a shining monument to the modern ___ walk by at dusk to

1. COEN'S STATE THEATER

Even if you don't plan to watch a movie during y___ stay in New Bordeaux, make your way past ___ majestic Coen's State Theater. The oldest — ___ biggest venue — in town is a testament to ___ Hollywood with its unique architecture. It's ea___ find at the north end of downtown, a few block___ from the French Ward.

2. GENERAL'S CIRCLE

At some point during your stay, take a long stroll past General's Circle. Under the watchful eye of the "Ol' General" you can see all walks of life pass through downtown. Besides watching passersby, artists are known to sketch or you might get treated to the occasional zydeco band.

3. ROYAL HOTEL

The Royal Hotel is easily the most exclusive place to stay in New Bordeaux. There's always a good chance that you'll be able to bump elbows with celebrities that often call this place home while travelling to town. Stop by for a Bourbon City Blinder and enjoy some of world-famous New Bordeaux hospitality.

PERFECT WAFFLE

PERFECT WAFFLE

| 1 | 0638 | SUSPICIOUS | An unoccupied vehicle running for at least two hours on the ███████ of ███████. The vehicle, a new Lassiter Courant, had a broken front passenger window. The owner has been contacted. No witnesses have come forward. |

| 2 | 1030 | GUN FIRE | Multiple weapons fired in the vicinity of the ███████████████ at corner of ███████████████ Police arrived at the scene to find 10 dead, five injured with clear scenes of a firefight. No statements given at the scene. |

| 3 | 1100 | FIRE | faulty machinery ignited at ███████ at corner of ███████ and ███████████ Resulting explosion did significant structural damage to crane. |

| 4 | 1200 | PROPERTY DAMAGE, FIRE | Report of a series of demolished fences, and a downed power line on fire at ███████ ███████ of ███████████ No witnesses have come forward. |

Live Jazz & Blues
...ve Jazz & Blues, New Bordeaux

L PLEASE CALL IF YOU THINK YOU WILL BE TOLD
TO SEND ME DOWN ROUTE 16 AGAIN. 3 YEARS OR
SO AGO YOU THOUGHT I'D STAY AND BE THERE JUST
SITTING, TWIDDLING THUMBS ON SOME PORCH. THE
FADED CHALK SIDELINES WITHERING AWAY WHILE TONY
AND I SIT AND WATCH THEM PRACTICE SOME FOOTBALL.
BURLY MOOKS, PULLING AND PUSHING PILES LIKE JUNK.
WALKING ALONG ON REMAINS OF THE OLD CROOKED STREETS,
YOU KNOW I'D KILL TO HAVE ANOTHER CHANCE, SAID TONY.
TOGETHER YOU'RE ABSOLUTELY, POSITIVELY NUTS, USUALLY
WHEN I NEED TO KNOW SOMETHING. ALL I'M SAYING, DO
NOT FORGET, YOU'RE SUPPOSED TO AGREE TO HELP
FAMILY GET TOGETHER. I'M INVOLVED AGAIN, NOW WITH
MY 2ND UNCLE'S NIECE. 3 AFFAIRS, LAST YEAR, BUT WHO'S
COUNTING? THIS TIME AROUND IS DIFFERENT, NO BULLSHIT.
NICE OF HIM TO CARE, CUTTING ME IN. ME AND TONY OUT EAST
SMELLING OF CIGARETTES AND THE LATE NIGHT ACTION.
WE'RE BUYING LOCAL BUSINESSES, OLD NEWS AS WE'VE
BEEN HERE BEFORE, SNIFFING THE AIR AROUND THE
WATERFRONT. LATELY TONY SAYS HE'S SAVING MONEY,
KEEPING IT FOR A RAINY DAY, LID ON TIGHT. ON
FRIDAY NIGHT IT WAS CLOUDY FOR HOURS, BUT NOW
IT'S SUNNY. VITO

T-4 · POST CARD SPECIALTIES, NEW BORDEAUX, LA.

— UNICOLOR · REPRODUCTION FROM ORIGINAL POTOGRAPH NEGATIVE·

POST CARD

Address

FOWLER & WEBB FINE TAILORS

LITTLE ITALY 25

EMPIRE BAY 03491

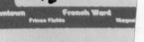

BENNY'S
Ristorante Italiano

Review: 4 stars

Opens Fri. Shows at 5pm, 7.15 & 9.30
Sun - 12.00 - 4.40 - 9.35

...but death

RACE!
In glorious Blood-o-vision

Swift

"Southern Soul Meets Little Italy at Benny's Ristorante"
By Bill Eakins

The sign of any good, neighborhood Italian restaurant is if you feel like you're at home. Especially, if that home includes an uncle sneaking you strong drinks and a mother that's generously serving up freshly-caught seafood,

the Mississippi from downtown, but tucked away just enough to keep out tourists, Benny's is a hidden gem. It's a great late-night spot for in-the-know locals that want a taste of Italy with some southern soul.

The classic Italian dishes on the

delivered on a bed of rigatoni, you know you're in for a treat. Word has it the owner, who likes to maintain his privacy, hails from Empire Bay where he perfected his craft in exclusive kitchens in Little Italy — he just wanted a change of scenery.

New Bordeaux

some "Bourbon City" classics. Make sure to order the Catfish Scaloppini or wrap your hands around a Po Boy Italiano.

And the drinks! While Benny's doesn't get credit for inventing the Bourbon City Blinder, the bartenders there have certainly made of point of delivering the most potent —

Bourbon City Blinder

The origins of the Bourbon City Blinder – like most alcoholic drinks – is a little hazy, at best. The way the local story goes, one bartender was done with a particularly rough shift working in the French Ward. Looking to unwind, he grabbed the first few bottles he could get his hands on and mixed them together into a mason jar he had sitting around. The bartender was so proud of his concoction, he spent the rest of the night stumbling around town, telling everyone of his creation. Word of that simple combination spread and has since become the signature drink of New Bordeaux, with several hot spots claiming to be the home of the original Blinder.

1 ounce of Humphrey's Bourbon

2 ounces rum -- dark rum

3 ounces ginger beer

2 dashes aromatic bitters

1 lime wedge

New Bordeaux
A Modern City with Traditional Southern Values

L-
ANWTWWFSKCWULGJWHJWKWFLXSEADQ
AFLWJWKLKFWPLOWWCAFUSDAXGJFASXG
JKGEWEMLMSDXJAWFVKGXGMJKAVGFLCF
GOAXLZAKAKMFUDWKAVWSGXSKWLMHGJ
AXZWKYGLKGEWLZAFYWDKWAFEAFVGFDQ
KSNAFYYJSUWGXLZAKLJAHAYGLGFWVSQLG
KWWLZWHGFAWKSFVESQTWDGGCMHKGE
WTGVQAGOWSNAKAL
-V

NEW BORDEAUX

NEW BORDEAUX, LA
JUN 14
1967
09631

JOHN F. KENNEDY
13¢ UNITED STATES

T.4 · POST CARD SPECIALTIES, NEW BORDEAUX, LA

L—
ive been asked to represent family
ANWTWWFSKCWULGJWHJWKWFLXSEADQ
interests next week in california fo
AFLWJWKLKFWPLOWWCAFUSDAXGJFASXG
rsome mutval friends of ours i dont kn
JKGEWEMLMSDXJAWFVKGXGMJKAUGFLCF
ow if this is uncle side a of a set up or
GOAXLZAKAKMFUDWKAVWSGXSKWLMHGJ
if they got something else in mind only
AXZWKYGLKGEWLZAFUWDKWAFEAFVGFDQ
saving grace o f this trip i got one day to
KSNAFYYJSUWGXLZAKLJAHAYGLGFWVSQLG
see the ponies and may be look up som
KWWLZWHGFAWKSFVESQTWDGGCMHKGE
ebody i owe a visit
WTGVQAGOWSNAKAL

—V

POST CARD

FOWLER & WEBB FINE TAILORS
LITTLE ITALY 25
EMPIRE BAY 03491

Lincoln Clay

Vito Scaletta

VISIT TODAY!

Gus Borelli

Vito Scaletta

NEW BORDEAUX TRI

NEW BORDEAUX, LA

NEW BORDEAUX'S PREMIER NEWSPAPER

VOL. 8302

66 PAGES, 5 SECTIONS

GUN RUNNING BUST IN THE BAYOU

BAYOU FANTOM – Superstitious locals have been saying that the ghost of Jean St. John continues haunting the Bayou, claiming lives. Apparently he never quit his gun running ways, either. Through a coordinated effort with the FBI and local authorities, a tipoff lead to the seizure of a huge weapons cache in the Bayou late last night. Where was all this hardware found? Near the wreckage of his supposed ship, The Grande Dame, hidden away in the Bayou Fantom. "Either ol' St. John has a taste for the Clipper 44 [handguns] or we c have some clever g gun runners taking advantage of a local legend to spook away trespassers," stated Police LT.

Clemen during confere ever th a bur that wind wron Bey cac fou

1. Baron Saturday's Fun Park

This theme park was opened briefly in the early 1950s, and for the short time it ran, it catered to the needs of the residents of Delray Hollow. Unfortunately, the park lost its funding and closed, but what remains of Baron Saturday's Fun Park is still worth taking a look at for all you explorers. While it isn't advisable to bring the kids to a half-completed construction site, it still is good for a couple amazing photos.

Cut this out. You obviously don't know how things work around here. Besides, no respectable tourist wants to go to that part of town.

NEW BORDEAUX TRI...

NEW BORDEAUX, LA

NEW BORDEAUX'S PREMIER NEWSPAPER

VOL. 8302

66 PAGES, 5 SECTIONS

GUN RUNNING BUST IN THE BAYOU

BAYOU FANTOM – Superstitious locals have been saying that the ghost of Jean St. John continues haunting the Bayou, claiming lives. Apparently he never quit his gun running ways, either. Through a coordinated effort with the FBI and local authorities, a tipoff lead to the seizure of a huge weapons cache in the Bayou late last night. Where was all this hardware found? Near the wreckage of his supposed ship, The Grande Dame, hidden away in the Bayou Fantom. "Either ol' St. John has a taste for the Clipper 44 [handguns] or we have some clever gun runners taking advantage of a local legend to spook away trespassers," stated Police LT.

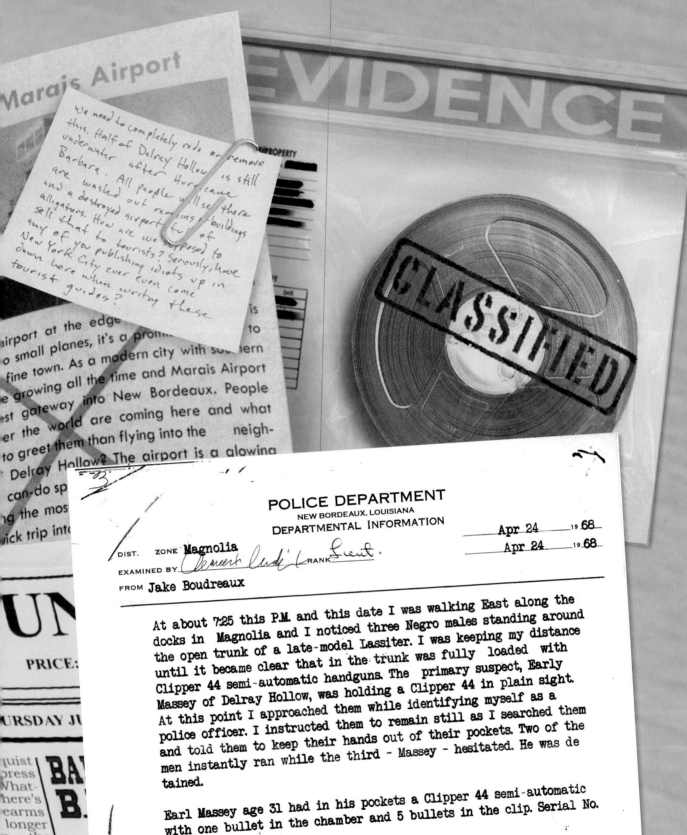

Marais Airport

We need to completely redo or remove this. Half of Delray Hollow is still underwater after Hurricane Barbara. All people will see there are washed out remains of buildings and a destroyed airport full of alligators. How are we supposed to sell that to tourists? Seriously, have any of you publishing idiots up in New York City ever even come down here when writing these tourist guides?

EVIDENCE

PROPERTY

CLASSIFIED

...airport at the edge...
...o small planes, it's a promi...
...fine town. As a modern city with sou...ern
...e growing all the time and Marais Airport
...est gateway into New Bordeaux. People
...er the world are coming here and what
...to greet them than flying into the   neigh-
...Delray Hollow? The airport is a glowing
...can-do sp...
...ng the mos...
...ick trip into...

UN...

PRICE:

...URSDAY JU...

BA...
B...

...quist
...press
...What-
...here's
...earms
...longer
...n   the
...”
...weapons
...pper 44s
...ne scene,
...a number
...smaller
...eing un-
...the area.
...cope of how
...l be recov-
...mains un-
...at   this
...cording to
...st.

POLICE DEPARTMENT
NEW BORDEAUX, LOUISIANA
DEPARTMENTAL INFORMATION

DIST. ___ ZONE **Magnolia** _____ RANK _Lieut_.

Apr 24 19 **68**
Apr 24 19 **68**

EXAMINED BY _Clement Judi'_____

FROM **Jake Boudreaux**

At about 7:25 this P.M. and this date I was walking East along the docks in Magnolia and I noticed three Negro males standing around the open trunk of a late-model Lassiter. I was keeping my distance until it became clear that in the trunk was fully loaded with Clipper 44 semi-automatic handguns. The primary suspect, Early Massey of Delray Hollow, was holding a Clipper 44 in plain sight. At this point I approached them while identifying myself as a police officer. I instructed them to remain still as I searched them and told them to keep their hands out of their pockets. Two of the men instantly ran while the third - Massey - hesitated. He was detained.

Earl Massey age 31 had in his pockets a Clipper 44 semi-automatic with one bullet in the chamber and 5 bullets in the clip. Serial No. 795812

Request that this gun be turned over to ballistics to be checked out.

Also request that Massey get checked out by the Gun Squad for potential leads on gun running outfits in the area.

NBPD

Baka

WHEN IN NEW BORDEAUX, VISIT BAYOU FANTOM

t the outskirts of New Bordeaux, nestled
ithin the Bayou Fantom, you'll find a cool
eeze sweeping through oak trees. Enjoy
e mystery of the marshland at the
uthern edge of our fair town – there's
   and undiscovered

1. Eaglehurst Plantation

Deep within the Bayou lies the Haunted
Eaglehurst Plantation. Local legend says that
eight people have died there. Some say more.
No one can seem to agree on the number
because there is no record of who originally built
the Eaglehurst Plantation. By all accounts, its
been there as long as anyone can remember
or before records were kept. The ancient estate
looks to be serviceable – even lived in – but the
property has remained empty for as long as
locals can remember. That, of course, lends itself
to ghost stories and visions of apparitions
sighted. And yet, nobody dares to go there at
night. Learn its long history during one of the local
day tours available of the plantation's grounds
and lower floors.

2. The Gh

While th
spoken
the Bay
legend
voodoo
that w
runner
War
some
Dame

Loses a Local Landmark, Gains Strip Club

The Perla Robinson Memorial Theater to be replaced by strip club.

DELRAY HOLLOW – The Hollow has been hit by hard times. Baron Saturday's Fun Park quickly shut its doors a few years back. Hurricane Barbara tore through the district, flooding out residents and permanently shutting down [Du]bois Airport. Now, residents lose more of the few [gath]ering places left [in t]he community. [It]'s closed its [door]s at the end of [the m]onth.

[This] news hits [espec]ially close to [home] for the locals [it w]as a tribute to [Perla] ...

orphans. She was married to Sammy Robinson who recently died under mysterious circumstances along with his son, Ellis. Efforts to investigate what was Perla's were met with resistance and dead ends in City Hall. The only leads to work off right now is a name, "Doucete" and the promise that it will be the ...

and centerpiece for the community, locals concerned. "The last thing this town needs is yet another strip club," said Father James Ballard. "You see, even though it was a jazz bar, Perla Robinson set up an office above it to help others in the neighborhood. I have a lot of respect for what they did for the community. So ...

memories, but families are continue to make it and here." Delray Hollo[w] a Local L[andmark] Gains Stri[p Club] Father Ba[llard] that he take his hall an[d] busine[ss] I alread[y] over signa[tures] resid[ents] ...

[tearing] down the bus[iness] ...

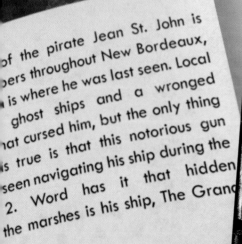

greetings from
New Bordeaux

CHOP SHOP BUST OUTSI

POINTE VERDUN — A tractor trailer, loaded with stolen car parts was stopped en route to the Tickfaw Harbor shipyards early last night. The driver, unidentified as of press time, fled the scene and escaped custody during a foot chase in Pointe Verdun.

The driver managed to make off with any records that were in the truck. As a result, there are no leads on where the cargo container was headed – or its point of origin. Still New Bordeaux Police Lt. Clement Lindquist is, "chalking this up as a big win" despite the fact that the truck had stolen plates.

Lindquist says, "While we don't have the ringleaders at this time, we are getting closer than ever to several suspects. Most important for now," he added, "we have effectively shut down one pipeline for the trafficking of stolen cars and car parts operating within our fair city."

The NBPD has racked up a number of successful busts lately throughout the city and while Lindquist is optimistic about zeroing in on the suspects, car thefts throughout the city these past few months. According to crime reports compared year over year, we're already seeing a 150% spike in car thefts in these first six months compared to all of

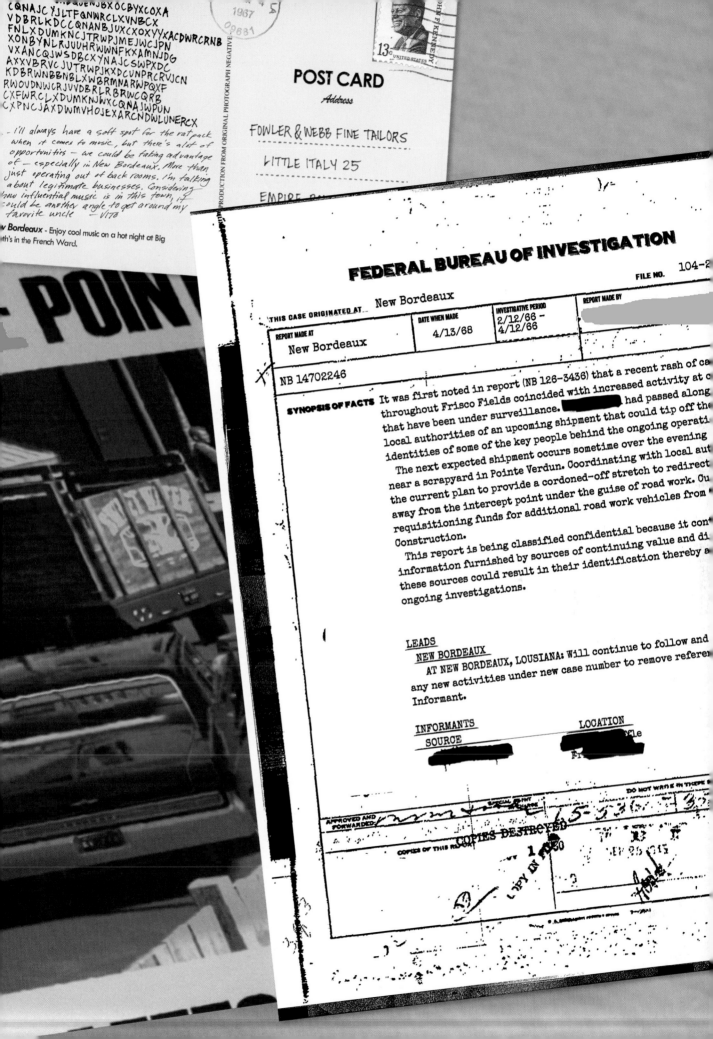

CQNAJCYJLTFQNWRCLXVNBCX
VDBRLKDCCQNANBJUXCXOXYYXACDWRCRNB
FNLXDUMKNCJTRWPJMEJWCJPN
XONBYNLRJUUHRWWNFKXAMNJDG
VXANCQJWSDBCXYNAJCSWPXDC
AXXVBRVCJUTRWPJWPJCSWPXDC
KDBRWNBBNBLXWBRMNARWPQXF
RWOUDNWCRJVVDBRLRBRWCQRB
CXFWRCLXDUMKNJWXCQNAJWPUN
CXPNCJAXDWMVHOJEXARCNDWLUNERCX

- I'll always have a soft spot for the rat pack
when it comes to music, but there's alot of
opportunities — we could be taking advantage
of — especially in New Bordeaux. More than
just operating out of back rooms. I'm talking
about legitimate businesses. Considering
how influential music is in this town, it
could be another angle to get around my
favorite uncle   — VITO

New Bordeaux - Enjoy cool music on a hot night at Big
...th's in the French Ward.

POST CARD

Address

FOWLER & WEBB FINE TAILORS

LITTLE ITALY 25

EMPIRE

FEDERAL BUREAU OF INVESTIGATION

FILE NO.   104-2

THIS CASE ORIGINATED AT	New Bordeaux			REPORT MADE BY
REPORT MADE AT	DATE WHEN MADE	INVESTIGATIVE PERIOD 2/12/66 – 4/12/66		
New Bordeaux	4/13/68			

NB 14702246

SYNOPSIS OF FACTS It was first noted in report (NB 126-3436) that a recent rash of ca
throughout Frisco Fields coincided with increased activity at c
that have been under surveillance. ▓▓▓▓▓ had passed along
local authorities of an upcoming shipment that could tip off the
identities of some of the key people behind the ongoing operati

The next expected shipment occurs sometime over the evening
near a scrapyard in Pointe Verdun. Coordinating with local aut
the current plan to provide a cordoned-off stretch to redirect
away from the intercept point under the guise of road work. Cu
requisitioning funds for additional road work vehicles from
Construction.

This report is being classified confidential because it con*
information furnished by sources of continuing value and di
these sources could result in their identification thereby a
ongoing investigations.

LEADS
NEW BORDEAUX
AT NEW BORDEAUX, LOUSIANA: Will continue to follow and
any new activities under new case number to remove referer
Informant.

INFORMANTS   LOCATION
SOURCE

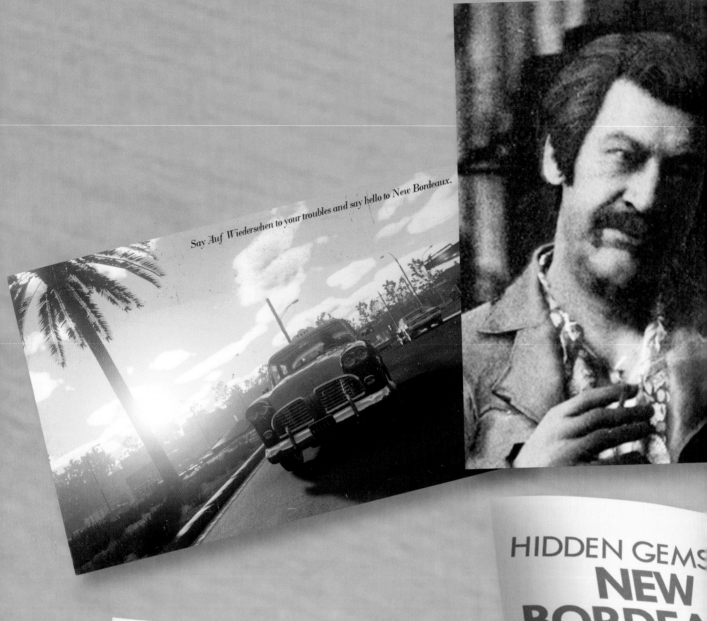

Say Auf Wiedersehen to your troubles and say hello to New Bordeaux.

L—
IT WORD HAS
UNCLE'S THAT
SOME HAS
EXPANSION AMBITIOUS
PLANS I'D — EVEN
HEARD TALK,
OF PLACES FAR

AS
FIND GERMANY I'LL
OUT
MORE NEXT
WEEK
—V

New Bordeaux - See something new in the Old South.

T.4 - POST CARD SPECIALTIES, NEW BORDEAUX, LA

NEW BORDEAUX, LA
MAR 11
1967
09881

13

POST CARD

Address

FOWLER & WEBB FINE TAILORS

LITTLE ITALY 25

EMPIRE BAY 03491

HIDDEN GEMS
NEW
BORDEA

Duffy's Irish Pub, '

There's this unassuming li
that's been serving up a
1903. Most joke that o
opened up, the Irish ca
it. Truth, though, is stre

Bordeaux?

BAYOU FANTOM – People are going missing in New Bordeaux, and the only thing found at each crime scene: A smoking, noisy voodoo doll – the "Screaming Zemi."

Up until now, the New Bordeaux Police Department has been trying to keep a lid on things, but when confronted recently, Police LT. Clement Lindquist confirmed, "There have been a number of missing persons reported in the past few months with Zemis found at the scene. We can confirm that most of those bodies are found 36-48 hours later in some _____ part of the Bayou Fantom, dead."

While there are few details being shared by the NBPD, we have learned from various sources that the victims so far seem to be men that have been abducted near brothels throughout the French Ward. Why these particular men are being targeted remains a mystery, the only calling card – the "Screaming Zemis." Local superstition connects the Zemi's with voodoo queens, ghost ships and vengeful spirits. But it's highly doubtful some _____ the French Ward. So, is there a copycat killer capitalizing on superstition roaming the streets of New Bordeaux? "Jean St. John....? Surely you're kidding," Lindquist laughed. "That's just some dumb ghost story to scare kids. There's nothing magical going on here – just some corner store voodoo dolls rigged to make noise and distract people from what's really happening." Lindquist refused to further speculate, saying, "This _____

Since this off-the-beaten path watering hole opened over 60 years ago, it's attracted all sorts of artists. Specifically, writers. In fact, more than five noted authors have sat in Duffy's for days, drinking and writing and claiming that the bar gave them their inspiration. It even became a second home to New Bordeaux's own Genevieve Fabry as she was writing her first collection of poems.

Fabry, known best for her razor wit and sharply written prose, made a habit of coming to Duffy's after selling her first pieces of writing. And she kept coming back to, "silence the critics in her head." If you get to Duffy's early enough in the evening, make sure to grab the booth closest to the bar. That's where she passed out and died after famously saying, "Well, that'd make 18 straight Bourbon City Blinders. I think that's the record."

It was.

Duffy's gives you an unfiltered look at the hardworking, simpler sides of New Bordeaux that usually don't appear in the guide books. Go early enough in the evening and you may still find aspiring writers, young and old, scribbling away in notebooks or napkins. Better yet, you'd still be able to meet the locals coming off shift at the nearby scrapyard.

_____ter's Haven

_____ New Bordeaux
_____e locals since
_____'s Irish Pub
_____moved in around
_____n fiction.

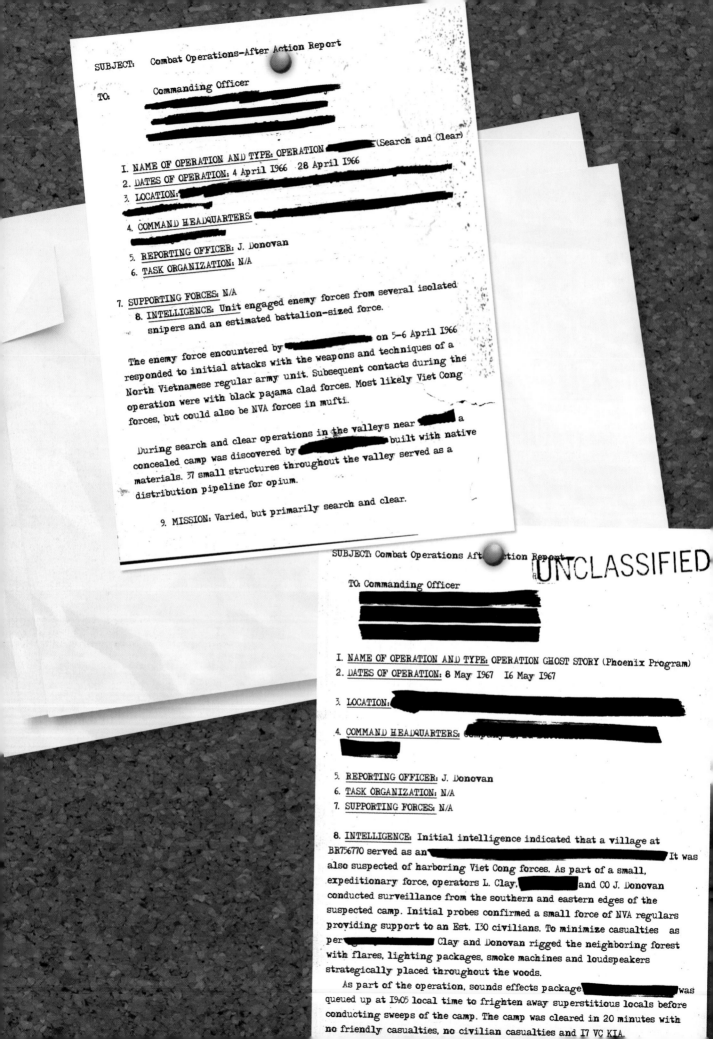

SUBJECT: Combat Operations-After Action Report

TO: Commanding Officer
███████████████████████████
███████████████████████████

1. NAME OF OPERATION AND TYPE: OPERATION ████████ (Search and Clear)
2. DATES OF OPERATION: 4 April 1966   28 April 1966
3. LOCATION: ████████████████████████████████
4. COMMAND HEADQUARTERS: ███████████████████
   ████████████
5. REPORTING OFFICER: J. Donovan
6. TASK ORGANIZATION: N/A
7. SUPPORTING FORCES: N/A
   8. INTELLIGENCE: Unit engaged enemy forces from several isolated
      snipers and an estimated battalion-sized force.

The enemy force encountered by ████████████████ on 5-6 April 1966
responded to initial attacks with the weapons and techniques of a
North Vietnamese regular army unit. Subsequent contacts during the
operation were with black pajama clad forces. Most likely Viet Cong
forces, but could also be NVA forces in mufti.

   During search and clear operations in the valleys near ████████ a
concealed camp was discovered by ███████████████ built with native
materials. 37 small structures throughout the valley served as a
distribution pipeline for opium.

   9. MISSION: Varied, but primarily search and clear.

SUBJECT: Combat Operations Aft██ ██tion Report   **UNCLASSIFIED**

TO: Commanding Officer
█████████████████████████
█████████████████████████

1. NAME OF OPERATION AND TYPE: OPERATION GHOST STORY (Phoenix Program)
2. DATES OF OPERATION: 8 May 1967   16 May 1967
3. LOCATION: ████████████████████████████████
4. COMMAND HEADQUARTERS: ███████████████████████
   ████████
5. REPORTING OFFICER: J. Donovan
6. TASK ORGANIZATION: N/A
7. SUPPORTING FORCES: N/A

8. INTELLIGENCE: Initial intelligence indicated that a village at
BR756770 served as an ████████████████████████████ It was
also suspected of harboring Viet Cong forces. As part of a small,
expeditionary force, operators L. Clay, ████████ and CO J. Donovan
conducted surveillance from the southern and eastern edges of the
suspected camp. Initial probes confirmed a small force of NVA regulars
providing support to an Est. 130 civilians. To minimize casualties as
per ████████████ Clay and Donovan rigged the neighboring forest
with flares, lighting packages, smoke machines and loudspeakers
strategically placed throughout the woods.
   As part of the operation, sounds effects package████████████ was
queued up at 19:05 local time to frighten away superstitious locals before
conducting sweeps of the camp. The camp was cleared in 20 minutes with
no friendly casualties, no civilian casualties and 17 VC KIA.

JOHN DONOVAN

E OF MANY of the new graduates
n Princeton's Class of 1953, John
ovan says that he's, "looking
ard to seeing the world and
king a difference."

I2. <u>RESULTS:</u>

	FRIENDLY FORCES		ENEMY FORCES
KIA	<u>22</u> ▇▇▇ Arty KIA (BC)		I67
	I ▇▇▇ KIA (Est)		248
	I ▇▇▇ WIA (cfm)		IO
	I8 ▇▇▇ WIA (Est)		Unk
WIA	<u>62</u> 3 ▇▇▇ Cav VCC		O
	<u>59</u> ▇▇▇		

Opium destroyed 4,000 pounds Est

MIA	O
Weapons	I53

I3. <u>ADMINISTRATIVE MATTERS:</u> There was one standout solider in this
operation. Cpl L. Clay performed admirably, controlling the battlefield
despite overwhelming odds. Clay ignored injuries in the field while
quickly retrieving ▇▇▇▇ and ▇▇▇▇ whom were both ▇▇▇
▇▇▇▇▇. Clay also
merits extra commendation for single-handedly leading two units into
a series of ▇▇▇▇▇
Recommend citation for Cpl. Clay and possible promotion. Recommend
bringing him deeper into the ▇▇▇▇

CAL PASTOR LOOKS BACK AT THE LAST ORPHANAGE

FRENCH WARD - Back in 1958, Saint Michele's Home for Colored Boys - the last orphanage in the French Ward - shut its doors for the final time. Since then, Father James Ballard has continued fighting to help the community and do his best to keep wayward children on the straight-and-narrow.

We recently caught up with Father James as Saint Michele's finally gets torn down to get some of his thoughts on the new Foster Care system, but clearly what once was still clearly weighed on his mind. "When I first came to New Bordeaux, I knew that Saint Michele's was in a bad way," Ballard started. "But what that building lacked in polish, it more than made up for in building the characters of boys that I saw grow into good young men in those hallways.

By all accounts, Ballard's time at Saint Michele's was marked with many improvements within the diocese including getting children off the streets. He fought hard for every opportunity -

helping poor black boys needed a home. He ever tioned City Hall to co supporting the work church and the Orpl At the end of the day, it just wasn't enoug we were doing goo community and hel up fine young me tinued, "but it jus God's plan."

Ballard ex when the city few funds s received, it spe the rundow Once the fu they only h they were f orphanage "It broke said. "Tr all those away ou lost in th and I r of the did a like l

Fat in d

"Nobody. No ... ...tion for the deat... ...ing ...weekend revel...
ot me..." fur-   the   their father. Another
cements   the   All   story tells of gam-
d of the

MORE INFIGHTING IN RIVE[R

RIVER ROW – Violent incidents continue to rise for the third straight week in the River Row district and there is no end in sight.

It started a few weeks ago with what seemed like a large, random street brawl between 20 some-odd union workers.

That incident ended in a dock-side drug bust.

Now, some are saying that organized

hasn't seen in over 30 years. If unchecked, do we risk the return to the days of the All-Saint's Day Massacre?

According to Police LT. Clement Lindquist, "The New Bordeaux Police Department feels confident that the problem is contained." Only problem is the eyewitness reports from locals that there's a heightened sense of danger on the streets. One River ... resident who

she saw several local known mobsters stepping up shakedowns of local businesses and even in-fighting among them on the streets.

"While nobody's gone shooting up the neighborhood yet, it's coming," she said. "You can tell from the dirty looks and angry conversations I hear at local restaurants like Benny's [Italiano Ristorante]. What I don't get is why the cops are letting this happen."

LT. Lindquist was quick to point out that,

"None of the repor... acts of violence vandalism have ...lated to criminal

In fact," He "there's been r... in citizens repo... rise in violenc... Run in over We aren't sa... aren't happ... are – bu... reporting it."

Wh... be ri... crim... ing in

Another night is about to heat up down in Bourbon City

NEW BORDEAUX   JAN 05 I

226 = 150 / 150
310 - 110 (90
_____
500

1/5/68

SAWNY'S

56267   7 18 61
HT 5 FT 10   WT 150
DOB 9 19 45   437

CASE # 06423B

POLICE LINES DO NOT CROSS
DO NOT CROSS
POLICE LINES

GANGS CLASH AGAIN IN THE HOLLOW

DELRAY HOLLOW – Earlier today, several men were found dead near the outskirts of Baron Saturday's Fun Park. The grisly scene played out in the shadow of the old Crazy Gatorroller coaster earlier this morning, according to police.

This is the latest in a long line of gang-related crimes boiling up all over town – especially coming from Delray Hollow. Bodies have been found shot up, or worse.

Despite the growing body count, no one is talking about it on the streets of The Hollow. They are too afraid to even call the police. A source within the New Bordeaux Police Department has confirmed that a new gang, comprised largely of Haitians, has been vying for control of the area. The only thing known about the gang is its shadowy leader, Baka. Even then, his ~~name only~~

This marks the tenth straight day of deadly gang fights breaking out in Delray Hollow. It's been an especially bloody battleground in the past week, leaving over 30 ~~people dead in its wake.~~

this rash of violence in The Hollow? So far, nothing except cleaning up the corpses.

The NBPD has been noticeably quiet about the growing gang violence despite ~~repeat~~

TTER TO THE EDITOR

Apology to Sal Marcano

By ~~rry~~ "Buddy" Bordelon

~~rea~~ders will notice ~~tha~~t we've recently ~~be~~en singling out an ~~up~~standing member ~~of~~ our community. Publicly calling out private citizens for alleged – even tangential – criminal activity is something that we do not take lightly here.

As much as we ferociously pursue the truth, we must ~~wei~~gh against it

the face of accusations levied against his business operations and personal life.

In light of the proof presented to me personally by Mr. Marcano, and lacking any evidence to indicate otherwise, we would like to take this opportunity to publicly apologize to Mr. Marcano in what must be difficult times for him. He is a respected business man and a pillar of our community and he deserves ~~nothing but our re~~ ~~for everything~~ ~~to our~~

MAFIA III
OFFICIAL STRATEGY GUIDE

Written by Rick Barba & Tim Bogenn

DK/Prima Games, a division of Penguin Random House LLC
6081 East 82nd Street, Suite #400
Indianapolis, IN 46250

ISBN: 978-0-7440-1733-5

Printing Code: The rightmost double-digit number is the year of the book's printing; the rightmost single-digit number is the number of the book's printing. For example, 16-1 shows that the first printing of the book occurred in 2016.

19 18 17 16   4 3 2 1

001-299357-Oct/2016

Printed in the USA.

Credits

DEVELOPMENT EDITOR
Matt Buchanan

SENIOR GRAPHIC DESIGNER
Carol Stamile

PRODUCTION DESIGNER
Justin Lucas

PRODUCTION
Beth Guzman

Prima Games Staff

VP & PUBLISHER
Mike Degler

EDITORIAL MANAGER
Tim Fitzpatrick

DESIGN AND LAYOUT MANAGER
Tracy Wehmeyer

LICENSING
Christian Sumner
Paul Giacomotto

MARKETING
Katie Hemlock

DIGITAL PUBLISHING
Julie Asbury
Tim Cox
Shaida Boroumand

OPERATIONS MANAGER
Stacey Ginther

Acknowledgments

Prima Games would like to thank everyone at 2K for their support and help in creating this guide.

The authors would like to add a special thanks to Ben Holschuh, whose gracious and good-humored liaison work made our stay in Novato not only productive but enjoyable. You rock, Ben.